A History of Denmark

Second Edition

Knud J. V. Jespersen

Translated by

Ivan Hill and Christopher Wade

palgrave
macmillan

First edition published 2004
Second edition published 2011 by
PALGRAVE MACMILLAN

Palgrave Macmillan in the UK is an imprint of Macmillan Publishers Limited,
registered in England, company number 785998, of Houndmills, Basingstoke,
Hampshire RG21 6XS.

Palgrave Macmillan in the US is a division of St Martin's Press LLC,
175 Fifth Avenue, New York, NY 10010.

Palgrave Macmillan is the global academic imprint of the above companies
and has companies and representatives throughout the world.

Palgrave® and Macmillan® are registered trademarks in the United States,
the United Kingdom, Europe and other countries.

ISBN 978–0–230–27341–2   hardback
ISBN 978–0–230–27342–9   paperback

This book is printed on paper suitable for recycling and made from fully
managed and sustained forest sources. Logging, pulping and manufacturing
processes are expected to conform to the environmental regulations of the
country of origin.

A catalogue record for this book is available from the British Library.

A catalog record for this book is available from the Library of Congress.

Contents

Preface to the Second Edition   ix
Acknowledgements   xi
Map 1   Denmark   xii
Map 2   Scandinavia   xiii

**1   Introduction: What is Denmark and Who Are
      the Danes?**   **1**
      A Description   1
      The Danes, According to Robert Molesworth   4
      Sir James Mellon and the Danish Tribe   5
      Some Principal Themes of this History   7
      The History of Denmark   9

**2   Foreign and Security Policy: From the Gatekeeper
      of the Baltic to a Midget State**   **12**
      The Collapse of the Baltic System around 1500   12
      Denmark as a Gateway   14
      Danish–Swedish Rivalry, 1563–1720   17
      The Wars with Britain and the Dissolution of the
          Dual Monarchy, 1800–30   21
      Denmark and the Unification of Germany, 1830–71   22
      From Neutrality to Membership of NATO, 1870–1950   26
      After the Cold War   30

**3   Domestic Policy, 1500–1848: The Era of Aristocracy
      and Absolutism**   **36**
      The Consensus Model   36
      The Coup of 1536 and the New Concept of Sovereignty   38
      From Domain to Tax State   41
      The Crisis of the State Council   44
      Coup d'État and Absolutism, 1660   46

From Estates of the Realm to Hierarchy   49
The Danish Law, 1683–45   51
Leasing Out the Power of the State   54
Struensee and Enlightened Absolutism   56
The Great Agrarian Reforms   58
The Reform of Military Conscription and the
     Emancipation of the Peasants, 1788   61

**4   Domestic Policy since 1848: Democracy and
the Welfare State   64**
Civil War and Revolution   64
The 1849 Constitution – Rupture or Continuity?   66
The Revised Constitution, 1866   70
Constitutional Struggle and Provisional Measures   72
Change of System and Parliamentarianism   75
The Century of Social Democracy   78
From Class Warfare to National Consensus   80
The Danish Model of the Welfare State   82
The Crisis of the Danish Welfare State   86
Goodbye to Welfare Democracy?   88

**5   The Church and Culture from Luther to
Postmodernism   91**
The Remote Church   91
The Reformation, 1536   94
The New Church   96
The Parish Priest as Civil Servant   99
The Church's Project – the State's Project   102
Pietism   104
The Enlightenment   108
Grundtvig   112
The Folk High School and the Danish Church   114
Grundtvig's Concept of Popular Democracy   116
Grundtvig's Legacy and the Danish Model   119

**6   Economic Conditions: The Old Denmark,
1500–1800   123**
Way of Life and the Economy   123
The Sound Dues, Denmark and the World Economy   125
The Old Agrarian Society   127

The Structure of the Landed Estates under Absolutism 132
The Agricultural Classes 134
Good Times and Flourishing Trade 136
The Agrarian Revolution Arrives in Denmark 138
The Great Agrarian Reforms 140
The New Rural Society 144

7 Economic Conditions: The New Denmark since 1800 148
Denmark and the Dual Revolution 148
'A small, poor country' 151
Grain Sales and Modernisation 154
The Co-Operative Movement – the Second
   Agricultural Revolution 156
The Beginnings of Industrialisation 161
The Policy of Regulation during the First World War 167
Land Reform and Bank Failure 170
The Crisis of the 1930s – Collaborative Democracy 173
In the Shadow of the Second World War 178
Agriculture in Retreat 180
The Second Industrial Revolution 182
The Welfare State and the Service Economy 184
The Danish Welfare State and the World Economy 186
The Reluctant Europeans 189
The Half-Hearted, Pioneering Country 192

8 The Danes – A Tribe or a Nation? 195
Danishness in the Looking-glass of History 195
The 'Farmers' Approach' 200
The Multinational State and Danishness 201
Danishness and Absolutism 204
The 1864 Syndrome and Danishness 208
The Prevailing Identity 211
Perceptions of Nationalism 215
When did the Danes become Danish? 218
Denmark and the Danes in 2000 222
Postscript: Denmark 2000–2010, a Brief Account 224
   Change of government – and a new political style 224
   The cartoon crisis 227
   The financial crisis and its consequences 229

CONTENTS

Notes   232

Select Bibliography   241

A Short Chronology Since 1500   246

Index   249

Preface to the Second Edition

Since the first edition of *A History of Denmark* was published in 2004 it has been adopted as a basic textbook in many higher education courses on Scandinavian history all over the world. However, seven years after its original publication, the book is not very easily available. For this reason it has been decided to republish it, and the publisher has, at the same time, given me the opportunity to revise and update the text where necessary.

Several reviewers and users of the book have, in the intervening years, given me many helpful comments on specific passages in the text, and some have also kindly pointed out themes that might have deserved a more elaborate treatment than they were given in the first place. Such comments and suggestions were received with gratitude, and they have given rise to several improvements in the present text, even if the basic, topical structure of the account remains unaltered. Minor errors and inaccuracies have of course been corrected in the process, but the most important amendments to the original text deserve to be mentioned specifically.

The second chapter on foreign and security policy now includes an extended description of Denmark during the Second World War, and at the end of the chapter there is a new section describing thoroughly the radically altered international position of the country after the end of the Cold War and also discussing the development of the new strategic concepts that, over the first decade of the twenty-first century, have led to a Danish military presence in Iraq and have made Denmark an active part of NATO's intervention in Afghanistan.

Chapter 4 on modern domestic politics now includes a more thorough discussion of the ideological battles of the 1930s, when parliamentarian democracy struggled to survive the frontal attacks from the totalitarian movements of Fascism, Nazism and Communism. A key figure in this struggle was the leading Social Democratic ideologist, Professor Hartvig Frisch, whose thoughts and activities proved to be decisive for the survival of democracy and also determined the framework of the subsequent Danish welfare society.

Chapter 5 on church and culture now includes a minor new section on the eighteenth-century Enlightenment on Danish soil, centred on its leading figure, the playwright, philosopher and historian Ludvig Holberg.

At the end of the concluding Chapter 8 is added a longer postscript outlining the most important events and trends in recent Danish politics – including the so-called 'cartoon-crisis' of 2006 that sent shockwaves through Danish society – thus bringing the account up to 2010.

An extra map showing Denmark in a larger European context has also been added to the new edition. The Notes and Bibliography have been updated to include all relevant references and works that have appeared since 2004.

It is my belief that the above-mentioned amendments fulfil most of the improvements that users of the book have suggested. As the account of the long history of Denmark is now also brought up to 2010, it is my hope that the new edition may still, for several years, fulfil its task as a suitable and up-to-date introduction for scholars, students and general readers, who would like to make themselves acquainted with contemporary Danish society and its historical roots.

Knud J. V. Jespersen

Acknowledgements

At the publication of the amended second edition of this volume I would like to repeat my thanks to the late Mr. Ivan Hill, MA for his translation of the first edition into English. I would also like to express my gratitude to my friend Mr. Christopher Wade for his willingness to undertake the task of translating the amendments to the original text in this second edition and for rewarding discussions in the process.

Knud J. V. Jespersen

Map 1 *Denmark*

Map 2 *Scandinavia*

Source: Maija Jansson, *Realities of Representation* (Palgrave, 2007). Reproduced with permission of Palgrave Macmillan.

I

Introduction: What is Denmark and Who Are the Danes?

A DESCRIPTION

Consulting a modern encyclopaedia under 'Denmark' would show that today this is the name of a state stretching from 54° to 58° north and 8° to 15° east. Denmark proper consists of *Jylland* (the Jutland Peninsula) and 406 islands, of which 79 are inhabited. The largest and most populous of these is *Sjælland* (Zealand), where the capital city, Copenhagen, is located, followed by *Fyn*. The Baltic island, *Bornholm*, is the easternmost part of the island kingdom. The total area is nearly 43,000 km². To this should be added Greenland and the Faroe Islands, which with Denmark itself form a national federation.[1]

Denmark itself has 7300 km of coastline and a 68-km land border with Germany. It is very definitely a low-lying country – the highest point is 173 metres above sea level – and well suited for agriculture, though poor in mineral resources. Approximately 64 per cent of the total land area is under cultivation. Twenty-two per cent is woodland, heath, moor, marsh, dunes and lakes. The remainder consists of buildings and transport infrastructure. The country is delimited to the west by the North Sea, while the Danish islands demarcate the Kattegat from the Baltic. Thus the country lies across the sea route from the Baltic to the oceans and the route from the Nordic countries to Central Europe. This position as a gateway has played a very important role in the history of the country.

The population of Denmark is around 5.2 million, of which 85 per cent live in towns. Only 5 per cent are employed in agriculture and fishery, while 27 per cent work in industry or construction. The remaining 68 per cent are in the public or private service sector or unemployed.

By European standards the country is small, of a similar size to Switzerland, Belgium or the Netherlands, but without their central location and occasionally decisive role in European history. As a small country on the edge of Europe, Denmark, along with its Scandinavian neighbours, Norway and Sweden, has traditionally been viewed as part of the periphery of Europe, just like the Eastern European countries and the Balkans. The following quotation from H. G. Koenigsberger's short history of Europe 1500–1789 illustrates this:

> Clearly, the history of Europe is comprehensible only if it is constantly seen in its relations to Europe's neighbours. For over a thousand years, after the end of the Roman Empire in the west, Europe was on the defensive: against the Muslim Arabs along its Mediterranean frontier in the south, against the seafaring Norsemen from Scandinavia in the north and west, and against successive attacks of different Asiatic peoples in the east, from the Huns, in the fifth century, to the Avars, Magyars, Mongols and, eventually and most persistently, the Turks.[2]

Here the Scandinavians, and thus the Danes, are considered as enemies of Latin Europe on a par with the Muslim Arabs, the Asians of the steppes and the Ottoman Turks. It was not until Christianity spread to Scandinavia over a thousand years ago that a process of assimilation started, slowly converting Denmark from being a hostile neighbour to that of being a part of European culture. Denmark's marginal geographical position in relation to the economic and cultural European core that is centred around the English Channel has also been of great significance in the more recent history of the country.

One other geopolitical factor deserves to be highlighted in order to understand the size of Denmark and why it has become what it is today. This is its ambiguous location. From a historical perspective the country is both a Baltic power and part of mainland Europe. The first entailed a strong preoccupation over many centuries with the balance of power in the Baltic and resulted in a centuries-long rivalry with Sweden, the other major Baltic power. The second, especially after the unification of Germany in the second half of the nineteenth century, has been of critical importance for the international standing of the country, and still is. A strong, powerful and united Germany to the immediate south forced Denmark to act according to German, and thus European, conditions to a much greater degree than before. In some ways Denmark's position from the middle of the nineteenth century resembles that of Scotland with its powerful neighbour, England, to the south.

From a longer historical perspective, the double position and role of Denmark can perhaps best be illustrated by the fact that the Danish kings were also Dukes of Holstein until 1864 and so had European interests to safeguard within the framework of the Holy Roman Empire until its dissolution in 1806, and afterwards in regard to Wilhelmine Germany. At the same time, right up to the middle of the nineteenth century, the kings obtained a significant part of their income from the Sound Dues, which were tolls levied on ships passing through Øresund. In itself this was a symbol of their dominance over the Baltic. So, the Danish kings were at one and the same time northern German princes and leading players in the Baltic region. This double position on the threshold of two very separate worlds has left an indelible mark on the historical destiny of Denmark.

Denmark's current commonwealth with the geographically remote Faroe Islands and the arctic Greenland is in many ways an anomaly, but it also serves as a reminder that the small, homogenous nation which is the Denmark of today is the product of a long historical development which can best be described as a process of reduction.

At the start of the period treated in this volume, the kings of Denmark held sway over a much greater territory than today, under the House of Oldenborg. First and foremost, after the personal union of 1380 the kingdom included Norway and its extensive North Atlantic possessions – Greenland, Iceland and the Faroe Islands. From 1536 Norway became formally integrated, virtually a province. The core area of Denmark also included the Scanian provinces on the southern tip of the Scandinavian peninsula and Gotland, the large island in the Baltic. The duchies of Schleswig and Holstein were also included in this huge state, of which Copenhagen was the capital, commanding the most important sea route into the Baltic, the Øresund.

In other words, this was an enormous North Atlantic–Baltic empire, stretching from the North Cape to the River Elbe in the south – a distance just as big as that from the Elbe to Gibraltar – and from the arctic Greenland in the north-west to Gotland in the east. This huge, unified kingdom extended over several climatic belts and ruled a very diverse population: Eskimos, Norwegians, Danes and Germans, each of whom spoke their own native tongue, lived in very different climates and had very different cultures. In reality the difference in lifestyle between the prosperous Scanian farmers and the hunters of Greenland was just as great as that between the olive farmers of sunny Italy and the foresters of the dense, dark Swedish forests.

The history of Denmark over the last 500 years is principally the story of how this extensive and diverse unified empire, held together by the sovereignty of the Danish crown and regular shipping, slowly disintegrated under the changing circumstances of the times, with the dissolution of the component parts resulting finally in there only remaining the small core area which is today called Denmark. This huge process of disintegration and reduction, critical to an understanding of modern Denmark, is one of the principal themes of this account.

THE DANES, ACCORDING TO ROBERT MOLESWORTH

Another theme is to attempt a historical explanation of the habits and mentality of the modern Danes. Both strands are, just like the country in which they live, the result of a long historical process, the course of which over the last 500 years will be traced here. However, describing oneself objectively is virtually impossible, and so perhaps a good place to start would be a brief description of the nature of the Danish lifestyle and 'national character' as observed by various foreigners at various times. It is probably most suitable to start with the best known historical description of Denmark and the Danish, Robert Molesworth's famous book *An Account of Denmark as it was in the year 1692*, which was published in 1694.

The Irish-born English diplomat Robert Molesworth (1656–1725) was British Ambassador to the absolutist Danish Court in Copenhagen for a few years around 1690. Shortly after his return home from his duties, which did not proceed exactly harmoniously, he wrote his Account, in which he collected his impressions of the country, its people and political regime. This was intended to be of instructive value for Molesworth's fellow countrymen, as shown by the following quotation:

Some naturalists observe that there is no plant or insect, how venomous or mean soever, but is good for something towards the use of Man if rightly applied: in the like manner it may be said, that several useful lessons may be learnt, conducing to the benefit of

Mankind, from this Account of Denmark, provided things be taken by the right handle.

As his choice of words suggests, he did not entertain a particularly high opinion of Denmark or the Danes, and this impression is confirmed elsewhere in the text – 'The language is very ungrateful,' he wrote, 'and not unlike the Irish in its whining complaining tone.' He described the Danes as desperately poor and oppressed by a tyrannical absolutist regime which in the course of just one generation had reduced the once free-born Nordic population to a condition of slavery. He found the climate quite simply odious, and described the capital of the country, Copenhagen, as a dirty little town with no sign of the character that distinguished other large European cities.[3]

The real purpose behind Molesworth's *Account* was evidently to use Denmark as a terrifying example in warning his countrymen against welcoming an absolutist regime and thus giving up the right of self-determination, and so his description of the conditions in Denmark can hardly be taken at face value. In addition, his own experience of Denmark was mainly limited to Copenhagen and its surroundings. Thus, his description cannot really be taken as comprehensive either of Denmark or the Danes in 1692. It should rather be seen as the hasty attack of a disappointed diplomat against a regime he detested and against which he wished to warn the political decision-makers of his own country. Even so, the substance of his critical observations ought not to be dismissed out of hand, and the discussion later on in this book about the conditions in Denmark in the late seventeenth century and the events which created them may be regarded as the present author's assessment of the extent to which Molesworth was justified from a scholarly point of view, and how far he overshot the mark.

SIR JAMES MELLON AND THE DANISH TRIBE

The same critical attitude cannot be considered to apply to another, later, account of Denmark and the Danes, written by another British Ambassador to Copenhagen long after Molesworth. This was Sir James Mellon, whose knowledge of the country came not only from his time as Ambassador in the 1980s, but also from a long period in the country as a student, especially at Aarhus University. Almost exactly 300 years after Molesworth's book, in 1992 Sir James published a very personal account of the country and its inhabitants as they appeared to a sympathetic, keen British observer. The book was called *About old Denmark . . . A Description of Denmark in the Year of our Lord 1992.*

Sir James introduced his account, both affectionate and perspicacious at the same time, with the statement that in his eyes marked the most significant characteristic of the Danes, and one which formed the underlying thesis of his book: 'The Danes are not a nation . . . they are a tribe, this is the strength of their fellowship and the reason that they have unshakeable trust in each other.' He continued to explain:

> When talking about the idea of a 'nation', this also involves the idea of fellowship, but a nation requires if not more, then at least something different. The Danes have certainly developed and adapted. They have travelled around the world and forged commercial and cultural links in all corners of it. But they have never found their way to a synthesis of dissimilar elements, which is what is required for a proper nation. Their unity as a people is in fact due to the emphasis on uniformity. So this is not 'both and', but 'either or'.[4]

So, according to Sir James Mellon, the Danes are not a nation in its normal sense, but a tribe, whose behaviour strongly reminded him of the tribal behaviour he saw amongst the Ashanti in Ghana during his posting to West Africa between 1978 and 1983. Amongst the Danes he found the same concern for the weaker members of society, the same propensity for consensus and uniformity, the same avoidance of conflict, and the same implicit faith that political results should be achieved through discussion and compromise rather than the face-to-face conflicts which are otherwise characteristic of parliamentary democracy. All of these traits, and most Danes would nod in agreement with his analysis, he attributed to the tribal awareness of the Danish population, which in his view make Denmark and the Danes quite special amongst modern European nations.

Of course, it is open to discussion quite how powerful an explanation this simple thesis ultimately is. As shown above, the historical Danish Empire was far from being homogenous, and conflict, both internal and external, has played as big a part in the history of Denmark as in that of any other nation. The strong tribal awareness postulated as an underlying element in contemporary Danish self-perception must therefore at least be considered as a relatively new cultural product and the result of a particular historical development.

However, there is little doubt that Sir James Mellon, in his entertaining way, has identified an important trait in outsiders' common perception of the country and its inhabitants: Denmark is a small, insignificant, comfortable country, peopled by a homogenous tribe whose members more or less all know each other, and even the most controversial political issues are resolved peaceably with the tacit understanding that we will still all be here afterwards.

It is a major concern of the following account to call into question and differentiate this stereotype. A significant aim of this history is to examine and explain from a historical perspective how far, how and why Denmark has become the country about which Sir James Mellon thought he could see and reflect upon so fondly and entertainingly in 1992. The account will describe how modern Denmark came into being, with special emphasis on some key elements in the process of modernisation which from 1500 on slowly transformed Danish society from being agrarian and always on the verge of famine to a prosperous, modern, industrial welfare society. The elements of particular interest – and so fundamental to the history – are sketched out in the next section.

SOME PRINCIPAL THEMES OF THIS HISTORY

The current modest size of the country is, as mentioned before, directly related to its historical position as the gateway between the Baltic and the North Sea. The centuries of rivalry with Sweden for supremacy in the North were to a considerable extent the result of this situation. This rivalry started as early as the dissolution of the Kalmar Union in 1523, but became more serious from the middle of the sixteenth century and can only really be said to have been resolved at the end of the Great Northern War in 1720–1. During these 200 years the conflict of interests with Sweden was by far and away the most important foreign and security policy issue and virtually decisive for Denmark's role on the international stage.

After the long, and for Denmark, relatively peaceful, eighteenth century, the emerging German nation state imprinted itself ever more strongly on the agenda for Denmark's foreign and security policy. The German moves towards national unity from the beginning of the nineteenth century led directly to the first Schleswigian War, 1848–50, and then to the national catastrophe for Denmark in 1864, when the duchies of both Schleswig and Holstein were lost. Since then, the relationship with its large German neighbour has been the predominant factor in Danish security policy, and this took on an even greater importance after the reunification of Germany in 1989. The current position of Denmark and its contemporary role on the international stage can only truly be understood on the basis of these historical changes in foreign policy.

It is also natural to take into account a range of psychological and material factors in the development of Danish society itself when attempting to test Sir James Mellon's tribal thesis and to put it into a historical perspective. In rough chronological order, the first influence to identify is the Reformation and the Lutheran Church organisation introduced in 1536, which left a deep mark, not just in terms of the growing mental distance from Catholic Europe, but also because of the strong emphasis on spiritual life and the attitude of the Danish people towards authority, both spiritual and temporal.

Then the 188 years of absolutist rule left a deep and still visible imprint on the country and its people. Absolutism as a form of rule was introduced through a bloodless coup in 1660 and was only removed in 1848, through an equally bloodless revolution which laid the foundations for the current democratic constitution. The consistent endeavours of absolutist rule aimed at uniformity and transparency in regard to the subjects are part of the inheritance which outlasted this period to become one of the foundation stones of the modern welfare society.

The same applies to the consistent egalitarianisation of the Danish landed-estate system. This was initiated in the second half of the seventeenth century, with a view to making the taxation system more efficient, but resulted in a unique structure of landed estates which extended through the entire country, with a very few exceptions. Around 600 roughly equally sized manor farms came into existence, each surrounded by a number of equally large tenant farms, which took care of most of the agricultural production. This created the typical Danish farm, which was the basic production unit for centuries, and, after the agrarian reforms at the end of the eighteenth century, provided the foundation for the rise of an independent class of land-owning farmers which, from the mid-nineteenth century, became the most powerful political force in the country.

The two most significant nationwide movements of the nineteenth century also had an impact. These were the movement for popular enlightenment, through the Folk High Schools, and the co-operative movement, each and both of which transformed the majority of the Danish population from being servile and inarticulate subjects to vocal politically involved citizens. It is virtually impossible to understand the nature of contemporary Danish society without considering these two movements which politicised the rural population.

It is also of considerable importance to include the late industrialisation of the country. Compared to other European countries, the industrialisation of Denmark was rather recent. It is only from the end of the nineteenth century that it makes any sense to talk about an industrial sector of any significance, and it was only the huge wave of modernisation in the decades after the Second World War that moved the country from the agricultural to the industrial. The relative lateness of the process of industrialisation is still seen in modern Danish economic life, as there is a very large industrial sector still based on agriculture and a predominance of small to medium-sized enterprises. Both of these factors had significant consequences for the living conditions of Danes and the way in which things are organised. The social divisions in Danish society are much smaller than in many other places.

This also applies to political divisions, which in turn leads to the last factor which has to be included as a fundamental element in this description of contemporary Denmark, and must also be kept in mind when assessing Sir James Mellon's tribal thesis. This is the fact that the Danish Social Democrats, unlike similar political parties in many other countries, have never been able to achieve an overall majority. This has been principally because the party has never really appealed to the agricultural lower classes, the smallholders and labourers, who have instead turned to the Social Liberal Party. This parliamentary reality has prevented the Social Democrats from implementing a hardline policy, and has forced them rather to build consensual alliances in order to form a government. This practically consistent style of negotiation by the parties in power during the twentieth century has had a decisive effect on the Danish political climate and on the peculiar nature of the Danish welfare state.

THE HISTORY OF DENMARK

The main themes of the following history are the result of a consideration of all the factors briefly outlined above, which together help to explain the way in which Denmark has developed. Chapter 2 deals with the change from being a medium-sized Northern European conglomerate state to the small nation state of today, and attempts to provide a historical explanation at the level of international politics for the current nature and size of the country. Chapters 3 and 4 examine the internal politics, from the aristocratic princely state which existed from around 1500 to the social democratic welfare state which completed its development in the late twentieth century. Chapter 5 looks at spiritual life in its broadest sense, with the evolution of the Church as the fulcrum. The following two chapters treat material development and attempt to trace that development from an agrarian society characterised by shortage and want, to the excessive affluence of the modern industrial society. The concluding Chapter 8 takes a wider perspective on psychological constructs, with a particular emphasis on trying to find the answer to the question of when Danes actually considered themselves as Danes, in regard on the one hand to the Germans or Poles, and on the other to simply being inhabitants of Jutland, Fyn or Zealand. There is also a discussion as to whether it is possible to identify a particularly Danish way of doing things. There is also a consideration of whether such a specially 'Danish way' is the result of the historical experience of the Danes, or whether it relates to an innate tribal awareness amongst Danes, such as that suggested by Sir James Mellon. The overall aim of these chapters is not to present a detailed and comprehensive history of Denmark in the traditional way, but to take a few, hopefully well-chosen, themes from the last 500 years of Danish history and try to depict modern Denmark and its inhabitants from a historical standpoint. That is the principal objective. If during the course of this endeavour other historical insights are presented which may be of interest in themselves to the reader, then this can only be advantageous.

This introduction should conclude with some remarks on the historical boundaries of this book. Naturally, these are not unimportant, and in themselves reflect definite interpretations and opinions of what is important in this context and what is not.

The later limit, the present day, is virtually obvious. The starting point of 1500 is, however, an expression of a definite understanding of the forces which have created modern Denmark. Even though the history of Denmark obviously has its roots firmly in the Middle Ages, it can be persuasively argued that the modern history of the country first truly began when the most powerful medieval institutions of the Baltic region – the Kalmar Union, the economic hegemony of the Hanseatic League and the dominance of the Teutonic Orders in the eastern Baltic – collapsed in the decades surrounding 1500. The result was that the region lacked a consistently organised power, and so opened up to the formation of new states in Renaissance style. Rivalry to fill the power vacuum arose, and this became the principal theme through the subsequent centuries, and thus an important part of the long process of modernisation which has marked out the history of both the Baltic region and the whole of Europe over the last 500 years. Therefore, if an arbitrary division has to be made, the year 1500 would seem suitable. From the start of the sixteenth century, the impact of these new dynamic forces, which we normally group together under the headings Renaissance and Reformation, was strongly felt, while at the same time the ideas, utopias and institutions of the medieval world slowly crumbled. Just as the history of modern Sweden is normally considered to have started with Gustav Vasa's definitive break with the Kalmar Union in 1523, so the history of modern Denmark can be said to have started at the same point.

This history therefore starts with this collapse. It could indeed be argued that it also ends with one – indeed in two ways: one the incipient collapse of the Social Democratic welfare state as we have known it since the 1960s, the other the erosion of the Danish nation state under pressure from the new world order resulting from globalisation and the rapid expansion of the European Union . There are many signs that these changes herald a completely new phase in the history of Denmark – a phase which may well one day mean that it becomes meaningless to talk of Denmark and of Danes as separate entities, just as it was in the Middle Ages. So the history which follows is in a certain sense the history of a limited period of half a millennium when a distinct country called Denmark existed and there was a distinct Danish state. This was only the case in a vague sense before then, and perhaps this will only remain the case in a limited sense in the coming millennium. Thus, perhaps in the truest sense, this is the history of Denmark.

2

Foreign and Security Policy: From the Gatekeeper of the Baltic to a Midget State

THE COLLAPSE OF THE BALTIC SYSTEM AROUND 1500

From many perspectives, the Baltic region around 1500 was closed off from the rest of the world and firmly rooted in medieval institutions. The three Scandinavian kingdoms had been united since 1397 in a typically medieval union – the Kalmar Union – which brought them together through a loose personal agreement under the regency of the Danish royal dynasty. From the very beginning of the Union, the assemblies which made political decisions in the three very different kingdoms recognised the sovereignty of the Danish House of Oldenborg, but this had little effect on their local policies.

The real power in the area was neither the King of the Union nor the local aristocrats. The true political and economic influence was the Hanseatic League, in itself another typical medieval institution, or more precisely the powerful merchants of the Wendic Hanseatic towns led by the rich and flourishing Lübeck.

This mighty cartel totally dominated the trade to and from the Baltic region. Large volumes of foodstuffs and raw materials from the Baltic region passed through Lübeck on their way to the Western European markets. There was a smaller flow in the opposite direction of refined and manufactured European products and imports from distant regions for sale on the modest markets of the Baltic. The Hanseatic towns actually maintained a strict political and economic hegemony over the whole Baltic region, treating it virtually as a 'back garden' with exclusive

access for Hanseatic merchants. In comparison with continental Europe, the Baltic region was a closed world. The Hanseatic barrier was in many ways as effective as the much later Iron Curtain.

Further to the east in the Baltic, and thus of less immediate importance for Denmark, another typical medieval institution held sway. This was the powerful Teutonic Order, whose organising influence reached from the centre in what are now the Baltic States far out into the Baltic and deep into Eastern Europe. This mighty feudal institution closed off the Baltic Sea region to the east just as effectively as the Hanseatic League did to the south and west.[1]

For centuries, these powerful products of the medieval world held both the Baltic region and the Scandinavian kingdoms in such an iron grip that it is hardly an exaggeration to say that the Danish kings of the Union did not so much rule by the grace of God as by that of the Hanseatic League and the rulers of the Teutonic Order. Around 1500, this world structure was on the brink of a downfall which was radically to alter the fundamental conditions for the Scandinavian kingdoms, including Denmark.

It is very difficult to isolate one particular cause of the decline which gradually took place over the decades after 1500. The collapse of the Hanseatic League and the Teutonic Order can in reality be seen as a local manifestation of the general development of Europe, which was experiencing an overall collapse of the existing system. There was a growing crisis in the Catholic Church, an imminent schism, and a weakening of imperial power at the expense of the nascent individual states. In short, there was a general breakdown of the central medieval utopia of united, universal Christianity, the republic of Christ, under the leadership of the Catholic Pope and the Holy Roman Emperor. This caused the feudal institutions throughout Europe to teeter, while the modern, territorially bounded princely states gradually took over. The end of the Kalmar Union, the drawn-out death throes of the Teutonic Order, and the weakening grip of the Hanseatic towns on the Baltic region were local symptoms of the overall dissolution of the old medieval European norms and values.

At a more concrete level, it is reasonable to point to the extensive redistribution of trade routes to, from and within Europe during these years which resulted from the Turkish blockade of the old trade routes to the Orient and the discoveries which opened sea routes to the Orient and America. From a wider European perspective, this meant that the old overland trading routes through Central Europe lost ground to the new sea routes along the European Atlantic coast. Over the longer term, this shifted the economic fulcrum of the world from northern Italy to Western Europe. The future belonged to the new seafaring nations of the Netherlands and England, and instead of Venice, Florence and Milan, the trading centres became London, Amsterdam and Antwerp.

As these cities and their hinterlands became centres of trade, they became highly urbanised, experienced an enormous growth in population, and accumulated power and wealth on a scale hitherto unseen. The rapidly growing densely populated areas became more and more dependent on importing food and raw materials. As early as the beginning of the sixteenth century, Europe exhibited a completely new economic distribution. Western Europe became a highly developed area of consumers, while Northern and Eastern Europe lagged behind as producers of food and raw materials. The flow of basic goods such as grain and shipbuilding materials from east to west increased dramatically in this period. This also spelled the death of the Hanseatic towns' monopoly on Baltic trade.

Neither Lübeck nor the other Hanseatic towns along the Baltic were capable of coping with this strongly increasing flow of goods with the means of transport they had available. Within just a few decades they had become a commercial sideline, and entered a long-term slump. The English and Dutch merchants took over more and more of the transport to and from the Baltic themselves. They were also able to take advantage of the great improvements in marine technology which had been made for sailing the Atlantic. A rapidly increasing number of English and Dutch commercial vessels sailed round the north of Jutland down into the Danish inner waters and continued through the Øresund to Baltic destinations. This became the principal shipping route for the following centuries, while the old route via Lübeck and Northern Germany slowly but surely fell into disuse. With the same inevitability, the Baltic gradually changed character from being an isolated area exclusively under Hanseatic control to being an open sea, freely navigated by vessels from the big Western seafaring nations. This new pattern gave Denmark a new role as a gateway.

DENMARK AS A GATEWAY

These huge changes in the European and local economic and political structure were of critical importance to Denmark. With the collapse of the old powers, the country, like its Swedish neighbour, was left to find its own place in the new world order. This in fact was the beginning of a costly and protracted process of modernisation which slowly changed the country from an isolated Hanseatic backyard into a modern European nation state.

The most visible political symptom of the new order was the fall of the Kalmar Union. The Union had actually been languishing in step with the decline in the power of the Hanseatic towns for a long time. The last Union king, Christian II (r. 1513–23) desperately tried to liquidate the Swedish elite hostile to the Union with the Stockholm Bloodbath in 1520, but in fact this just hastened the process. When Gustav Vasa (r. 1523–60), the leader of the Swedish separatist movement, was hailed as king of Sweden in 1523, the Union died completely, despite later Danish attempts to resuscitate it.

It was replaced by two independent sovereign states, the new Vasa Sweden and the rump of the Union, the twin monarchy of Denmark and Norway. Each had important and essentially opposing interests in the Baltic and so treated each other as mortal foes. The struggle between Denmark and Sweden for mastery of the Baltic – *dominium maris Baltici* – was to become from then on for the next two centuries the most dominant factor in the foreign policies of both countries.

Also, because of the changes in international trade routes mentioned earlier, Denmark suddenly found itself in an unfamiliar key position in the European political landscape. As we have seen, the new patterns of trade made the main Danish sea passage, the Øresund, the principal route for Baltic trade, and thus Denmark held the keys to the Baltic. This geographical position gave Denmark the function of a gatekeeper. For good and ill, this made a deep mark not only on the future destiny of the country, but even on its nature and extent.

Denmark now gained a role in wider European politics completely different and more exposed than previously. This new position was emphasised further as the Baltic changed from being fairly insignificant in a European context to being an area of great strategic importance. The region also took on a new significance in providing resources for the growing Western naval powers.

To suggest a modern parallel, the role of the Baltic in European politics might be compared to that of the Persian Gulf in contemporary global strategic thinking. The surrounding region contains one of the modern world's key resources, oil, in easily accessible and abundant quantities. The Western industrial nations cannot function without oil. Without access to this essential resource, even the world's only remaining superpower, the United States, would soon collapse. This naturally means that the Middle Eastern oil-producing region is extremely sensitive and that powerful interests clash there.

The Baltic region took on a similar strategic importance in early modern European politics. Reasonably unfettered access to, and a certain control over, the resources of the region, such as basic foodstuffs and shipbuilding materials, was critical for the naval powers. The English fleet, which was fortunate in defeating the Spanish Armada in 1588, was to a great extent constructed of materials from the Baltic region. Without the constant supplies of grain from the Baltic, the populations of the Netherlands and England would have perished of famine. Thus, what happened in the Baltic, and how the power balance developed, was more than just a local issue, but a matter of the utmost strategic importance for the Western naval powers. During the sixteenth century this meant that the Baltic was a sensitive strategic area from a European-wide perspective and it could not be left to its own fate or to the discretion of the regional powers. Denmark was by no means of the least interest in this regard, due to its strategic location at the neck of the Baltic. In other words, the collapse of the Hanseatic League and the opening up of the Baltic gave Denmark great significance in European politics. The process of Europeanisation, alongside the process of modernisation already mentioned, became a powerful dynamo in transforming Denmark from a medieval ecclesiastical province into a European nation state.[2]

In step with this development, the Western naval powers in turn took precedence as the controlling power in the Baltic in the vacuum left by the collapse of the Hanseatic hegemony. First, it was the Dutch who played an active role in Baltic politics up to the end of the seventeenth century and for long periods exercised effective hegemony. Then it was the turn of Britain. This was perhaps most clearly and dramatically demonstrated by the British attacks on Copenhagen in 1801 and 1807. The constant attention and occasional direct interventions of the big powers were critical for Denmark's position and role as well as for the establishment of the contemporary political geography of Scandinavia. The true dynamic force in this process of change was in the first instance the virtually permanent state of war between Denmark and Sweden up to 1720.

DANISH–SWEDISH RIVALRY, 1563–1720

These conflicts, played out in the shadow of the increasing interest the big powers were taking in the region, came sharply into focus the moment the Hanseatic League's loss of hegemony became obvious, which it did after Lübeck unsuccessfully intervened in the Danish Civil War, 1534–6, commonly known as the Counts' War. The initial cause of the conflicts was the question of which of the two Scandinavian powers – the new Swedish Vasa state or the remains of the Union, Denmark and Norway – should dominate the Nordic region and take mastery of the Baltic. For the Danish king, this was principally a matter of coercing Sweden back into the old Union, whereas for the young Vasa state it was a question of ensuring survival against its Scandinavian neighbour, which had the country locked in on three sides and was blocking its access to the west. As the rivalry continued, and the Swedish military superiority became obvious by 1630, it changed into a struggle for Denmark to survive in the shadow of the temporary Swedish great power built up by Gustavus Adolphus II (r. 1611–32) and his successors. It was only with the peace treaty of 1720 after the Great Northern War that a new balance emerged between the formerly mighty Sweden and the greatly diminished Denmark.

The long-lasting confrontation between Denmark and Sweden falls into three clearly divided phases.[3] In the first, marked by two wars – the Nordic Seven Years War (1563–70) and the Kalmar War (1611–13), both started by the Danes – the Danish intention was to force Sweden back into the Union. They did not succeed. Both ended as pure wars of attrition, and neither produced any changes in the borders.

The second phase started after Christian IV's (r. 1588–1648) unfortunate venture of 1625–9 into the Thirty Years War, which can be interpreted as the Danish king's decisive strategic response to the Swedish expansion of power along the Baltic coasts of what is now Finland, the Baltic States and Poland. Gustavus Adolphus's systematic conquests along the Baltic coast were a patent threat to Danish control of the Baltic, and indeed to Denmark itself, but Denmark had been so enfeebled by the fiasco in Germany that the Danish king was hard put to find a response. Sweden was clearly in the ascendant, while Denmark was definitely on the way down. So to a large extent, the critical issue in the second phase of the conflict from 1630 to 1660 was actually whether Denmark could survive as a sovereign state, or whether it would simply be annexed by the Swedish Baltic Empire.

This phase was similarly marked by two, or, it could be said, three, wars. These were Torstensson's War, 1643–5 and the Karl Gustav Wars, 1657–60. The first was an unexpected lightning attack by Sweden on Denmark with the aim of snatching the mediating role of the Danish king at the peace negotiations in Westphalia which were an attempt to bring the Thirty Years War to an end. The Swedish attack was completely successful. The action effectively stopped Christian IV's mediation, which he was attempting to exploit to rob the Swedes of the gains they had won by force during the Thirty Years War. In addition, Denmark had to cede the province of Halland to the Swedes. Just as seriously, the previously powerful Danish fleet had been so depleted in the naval battles of the war, that it could no longer defend Danish territory and royal possessions against attack. Denmark thus slipped down a rung in the table of European powers. This demotion proved to be permanent.

The Karl Gustav Wars, which ironically were again declared by Denmark, fully confirmed this come-down. The astonishing boldness of the Swedish king in fording the ice-covered Danish waters in the harsh winter of 1658 and his subsequent siege of the capital seemed to have sealed Denmark's fate. Only the unexpected death of Karl X Gustav (r. 1654–60) in 1660 and the intervention of the Western powers prevented the country's complete demise as a sovereign state. The price was the surrender to Sweden of the old Norwegian regions of Jämtland, Härjedalen and Bohuslän and all of the Scanian provinces, an area amounting to around a third of the monarchy's total territory.

Thus, the border between Denmark and Sweden was no longer the extensive forests of Småland, but the narrow sea passage of the Øresund, which correspondingly changed its status from that of an inland Danish strait to an international waterway. This shift has led to the situation today, where the capital of the country is on the border. The Western naval powers, with the Netherlands in the vanguard, thus achieved a solution in terms of Scandinavian political geography which was optimal for them, namely that the most important sea passage to the Baltic was no longer controlled by one powerful gatekeeper, but by two rival powers. This meant that the Baltic was now properly opened up for the naval powers and there were ideal opportunities to control it over the heads of the local powers. There is an old saying that when two people fight, a third person laughs. The two contestants, Denmark and Sweden, had weakened each other through their constant rivalry over the centuries, and in turn invited the naval powers to form alliances, so that in the end they called the tune of Scandinavian politics. The naval powers, and especially the Netherlands, could well laugh. The permanent conflict in Scandinavia had given them a wonderful opportunity to bring the Baltic in under their own mercantilistic policy, which was the foundation of their power. Just as the local wars around the Persian Gulf often force the great powers to intervene and virtually put the local leaders under tutelage, the final outcome of the long rivalry between Denmark and Sweden was that by the middle of the seventeenth century, the Baltic region was virtually a colony of the naval powers to the west.

Given that the situation after the peace accord in 1660 was favourable to the naval powers, it is no surprise that despite all the exertions and sacrifices, the final phase of the conflict between Denmark and Sweden ended with the status quo. This phase, which continued until 1720, was also marked by two wars, the Scanian War, 1675–9 and the Great Northern War, 1709–20, or once again three wars, if the short pointless skirmish of 1700 is included. Both of the wars were overshadowed by the two large European conflicts waged by Louis XIV (r. 1643–1715) – the Dutch Wars and the War of the Spanish Succession, and can in many respects be considered as reactions to these.

Both started with Danish declarations of war and can be interpreted as a Danish attempt to reconquer the territories lost to the now ailing Swedish great power under cover of the turmoil in Europe. Although there were some moderate military successes, the overall project did not work. The borders of the Nordic countries remained where they were set in 1660 when the great powers intervened. This meant that Denmark had now been definitively driven out of the Scandinavian peninsula. On the other hand, Sweden was in ruins as a result of the desperate and unsuccessful attempt by Karl XII (r. 1697–1718), the warrior king, to re-establish a Swedish sphere of influence in Eastern Europe to replace the precarious alliance with the now weakened France. Sweden was once again reduced to the position of a medium-sized power, in the same league as Denmark, which thus no longer needed to feel threatened by its neighbour.

After 1720, the long rivalry between Denmark and Sweden gave way to a completely new balance of power in the Baltic, which brought a stability which had not existed since the Middle Ages. In the sixteenth and seventeenth centuries the incessant conflict between Denmark and Sweden, along with the constant surveillance and occasional direct intervention of the Netherlands, had dominated the agenda for the region. This agenda was radically different after 1720. Now the latent threat to both Sweden and Denmark was the new Russia under Peter the Great's energetic leadership. The emergence of the new expansionist Eastern power, which had become a significant power in the Baltic during the Great Northern War, was manifested by the foundation of St Petersburg in 1703. This made the earlier disagreements between Denmark and Sweden pale into insignificance, and pushed the two countries into a peaceful relationship in which they abandoned their territorial ambitions towards each other. Except for a single trivial episode in 1788, a bloodless state of war 1808–14, and the occasional clashes around international football games, these peaceful relations have continued unbroken to the present day.

For Denmark, the rivalry with its Scandinavian neighbour had proved painful and expensive. A lot of the Norwegian border territory and the Scanian provinces had been lost. The Danish dream of mastery over the Baltic had been completely crushed. Instead, Denmark was slowly forced to retreat from the eastern Baltic, where the Danish kings' merchant navy had previously sailed as in home waters. The remaining Danish sea territory was now reduced pretty much just to the Baltic west of Bornholm and the inner Danish waters. Even this could hardly be defended without external help. Denmark had now really become a sparrow amongst hawks in European terms.

Russia's appearance in the arena of European power politics left Denmark's foreign policy in a permanent dilemma, although this was not insoluble for so long as the world order established by the Peace of Westphalia in 1648 remained in place. In fact it did so until the French Revolution and the Napoleonic Wars. Denmark's location by the access routes to the Baltic also meant that it was precariously situated exactly where Russian and British interests ran up against each other. This required a finely judged foreign policy to balance the now dominant naval power to the west against the new strong land power in the east. Denmark's survival was dependent on maintaining friendly relations with both. Within the ordered world following the Peace of Westphalia, this balancing act was so successful that after 1720 the country enjoyed the longest continuous time of peace in the whole of its history. The system only collapsed in the chaos wrought by the Napoleonic Wars, when Denmark lost this balance, and so lost yet more territory.

THE WARS WITH BRITAIN AND THE DISSOLUTION OF THE DUAL MONARCHY, 1800–30

Far into the eighteenth century it seemed as if Denmark could succeed in keeping out of the conflicts between the big powers which otherwise characterised the European history of the century. By a whisker, the country managed to avoid being drawn into the Prussian Seven Years War (1756–63), and during the colonial wars between Britain and France, Danish merchants profited handsomely by transporting goods for the warring powers under the country's neutral flag. However, just how fragile this policy of neutrality was became painfully clear in the subsequent seismic clash between Napoleon and Britain. The entire foundation of neutrality was finally shattered when in 1801 the British government decided to smash the neutrality pact between Denmark, Sweden and Russia to gain access to the Baltic.[4] When the British fleet under Admiral Nelson appeared in the Øresund off Copenhagen, quickly brushing off the Danish fleet and threatening to bombard the Danish capital, Denmark had no choice but to leave the neutrality pact and accept neutrality on British terms. Britain thus clearly showed that Denmark, and not least the straits of Denmark, fell within the British sphere of influence, and so there were very clear limits to the country's neutrality.

With Napoleon's apparently unstoppable advance across the European continent in the following years, Denmark's dilemma became ever-more pronounced. In 1806, when Napoleon started to blockade the continent against Britain, Denmark was quite literally caught between the devil and the deep blue sea. If Denmark chose to accede to the French demands to join the blockade, it would incur the wrath of Britain, and 1801 had already shown what that could mean. Defying France would be to risk the imminent invasion of Jutland and Sweden might take the opportunity to conquer Norway. This would have dismembered the dual monarchy.

The British were worried that Napoleon could take the not insignificant Danish fleet and turn it against them. To eliminate this risk, Britain struck again in 1807. A large British fleet once again appeared in the Øresund, with a strong expeditionary force on board. It landed to the north of Copenhagen without meeting any resistance worthy of mention and within a few days had Copenhagen encircled. Then Copenhagen was heavily bombarded, suffering extensive destruction and loss of life. After several days under fire, the city surrendered and the troops left again, taking the whole Danish fleet with them. From that point on,

Denmark ceased to be a Baltic power of any importance. The necessary means – the fleet – had gone and would never be the same size again.

After this humiliation the Danish government had absolutely no choice but to throw in its lot with Napoleon and simply hope that he won. On the other hand, Sweden joined an alliance with Britain. Once again, as so often before, the two Nordic countries found themselves on opposite sides of a large European conflict. From 1808 they were formally at war with one another, but no military operations took place during this formal state of war.

The fate of the Napoleonic Empire was sealed with the catastrophic Russian campaign of 1812, and when the peace treaty was signed in 1814–15, Denmark was an ally of the losing side, and one of those who lost most. The de facto British dominance of Danish waters during the war had severed the two main territories of the monarchy, Denmark and Norway. With the peace, Sweden demanded control over Norway in compensation for losing Finland to Russia in 1809. The result was that Norway left the old union with Denmark and made a personal union with Sweden which lasted until 1905. The meagre compensation Denmark received for this huge loss was the tiny north-German county of Lauenburg.

Ignoring the distant and sparsely populated North Atlantic possessions of the Faroes, Iceland and Greenland, the upshot of the upheaval of the Napoleonic Wars for Denmark was that the multinational conglomerate state had disappeared, and Denmark had become a tiny bi-national statelet at the top of the north-German plain. The triangular national balance which had ensured stability for so long was no more. Remaining inside the borders of the state were just the dominant Danish population and a significant number of Germans in the prosperous and culturally advanced duchies. The steadily growing confrontation between these two parts of the population under the pressure of the increasingly aggressive nationalist movements in both Denmark and Germany formed a key part of the background to what many Danes, even today, consider the definitive national trauma: the loss of the duchies to Germany in 1864.

DENMARK AND THE UNIFICATION OF GERMANY, 1830–71

The nationalist revivals which swept through Europe in the nineteenth century, along with the waves of popular revolution in 1830 and 1848, were of critical importance for the remains of the conglomerate state under the House of Oldenborg, and led to its final dissolution.

One particular feature of the Westphalian system which collapsed in the wake of the Napoleonic Wars, but revived in a slightly altered form with the Vienna Congress in 1815, was the strong division of states in the German area. The existence of numerous small and medium-sized German states was virtually a condition for the system to function, as they served as a buffer between the great powers. The division of Germany was also a security advantage for Denmark, as it reduced the threat from the south and so allowed the Oldenborg state a dominant position in the north-German region.

This fundamental geopolitical situation radically changed with the unification of Germany during the nineteenth century. The movement towards unification began in the field of economics with the formation of the Customs Union in 1834, continued with the demands for national unity carried forward by the ever-more vocal nationalist movements and was finally completed at a political level by Bismarck and his *Realpolitik*. The culmination was the establishment of the Wilhelmine Empire in 1871.

This development created almost insurmountable problems for the Danish conglomerate state and its conservative, absolutist government. The new national consciousness created a previously unknown rift between the Danish and German inhabitants. The German section of the population impatiently followed the liberal-inspired triumphal progress of nationalism in Germany and wished to share in the democratic reforms which the German liberals championed. In other words, they wished to sever the link with the Danish-dominated conservative Oldenborg state and join the new big German national community.[5]

This led to the first Schleswigian War, 1848–50, which was actually a civil war in the Danish monarchy. This war ended with the defeat of the insurgents in Schleswig-Holstein, but in no way resolved the underlying conflict. In fact, this victory encouraged the Danes to overestimate their strength and power. This arrogance spread to the very heart of government, and so paved the way for the humiliating defeat in the Second Schleswigian War of 1864.

The full story of this brief but, for Denmark, momentous war contains an element of tragic inevitability. This stemmed from the radically changed circumstances that both the Danish and Prussian governments contended with in conducting foreign policy due to pressure from the nationalist movements and their ever-louder demands to influence matters which were previously the exclusive business of government cabinets.

In Berlin, Bismarck was embattled in a constitutional struggle with the liberal elements in the Prussian parliament. The defence budget was an important factor in this struggle, and Bismarck was anxiously seeking an opportunity to wage a victorious war to cut the Gordian knot and bring the liberal majority to heel. Such an opportunity arose in 1863, when the Danish government, under great pressure from a public still heady with the victory in the First Schleswigian War, felt compelled to extend the Danish constitution to include Schleswig in order to truly incorporate the duchy under the monarchy. This decision was a complete volte-face in regard to the international accords that Denmark had made at the end of the First Schleswigian War. The provisions of these were that both duchies should continue to recognise the sovereignty of the Danish king, but remain constitutionally separate from the monarchy.

Extending Danish sovereignty to include Schleswig put the Danish government in breach of all international law. This invalidated the guarantee of the great powers for the peace treaty of 1852, and left the door open for a German military intervention. In other words, the Danish politicians, pressed by public opinion, handed Bismarck the excuse for the quick and easy war he wanted on a silver platter.[6]

He took it with determination and skill. In the winter and spring of 1864, he and his Austrian ally drove the outnumbered Danish forces out of both duchies. The Danish government was isolated and in a state of panic and their only option was to sue for peace on the best possible terms. The defeat was crushing and the Danish government was totally isolated. The support that Norway and Sweden had promised never materialised when the crunch came. So even the best possible conditions were harsh. Both duchies, including the 200,000 Danish speakers and sympathisers in North Schleswig, were incorporated into Bismarck's new Germany.

At a stroke, the Danish–German border moved several hundred kilometres north and cut across almost half of Jutland. The old border between the monarchy and the duchy of Schleswig, which ran along the course of the River Kongeå, now became the national boundary. This remained the case until the plebiscite of 1920, resulting from the Treaty of Versailles at the end of the First World War, when the northern part of Schleswig voted itself back into Denmark. This plebiscite created the current Danish–German border, and despite some tentative efforts from both sides, it has not moved since. The border also mirrors as precisely as is possible the true boundary between Danish and German, both in terms of language and disposition. What little remained of Denmark was as close-knit as could possibly be imagined in terms of a perfect nation state. There was a single nationality with a single language: Danish. The modern small, homogenous nation state of Denmark is thus the product of the catastrophe of 1864.

However, the price was nearly intolerable. The territory was reduced by a third and the number of inhabitants by two-fifths. It is therefore no wonder that the Danish government found it more than difficult to accept that this disaster was final. In the years immediately following 1864, people clung to the slender hope that there could be a resurgence with the help of the French. Once Bismarck routed Napoleon III in the Franco–Prussian War of 1870–1, this hope was finally shattered. It was only the rapid and total collapse of France that stopped Denmark from entering the war in support of the French. Had it done so, this would almost certainly have marked the end of Denmark as an independent state.

Indeed, after the defeat of France, many thoughtful observers wondered whether Denmark could survive at all in the long term as an independent state. Several of them predicted that Denmark would be divided up between Germany and Sweden, thinking that the western territories would be subsumed by Germany and the eastern by Sweden.

As is patently obvious, this did not actually happen. Nonetheless, this defeat had profound long-term consequences for Danish foreign policy over the next 70 years. We will return to this subject later. There were also significant consequences for Danish self-perception. These years of adversity gave birth to the peculiarly Danish image of Denmark as Lilliput, with a small and insignificant role to play, and which could do best by turning its back on the world. The sceptical attitude to the European Union and the fear of contact with the rest of Europe which subsequently dominated the debate about Europe in Denmark after the Second World War was born in these years.

So was the predominant historical understanding that Denmark's long fall from being a major Northern European power to becoming a tiny insignificant state was both unavoidable and inevitable. The generation of historians who dominated Danish historiography in the decades after the defeat of 1864 saw it as just the most recent of a long line of inevitable defeats which Denmark had suffered since Christian IV's defeat by general Tilly at Lutter am Barenberg in 1626. The lesson they drew was that wise political leaders in Denmark should adapt their policies to the fact that things always went wrong when the Danes tried to box above their weight. The historians' interpretation supported the easily despairing small-country attitude which became the salient feature of Danish politics and self-perception during the whole of the first half of the twentieth century. This mentality was summarised with a clarity bordering on cynicism by Erik Scavenius (1877–1962), who was Minister of Foreign Affairs (1913–20 and 1940–3) and for a short period (1942–3) Prime Minister during the German occupation of Denmark in 1940–5, when in 1948 he published his apology for the policy of concession to the German occupying forces of which he was one of the staunchest proponents. He started his book with the following statement:

There is a widespread perception in this country that Denmark's foreign policy is determined by the Danish government and parliament. However, that is only correct in so far as the formal decisions through which policy is expressed appear to be decisions of these bodies. In fact Danish foreign policy is determined by factors over which the Danish government and parliament can exert very little influence. The principal role of Danish foreign policy is thus to stay abreast of these factors and their interaction, and on this basis estimate the right moment to step in and try to benefit from the situation existing at any given time in promoting Denmark's interests.[7]

The power of the small state, or rather lack of it, could hardly be expressed more clearly. Nor could the basic doctrine of Danish foreign and security policy in the decades between 1864 and the Second World War be more concisely formulated.

FROM NEUTRALITY TO MEMBERSHIP OF NATO, 1870–1950

Defeat at the hands of Bismarck's Germany in 1864 left Denmark deeply dependent on the new German great power. From then on it was no longer possible for Denmark to pursue a foreign policy which conflicted with German interests, and changing governments right up to the fall in 1943 of the government during the German occupation, 1940–5, acted accordingly. When Germany subsequently established the strong naval base in the Baltic at Kiel, and then opened the Kiel Canal in 1895, making it possible to move naval forces rapidly from the

North Sea to the Baltic, there was no doubt at all that Germany was the dominant naval power in the western Baltic.

Fortunately for Denmark, the construction of the Kiel Canal also meant that the Danish straits became less strategically important to Germany. So blocking the Great Belt with mines in 1914 was a gesture sufficient to prevent the Germans taking matters into their own hands by invading Danish territory. This mine-laying, mainly aimed at the Western Allies, effectively eliminated the exposure of Denmark at the mouth of the Baltic, and allowed the country to remain uninvolved in the First World War. The weak defence measures between the wars, little more than a symbolic statement of neutrality rather than a serious effort to prevent its violation, were also dictated by the desire to avoid provoking Germany in any way. This desire took on extra weight with the return of Southern Jutland to Denmark after the plebiscite of 1920. With this, Denmark achieved what was felt to be possible in regard to Germany.

The Second World War eventually caused fundamental changes in the underlying principles of Danish defence policy. The German invasion of 9 April 1940, which led to the occupation of Denmark and Norway, hit the Danish government and people quite unprepared. Within a matter of hours the government and the king decided to capitulate and to agree to the German demand for a cessation of all military resistance. In return, the German government undertook to respect Denmark's political independence. So far as the Germans were concerned it was a 'peaceful occupation' with a view to securing the continued neutrality of Denmark. A few days later, British forces occupied the Faeroes and Iceland, and Greenland subsequently came under the effective control of the United States. As a result, for the remainder of hostilities, the territory of the kingdom of Denmark was controlled by three world powers that were at war.

In Denmark itself, the government's acceptance of the German ultimatum was the beginning of the so-called policy of collaboration that prevailed until the popular uprising in August 1943 which led to the resignation of the government and an end of official co-operation. It was a policy that enabled Denmark to retain her status as a formally sovereign, neutral state, whose relations with Germany were maintained through the respective foreign ministries, and where responsibility for the country's internal affairs remained with the Danish government. In other words, the fiction of neutrality was maintained, and it had the advantage that, unlike other occupied countries such as Norway and Holland, Denmark avoided the imposition of Nazi ideology in civic affairs. It also meant that the Danish National Socialist Party, the DNSAP, was politically irrelevant and that, from the outset, the main political parties entered into close co-operation to retain the democratic values on which society was based.

The cost of this unusual position was that the Danish economy had to adjust to the wartime needs of Germany. Effectively, all Danish exports of food products during the war were destined for Germany and it has been estimated that, on an annual basis, these exports corresponded to one month's need in that country. In a number of other ways it soon became clear that the pretence of neutrality was a complete fiction. Time after time the government caved in to new German demands. These included restrictions on the freedom of the press, the removal of openly anti-German politicians such as the Conservative Minister of Commerce, John Christmas Møller, and the leading Social Democrat, Hans Hedtoft, and the delivery of a number of motor torpedo boats to the German navy. The screw was given another turn after the German invasion of the Soviet Union on 22 June 1941, when, regardless of the constitution, the government banned the Danish Communist Party and interned its leaders after German pressure. At the same time, the government approved the formation of a voluntary army corps, the *Frikorps Denmark*, which, under German command, was put into action on the Eastern Front and, in Berlin in November 1941, Denmark signed the Anti-Comintern Pact.

At the same time as this string of humiliating concessions took place, there was a growing public scepticism about the government's policy of co-operation and, from 1942, it came under increasing pressure from a growing resistance which took the form of illegal activities directed against the occupying power and its Danish supporters. In the spring of 1942 the leader of the Conservative Party, Christmas Møller, escaped to England and for the remainder of the war his broadcasts through the BBC encouraged active resistance amongst his fellow Danes. At about the same time, the British Special Operations Executive (SOE), which was formed in 1940 in order to support and coordinate resistance in German occupied countries, at long last managed to achieve a foothold in Denmark. With the support of the SOE, the resistance gradually took the form of an armed illegal struggle against the occupying power and, during 1942–3, there was a gradual increase in the number of sabotage attacks.

This sabotage activity increased dramatically during the summer of 1943 and, at the same time, there was an outbreak of strikes in a number of provincial towns and cities which, more often than not, were orchestrated and led by members of the illegal Communist Party. In August this led to German demands for such strong countermeasures that the government decided to resign. On 29 August, in a wide-ranging response, the Germans disarmed the remainder of the Danish army and interned its officers, both commissioned and non-commissioned. The Danish navy was able to scupper most of its fleet and thereby prevented it falling into German hands. These dramatic events marked a very decisive end to the policy of collaboration. Thereafter, under the leadership of the illegal Danish Freedom Council, *Danmarks Frihedsråd*, which was formed in September 1943, to co-ordinate the armed struggle against the occupying power, Denmark found itself effectively at war with Germany and was thereby associated in all but name with the Western Allies. For the remainder of the occupation, the Freedom Council functioned as Denmark's unofficial government.

The general will to resist was strongly encouraged at the beginning of October 1943, when, contrary to all agreements that had been made, the Germans sought to intern the Danish Jews and transport them to concentration camps in Germany. In the event, the German plan was almost a complete failure. Through an enormous effort by many ordinary Danish men and women, in the days and weeks that followed, the great majority of the Danish Jews – over 7000 – were safely evacuated to neutral Sweden, and only a few hundred fell into German hands. That action alone opened people's eyes to the true nature of the German regime and caused the numbers in the active resistance groups to increase dramatically. It has been estimated that, by the end of the war, the resistance movement under the operational leadership of the Western Allies was about 50,000 men and women.

During 1944–5 there was a gradual rapprochement between the resistance leaders and the politicians. This easing of tension between the two groups was, to a large extent, the result of pressure from Britain in an endeavour to avoid something approaching civil war at the time of the liberation. During the final phase of the war, both Britain and the United States actively sought formal recognition of Denmark as an allied nation, but these efforts foundered in the face of opposition from the Soviet Union, which had not forgotten the earlier Danish government's dissolution of the Danish Communist Party or its endorsement of the Anti-Comintern Pact. However, the efforts of the Western Allies were not completely without success in that the first Danish government after the liberation became a coalition consisting of an equal number of representatives from the resistance movement and from the old political parties under the leadership of the former Prime Minister, the Social Democrat Vilhelm Buhl. Representatives from that government were invited to represent Denmark at the inaugural meeting of the United Nations in 1945. And so, despite the country's equivocal position during the war, it managed, after all, to emerge as a *de facto* ally. In the years of the Cold War that followed, as the world became divided between a Communist world on the one hand and a non-Communist world on the other, it became increasingly clear that Denmark could no longer pursue its traditional policy of neutrality, but would need to place its security in the hands of the Western Alliance that had liberated the country from the German occupation.[8]

This recognition led to Denmark joining NATO in 1949, a move which was an extension of the agreement with the United States over military bases in Greenland which had already been made by the Danish Ambassador to Washington, Henrik Kauffmann, during the war. Joining the Western Defence Alliance met Denmark's need for security against the Soviet Bloc and the threat it posed at frequent intervals. Also the division of Germany, first into occupied zones and later into East and West Germany, made the threat to security from that direction much weaker than it had been since Bismarck. The Copenhagen–Bonn accord in 1955 also ensured that any problems in the Danish–German border area could be resolved peacefully as they arose. From the point of view of security, Denmark had never been better placed than in the years following the Second World War, strongly rooted in the Western Alliance and enjoying the extra protection of the US nuclear umbrella.[9]

The entry of Denmark into the European Community alongside the UK in 1973 secured the free access for business and, especially, agriculture to the large European export markets so essential to economic growth, albeit after some years of painful insecurity. Although very controversial, Danish membership of the EU has subsequently been the cornerstone of Denmark's relations to the rest of the world. There will be occasion to return to this theme later in this history.

AFTER THE COLD WAR

The Cold War between the Soviet-led Warsaw Pact and the American-led NATO alliance ended dramatically and unexpectedly with the fall of the Berlin Wall in November 1989, the reunification of Germany, and the collapse of the Soviet Union a few years later. These events fundamentally changed the rule of the game and the balance of power in international politics, and also led to remarkable changes in Denmark's security and foreign policy. The most significant difference was that Denmark very clearly abandoned the hesitant and insular position that, despite changing circumstances, had dominated Danish defence policy since 1870 and, in its place, adopted a far more active and less ambiguous course, a course that is still followed today.

However, even before that time, there were clear signs in Denmark that the broad political consensus on defence matters that had prevailed during the Cold War was beginning to fall apart. These differences of opinion began to appear during the so-called 'footnote period' from 1983 to 1988 when, within NATO, Denmark's loyalty to the alliance was viewed with some scepticism. The underlying reason was NATO's so-called double-track decision, in December 1979, to install almost 600 medium-range missiles in Western Europe in response to the positioning of a number of SS-20 nuclear missiles by the Soviet Union in Eastern Europe directed against targets in the West. At the same time, NATO offered to enter into discussions with the Soviet Union on a mutual reduction of armaments – a typical move in the arms race that was so much a part of the Cold War.

The non-Socialist coalition government was inclined to support this decision within NATO but, at variance with its earlier loyalty to the alliance, the Social Democrats, who had recently had a change of leadership, were opposed and made their continued support subject to the commencement of negotiations with the Soviets before positioning these missiles. Without a majority in parliament on this issue, a reluctant foreign minister had the unenviable task of advising NATO that Denmark could only partially support the decision. It was a task that was repeated 23 times during the years that this 'double-track' line of thinking was part of NATO policy, and it not only undermined NATO's collective credibility, but also weakened Denmark's position within the alliance. It was not until 1988, when the Conservative Prime Minister at long last took the bull by the horns and called an election on the issue, which he won, and the majority in favour of the alternative defence policy was overturned, that Denmark was once again able to play the part of a legitimate member of the alliance.

That policy of the Social Democrats, which for quite a long time harmed Denmark's reputation within NATO, was probably determined first and foremost by internal politics – as a means to weaken or over-throw the government – but it also showed that the new generation of leaders in the country's largest political party felt less commitment to Cold War tenets and that it was time for a more active and independent defence policy. In other words, earlier fears of a Russian attack had gradually receded and, particularly when Mikhail Gorbachev became General Secretary of the Soviet Union in 1985, it was felt that the wind from the east had become less hostile. At the same time, especially within the left wing of the party, there was a widespread dislike of President Ronald Reagan's conservative and – in their eyes – confrontational approach. In more recent times this episode has generally been regarded as an instance of irresponsible behaviour by the Social Democrats and a low point in the history of Denmark's membership of NATO; but it was also an early sign that the concept of Denmark's role and potential was beginning to change in a world that was itself in a process of rapid transformation.

This change of attitude became clear shortly after the fall of the Berlin Wall when, in 1990, Denmark agreed to provide a warship as part of the UN blockade of Iraq prior to the response by coalition forces to Iraq's invasion of Kuwait. In the event, the Danish frigate was not directly involved in military action; but, nevertheless, it was the first time for centuries that a Danish warship had been part of a military operation so far overseas, and it was a clear signal that Denmark was prepared to take part in military actions when called upon by the UN or NATO.

This more resolute foreign and defence policy, which once again enjoyed broad parliamentary support, materialized at the same time in connection with the three Baltic states that were emerging from the collapse of the Soviet Union. Denmark had never formally recognised the annexation of these countries and, on that basis and because of their proximity to Denmark, the Danish government felt a special responsibility to actively support their liberation. As a small country, Denmark was in a better position to do so than the larger NATO countries, whose undisguised support might well have caused unwelcome tremors at a critical time in international affairs. There is no doubt that this Danish initiative was viewed favourably by these larger NATO partners and, at that vital time, Denmark invested considerable resources in the form of material aid as well as diplomatic and military advice. This active political involvement on Russia's doorstep was something that had not happened since the 1700s.

The break-up of the former Yugoslavia as a consequence of the collapse of the Soviet Union led to embittered infighting and genocide and also caused an increase in Denmark's involvement in international affairs. In 1992, the government sent a force of about a thousand soldiers to Croatia as part of the UN peacekeeping operations in the area. The following year this contingent was reinforced with a tank squadron, and Denmark's involvement relative to the size of the country thereby became considerable and, for the first time in modern history, Danish forces were actively engaged in military operations beyond the country's borders. This action in the Balkans enjoyed wide political support in Denmark, which showed how accepted wisdom on defence matters was undergoing rapid change. The collapse of the Soviet Union had removed any direct threat against Danish territory and a military preparedness to meet such a danger no longer appeared relevant. In its place, the line of thinking was that Denmark's military resources should be readily available to the international community in areas of conflict – such as the Balkans – which posed a wider threat. Denmark's defence would no longer be secured at its borders, but Danish troops would endeavour to ensure the safety of the country by playing their part in suppressing disturbances that threatened international stability. This was the key element in the reformulated defence doctrine that has prevailed since the end of the Cold War.

Another significant development in Denmark's external affairs during the past decade has been an improved relationship with the United States at the cost of its links with allies in mainland Europe. It began with the terrorist attack on the World Trade Center in New York on 11 September 2001, an attack that sent shock-waves through the world and, also in Denmark, prompted a wave of sympathy for the Americans and, at the same time, a serious concern about Islamic terror. The Social Democrat Prime Minister, Poul Nyrup Rasmussen, declared that Denmark would stand 'shoulder to shoulder' with the United States and would be with the Americans 'the whole way' in the impending struggle against terrorist networks. However, shortly afterwards, he lost the parliamentary balance of power to a non-socialist coalition under the leadership of the Liberal Anders Fogh Rasmussen, who became the new Prime Minister. But this change of government further strengthened the relations with the United States and, in the following years, led to the former Prime Minister's declaration of solidarity being transformed into a military reality, the extent of which led to political divisions in parliament.

In 2003, with a narrow majority, the government agreed to join the American-led 'coalition of the willing' together with the UK, Australia and Poland, to support President George W. Bush's invasion of Iraq which was intended to bring an end to Saddam Hussein's regime of terror and bring democracy to the country. During the following four years a sizeable Danish contingent operated in the Basra region under British command. During this operation one soldier lost his life and 19 were injured. By this step the Danish government demonstrated that it was prepared to go for it alone, unlike other European allies such as Germany and France. It was thus a further step away from the insularity that had characterized Danish defence strategy in the past.

The strong Danish involvement in the ongoing American-led military operations in Afghanistan is further evidence of the country's new role on the international scene and of its close co-operation with the United States. Denmark was actively involved from the start of this conflict in 2001 and, in 2010, a reinforced battalion still remains part of the coalition force in the dangerous Helmand province in the southern part of the country. So far, 33 Danish soldiers have lost their lives in this conflict and a larger number have been wounded.

Contrary to what one might expect from a population that, for generations, has been unused to losing its young men on the field of battle – and certainly not on a field as far distant as Afghanistan – these losses have been received with quiet resignation, and there have been no shrill demands to bring the troops home. This can be interpreted as a reflection of a change of attitude amongst the population – a general understanding and acceptance of the movement away from insularity that began at the end of the Cold War. For a similar reason, the election of Anders Fogh Rasmussen, the Prime Minister, as NATO's new Secretary-General in 2009 was met with appreciation and pride in Denmark – an election that may be regarded as recognition by the NATO alliance of Denmark's change of course and of its new international involvement. It is still too early to say where this course might lead in the long term but, to some extent, it is a return to the situation that prevailed in the eighteenth century. However, what is already clear is that, during the past twenty years, Denmark's foreign policy has changed faster and to a greater extent than anyone a generation ago would have believed possible.[10]

For the most part, the history of Denmark's foreign policy from 1500 to the present time is, on the one hand, a sad account of a constant loss of territory and gradual withdrawal from the Baltic. However, on the other hand, it is also to some extent a success story, of how a state came into being on the periphery of the European mainland, whose borders contained a nation, neither more nor less. This was, and is, unique in the world and an important factor in Danish self-perception. Only now, in the age of globalisation, has this understanding become less certain – a theme we will return to later on.

3

. . . .

Domestic Policy, 1500–1848: The Era of Aristocracy and Absolutism

THE CONSENSUS MODEL

In September 1973, a couple of months after what was called the landslide election which permanently changed the usual pattern of Danish politics, Jens Otto Krag (1914–78), a former Prime Minister, wrote a newspaper article analysing the political situation at the time in Denmark. The year before, Krag had unexpectedly resigned as leader of the minority Social Democrat government soon after winning the referendum about Denmark's affiliation to the European Community. Krag had been active as a social democrat since the 1930s, and immediately after the Second World War he became part of the party's inner circle. In the 1950s he held various key ministerial posts and was Prime Minister from 1962 to 1968 and again from 1971 to 1972. He therefore had a great deal of knowledge and experience of Danish political life.

In this article, one of his last public contributions to Danish political life in his long involvement with it, he took the opportunity to look back over Danish politics during the twentieth century and to offer some reflections on the patterns within the political system. Some of the points he made were:

> In many elections over the years, the battle in most of the country has been directly between the Social Democrats and the Liberals. The two parties nonetheless have been to some extent symmetrical.

Perhaps this symmetry has been lopsided, but the fact remains that in the old days the workers and the farmers were the core of the Danish population.[1]

With this comment, the experienced politician expressed a striking characteristic of modern Danish democracy as it had developed since the change of system in 1901. This was that the popular negotiated democracy rested on the two most significant groups of the population, the farmers and the workers, who respected each other and conducted a running political dialogue which stretched across all boundaries of class and economic interests.

What Krag was in fact describing was the modern Danish model of political consensus – collaborative democracy – which distinguished Danish political behaviour for most of the twentieth century. It was perceived as a measure of good political skill to be able to reach an understanding about issues and, while respecting the whole, be able to reconcile interests to achieve an acceptable solution without creating destructive social conflicts.

Krag clearly identified the workers and the farmers as the key groups in Danish political life. He did not depict them as irreconcilable forces, but as a symmetrical pair who together supported Danish popular democracy. In other words, for him, as for most leading Danish politicians after the war, the political ideal was a responsible collaboration between the representatives of these two groups in the interests of the whole of society, thus making Danish democracy truly national. The fact that this ideal was rarely achieved is another matter. The key thing is that this ideal of true popular democracy remained the goal. It was this ideal, and the political behaviour aimed at meeting it, which led Sir James Mellon to talk of tribal awareness in his charming portrait of the Danes of the late twentieth century.

The key element in this behaviour is the concept of *folkelighed*, meaning a kind of popular democracy, but with connotations that are virtually untranslatable. In English, 'popular' has negative resonances which do not attach to the Danish word, and the German *völkisch* has uncomfortable echoes from the Nazi period. It is also worth noting that even though Krag identified the workers and the farmers as the bearers of Danish culture and politics, he was in no way talking about the kind of totalitarian worker and farmer culture of the now defunct German Democratic Republic. This grotesque manifestation of socialism was in fact a bugbear, a concrete expression of what could go wrong when the class struggle reigned supreme and the duty to safeguard the interests of society as a whole, through a popular democracy, was ousted from political life. In comparison with the DDR (former East Germany), there was virtually no ideology of class struggle, but instead a binding concept of popular equality. This formed the basis for Danish political life during the twentieth century, as it developed along lines of consensus rather than the conflict which has characterised some other democratic societies.

This does not imply that the Danes are by nature more peaceful and socially responsible than other nations. Far from it. The particular nature of Danish politics is best understood as being a product of the experience of politics rooted way back in the past, at least to the start of the sixteenth century, when it first became meaningful to talk of a Danish state and Danish power. This chapter and the next attempt a kind of archaeological exploration of these roots in order to identify the most significant elements in the long political history which has led to the contemporary nature of Danish politics. It all started, paradoxically, with a coup d'état in 1536.

THE COUP OF 1536 AND THE NEW CONCEPT OF SOVEREIGNTY

The death of King Frederik I (r. 1523–33) in 1533 triggered a violent civil war in Denmark which raged until 1536. The Rigsråd, or council of state, decided to postpone the selection of a new king indefinitely, and took over the government itself in the interim. According to the constitution, Denmark was an elective monarchy, and the state council of higher nobles had the right to appoint the new king, although there was a long-established precedent of choosing the oldest son of the deceased king.

However, Duke Christian, the oldest son of Frederik I, was known to be a passionate adherent of Luther's teachings and had already taken steps to introduce the Reformation in several parts of his Southern Jutland duchy. Many people, and not least the Catholic-dominated council of state which included the bishops, considered that choosing him as his father's successor would put the existing social order in jeopardy, which in spite of the powerful movement for reformation was still based on the Catholic Church. It was for this reason that the appointment of a new king was postponed, and the council took over until a suitable Catholic candidate could be found. This turned out to be a fatal decision.

It brought all the social, religious and political tensions which had long been bubbling under the surface to a head, exploding in a bloody civil war in which the townspeople and the peasants, supported by the Hanseatic town of Lübeck, were on one side, and the state council, the Catholic Church and the powerful nobility were on the other. For two years after 1533, the entire country was plunged into anarchy and chaos no less extensive or violent than the peasants' revolt which had shaken Germany a few years before in the wake of the reformations.

As a result, the only stabilising factor in the country was actually Duke Christian, whom the state council had refused to elect king. On the strength of his duchy, and with the help of an army of highly effective German mercenaries, he launched a systematic campaign first to take control of Jutland and then to be elected king by the provinces. His forces then drove eastwards with such success that finally only Copenhagen resisted him. After a long siege, the inhabitants of Copenhagen capitulated too, and by the summer of 1536, Christian was in total control of the whole country. Thus, he could take the title of Christian III (r. 1534–59), with the authority of a conqueror. Shortly afterwards he set in train both ecclesiastical reformation and a fundamental and enduring transformation of the religious and political structure of the country.

In August 1536, the king had the Catholic bishops imprisoned and charged with high treason on the grounds that they were the motivating force behind the decision of the state council to postpone the election of the king, which in turn had provoked the savage civil war. This was a drastic measure, and a critical break with the past, as the leaders of the Catholic Church were, until their arrest, the most prominent and powerful faction in the state council, which, alongside the king, formed the true political leadership of the country. The previous leaders of the Church were now constrained to renouncing their political and spiritual offices, and the Danish Church changed from being a Catholic ecclesiastical province to a Lutheran princely Church. The king became the secular head of the Church, in rather the same way as Henry VIII did in England around the same time. We will return to a closer examination of the reformation of the Church in a later chapter. For now, it is enough to emphasise that with this coup, the king removed the religious element in the leadership of the state at a stroke. From then on, ruling was a purely secular matter for the king and the non-ecclesiastical remains of the state council, which now consisted of 15–20 secular councillors. At the same time, the king confiscated the extensive estates of the Catholic Church, which in itself greatly increased royal power, as these accounted for a third of the cultivated area of the country.

To ensure the success of the new arrangements, the king forced the secular members of the state council to issue a solemn declaration, where in unambiguous sentences they swore eternal loyalty to the new king and promised never to reintroduce a spiritual regime to Denmark. This was intended to establish the new conditions of power once and for all – and it succeeded.

A few months later the new order was enshrined in a legally binding form, and the new power structure became formalised. The result was that the concept of sovereignty took on a completely different meaning in Denmark, and this laid the foundations for the development of the later strong state. In the constitutional documents of 1536, this new sovereignty, or perhaps this new concept of a state, was linked to the expression 'The Crown of Denmark', which in the terminology of the age was used as an overall description of the authority which the king and the council of nobles together represented. The radical change in this new invention was that the concept of sovereignty was liberated from being unilaterally bound to one or other of the central institutions of power – the monarchy or the state council – and was instead linked to an impersonal, abstract and permanent concept, that of 'The Crown'. This concept was the overall description of the authority represented by the king and the nobles together. These two authorities together constituted 'The Crown of Denmark' in an abstract, permanent sense. Kings could die, the members of the council could change, but 'The Crown of Denmark' – the fulcrum of sovereignty and the state – existed independently.

This in turn created the necessary legal framework for the expansion of the power of the state in the following centuries, for establishing a power of the state which virtually took on its own life beyond the reach of society. It existed, so to say, for itself and by virtue of itself. The early modern Renaissance state thus came into existence in Denmark. In essence, this development was very similar to that in England around the same time, where the Tudor revolution replaced 'King and Parliament' with 'King-in-Parliament' as an expression of the fact that the highest level of sovereignty was manifested through statutes resulting from the formalised co-operation of the king and the parliament. The historian G. R. Elton identified this change in the perception of sovereignty as the reason for the strength and dynamism of the Tudor state in England.

So, after the revolution of 1536 in Denmark, royal power and the state council were no longer seen as constitutional opposites or alternatives, but as complementary components of the same body politic. After this, it no longer made any sense to talk of either the king or the state council. Now, both the king and the state council together formed 'The Crown of Denmark' in constitutionally carrying the highest level of sovereignty. This permanent alliance could ensure the unhindered exercise of power in perpetuity, regardless of changes of monarch or members of the state council. This configuration in Denmark was called a dyarchy – a two-headed state – and, as in England, it opened the gates for a previously unknown dynamic exercise of power and the systematic construction of extensive powers for the state.[2]

This new role grew gradually over the ensuing centuries along with increasing demands for the state to provide both foreign and domestic security. Thus, it is by no means incorrect to maintain that the strong and pervasive power of the state which characterises modern Denmark had its earliest beginnings as long ago as the constitutional revolution of 1536. It has had more extensive ramifications than were probably foreseen by its architects, when they created it as a concrete expression of the alliance between king and nobles principally intended to prevent any recurrence of the bitter and violent civil war. This alliance, with the principal aim of keeping the lower classes under control, continued up to 1660, when the monarchy decided to turn its back on the now enfeebled nobility and form an alliance instead with the lower classes to carry out the next big coup in Danish history: the transformation of the constitution from dyarchy to absolutism.

FROM DOMAIN TO TAX STATE

The elimination of the Church as an independent power and the suppression of the revolt of the lower classes left the king and the nobility solidly in possession of all the political and economic power in Denmark in 1536. As explained previously, they had created a constitution which not only knitted them together but also assured them of a permanent grasp of power. They also had virtually total control over the most important means of production in the country: cultivable land.

In the middle of the sixteenth century the Crown estates accounted for around half of all the agricultural land, the nobility owned approximately 44 per cent, and only the remaining 6 per cent was cultivated and owned by freeholders.

By far the majority of agricultural production – the only significant production of the country as a whole – thus took place on the estates of the Crown and the nobility, through a system of peasant tenancies. Peasant farmers constituted about three-quarters of the entire population. Over the following years, the king and the council built up a system of power mainly intended to preserve this production structure and used legislation to maintain social inequalities, still with a view to keeping and consolidating the political and economic social order resulting after the civil war and the coup of 1536.

This system worked without any friction so long as the few, and very prosperous, nobles could continue to exercise power and enjoy their privileges without any serious challenge from the population at large, and for so long as the state was in a position to finance its own activities, using the income from the Crown estates and various customs duties, and without any need to impose any significant direct taxes on the lower orders. However, both these circumstances changed in the first half of the seventeenth century, and the system imploded.

The aristocracy of the sixteenth century was an exclusive but very small class – fewer than 2000 people in all in a population of nearly 800,000. Conversely, this group enjoyed enormous privileges, paid no taxes, enjoyed the exclusive right to own agricultural estates and had a monopoly on all the influential and well-paid public offices.[3] These extensive privileges were the result of the historical role of the nobles as the defenders of the realm. The lance-bearing knights in armour historically had had the sole responsibility for protecting society against enemies from without and within, and the privileges were originally a form of economic insurance that they had the means to fulfil this expensive duty. One of the most prominent of the nobles, Lord Admiral Herluf Trolle (1516–65), expressed this self-perception of the nobility very concisely in 1565, in the middle of the Nordic Seven Years War, when a close friend tried to persuade him against once again putting his life at risk by fighting the Swedes:

Do you know why we are called knights, why we wear golden chains, own estates and have superior breeding to the others? It is because, when the king, the nobles, the country and the kingdom need it, when the enemies of the realm need to be repelled, we, above all others have the honour of protecting and shielding our ancestral kingdom with all our power and resources, so that our subjects may live in peace and tranquillity. If we want the sweet things of life, then we must also accept the bitter ones.

It would hardly be possible to express the old ideal of knightly service better than this.

Yet even at the time when Herluf Trolle uttered these bold words, military technology had so developed as to make them woefully out of date, transforming the noble knight on his charger into a figure as comical as that of Don Quixote. Neither in Europe nor the Nordic region were wars conducted any longer by noble champions on their steeds, but by huge infantry formations of mercenaries armed with muskets or other small arms. This meant that, just like their counterparts throughout Europe, the Danish nobles slowly but surely lost their military function, and with it, the justification for their substantial privileges. This threw the whole class into a prolonged crisis of identity which seriously damaged their self-confidence and drive. In tandem, more and more voices, especially those of the commoners, were raised, making ever-keener criticisms of the privileged position the nobility continued to enjoy. This crisis of trust and self-confidence intensified through the seventeenth century and culminated in a radical change in 1660, when the nobles gave up their economic privileges and political influence with virtually no resistance as they were squeezed between a decisive king and the ever-more confident commoners and clergy.

Another critical factor in this development was that during the first half of the seventeenth century, the Danish state changed from being virtually self-financing under the Crown to raising more and more revenue through direct regular taxation.[4] The new methods of warfare already mentioned played a part here, as the state took over responsibility for the mass industry which had replaced the outmoded artistry of the knights of old. The numerous wars of the period against the arch-enemy Sweden, and not least Christian IV's disastrous adventures between 1625 and 1629 in the Thirty Years War, made hitherto unprecedented demands on government finances and meant that the traditional sources of income had to be supplemented by increasing levels of direct taxation. Certainly, at first these were called extraordinary taxes, but they quickly became permanent.

THE CRISIS OF THE STATE COUNCIL

All this threw one of the main organs of state, the aristocratic state council, into an insoluble dilemma because of its dual role, representing the nobility on the one hand, but on the other being responsible for the state as a whole. In the latter role, the council had no choice but to demand direct taxation to alleviate the almost chronic financial situation. Yet in the former role, the council was the guardian of the privileges of the nobility, as painstakingly described in the coronation charters and other legislation. Of all these privileges, exemption from taxation was the most important, and so the nobles naturally expected that this would be maintained despite the rapidly increasing taxation of the Danish population in general – the peasants, the commoners and the clergy.

As the tax burden rose, it became ever-more unreasonable that the richest group of the population should insist on exemption as one of their privileges, for which the justification had become lost in the mists of time. Public criticism of the nobility and the state council grew, and not even the council could maintain its position for long. From the 1620s onwards, the nobility were repeatedly called upon to shoulder part of the tax burden. For the sake of honour, their contribution was not called taxation, but a voluntary contribution – but it was tax in all but name.

Through this concession, the state council effectively decided to place its role as an organ of the state above that of representing the nobility. This underlined the responsibility the council felt for the realm as a whole, and this is to their credit. However, it created a breach of trust between the council and the ordinary nobles. This rift widened as it became obvious that the nobles' own representatives in the government were willing to sell out their privileges. In other words, the state council was cast into a political vacuum, and so was easy to sacrifice when in 1660 the alliance between the king and the non-noble classes made a decisive assault to end the dominance of the nobility on Danish political life.

In brief, the new tax regime made the old political system unsustainable, as it was simply not designed to cope with the new financial realities. These required either a broad representation of social classes in the political leadership, or a monolithic leadership which could rise above all sectional interests. In truth, there were only two ways out of this deadlock for the state council. One was to accept being supplemented by a broader representation of commoners in the government of the country – but that would have been almost the same as signing their own death warrants, and could hardly have been expected or demanded of the council. The other was to try to drive the king out of the government system completely and establish itself as a kind of *alter rex*, with full control over the apparatus of state.

It was exactly this latter that the state council tried to achieve in the 1648 negotiations over the royal charter following the death of Christian IV. As the price for electing his son, Duke Frederik, as king, the council prescribed the most restrictive coronation charter that any Danish king has ever signed. It made the new king, Frederik III (r. 1648–70), totally dependent on the state council, which established itself as the real centre of power. Thus, the once so harmonious collaboration between the king and the council was transformed into a bitter struggle for existence between the two organs as a result of the advance of taxation.

The aristocratic state council was apparently at the height of its powers in 1648 – but only apparently, as just 12 years later the council meekly handed over all its powers to the very king it had tried to bind hand and foot in 1648. Quite how this reverse happened has been one of the classic issues of Danish historical research. However, in the light of the structural challenges explained above, it is not really so mysterious. Although it was probably hard to see in 1648, the king actually had a number of winning cards in his hand in the struggle for existence with the council in the years which followed.

In point of fact, at that time the monarchy was an old, well-established institution. Christian IV, the father of Frederik III, had earned the unanimous popularity of his people through his 60-year reign. Thus, the new king had a great deal of popular sympathy to draw upon, increased by his fearless patriotic conduct in the defence of Copenhagen, when the Swedish troops laid siege to it in the last Karl Gustav War of 1658–9 and attempted to storm it. In sharp contrast to the frightened and irresolute state council, the king stood as a focus for the people at this fateful moment, and was himself a symbol of resistance to the invading enemy. In addition the king was not saddled with the agonising problem of representing the different social classes in the country, which had proved to be the Achilles' heel for the council. The king was the king of the entire nation, whereas the state council ended up representing only itself. The influential ideas of the French political philosopher Jean Bodin (1530–96), who emphasised the indivisibility of sovereignty and the divine nature of kingship, also served to benefit the king. Lutheran theologians were praising the thesis of the sanctity of all authority, backed up by sermons in every pulpit on every Sunday.

All of these factors, coupled with the need of the new bureaucratic tax-state for a unified government and a more streamlined political decision-making process, worked to the advantage of a powerful monarchy which took its authority from God rather than the people. And yet another factor was that the only real rival to the king was the privileged nobility, and they were suffering a deeper and deeper crisis of identity after losing their original military role. All in all, that the monarchy triumphed in 1660 is no great surprise.

COUP D'ÉTAT AND ABSOLUTISM, 1660

The transformation of Denmark in the autumn of 1660 from an elective to a hereditary monarchy with a new constitution which replaced the state council with an absolutist regime was the result of a train of events sparked off by a deep national political and financial crisis. This in turn was the consequence of the destructive wars with Sweden, 1657–60, which threatened the very existence of the country and led to the surrender of all the old Danish provinces on the Scandinavian peninsula east of the Øresund – nearly a third of Danish territory and a corresponding proportion of the population. For nearly three years, the Danish people had to foot the bill for the devastation and plunder of the Swedish occupying forces, and this brought the country's economy to a state of collapse, and the government finances were in ruins.[5]

In order to re-establish order and bring the government finances under control as quickly as possible after the peace accord, in the late summer the king convened a general assembly of the estates of the realm in Copenhagen. The three principal estates, the nobility, the clergy and the commoners, were represented. No one thought of inviting the peasants, who accounted for more than three-quarters of the population. The objective of the meeting was to agree on new taxes to plug the gaping hole in the state coffers. However, on the initiative of the leaders of the clergy and the commoners, the discussions soon turned to the constitution itself and the traditional role of the nobility in it, and the commoners' complaints were founded on the refusal of the nobles to shoulder the burden of taxation to the same extent as the other estates.

In an attempt to force the nobility to concede, the lower orders played a trump card at the beginning of October by introducing into the negotiations a proposal that the monarchy become hereditary instead of elective, as it had been until this point. This proposal hit the nobles and the state council in their most sensitive spot. If the monarchy did become hereditary, the succession would be automatic, and there would be absolutely no need for the king to sign a coronation charter on accession to the throne. At a stroke, this would sweep away the old contract and the traditional division of power between the king and the nobles. Unsurprisingly, the state council and the representatives of the other nobles refused to accept the proposal, but in return gave more concessions in the area of taxation. However, this was too little, too late.

A few days after the proposal was made, Frederik III, who had up to then been very carefully remaining in the background in the first phase of the negotiations, now entered the picture at full strength. Using loyal troops, he blockaded Copenhagen and made it clear to the confined representatives of the nobles that they had no choice but to agree to the proposal. In other words, he virtually staged a coup, and took the state council and the other nobles hostage during this phase. Confined in Copenhagen, where they had few supporters or friends, the representatives of the nobles had no option but to put a brave face on it and accept the proposal of heredity.

So, on 13 October 1660, all the representatives of the estates, including those of the nobility, joined a procession to the royal palace to offer the king heredity. He, not surprisingly, graciously accepted the offer. At the same time the restrictive constitution of 1648 was declared void, and the representatives simply requested the king to draw up a new one which would take suitable account of the needs of the country and the interests of the people. In effect, the representatives gave the king a free hand to establish a completely new constitution for Denmark, as he thought fit.

The king did not let the grass grow under his feet. As soon as 18 October he had arranged a magnificent ceremony of homage in front of the royal palace, at which the representatives one by one swore an oath of allegiance to the hereditary king on behalf of the estates they represented. Just to make the whole picture complete, a number of peasants from the area surrounding the capital were rapidly recruited so that they, albeit rather perplexed, could also swear fealty to the new hereditary king on behalf of all the peasantry in Denmark. And so for now, the deed was done. Under circumstances reminiscent of a coup, Denmark had a new hereditary king and the old dyarchical constitution was shredded up. What would replace it was still completely unclear. Only one thing was certain, that the centuries of political dominance that the nobles had enjoyed had come to an abrupt end as a result of the new strong alliance between the king and the lower classes.

The uncertainty did not last for very long. Before the end of the year there were clear indications that the king and his small conclave of advisers were aiming to introduce absolute monarchy in Denmark on the pattern of current absolutist ideas in continental Europe. These conjectures were confirmed when on 10 January 1661, the king distributed the Act of Sovereignty for signature by the representatives of the estates. This distinctive act was formulated as a proclamation from all the king's subjects by which they unconditionally handed over all power, all sovereignty and all royal prerogatives to the king and his descendants. Once the 1600 or so representatives of the estates of the realm had signed this document during the winter, absolute Danish monarchy became a full reality, and the somewhat dubious circumstances concerning the introduction of heredity during the autumn were given the seal of legal approval.

Uniquely in the history of European absolutism, just five years later, on 14 November 1665, the king issued a special *Lex Regia* – the Act of Succession – which detailed the circumstances of the transfer of power in 1660, and confirmed that the king had unlimited powers, while also establishing the rules of royal succession. Even though the existence of this law and its wording was treated as a state secret for many years (it was first printed in 1709), in practice it served as the absolutist constitution right up to the demise of absolutism in 1848. Some of the clauses, concerning the order of the royal household, remain in force to this day. The Act of Succession reflected as precisely as possible the perception of absolutism as a divine institution rooted in popular support, where the king was appointed to rule the Danish people answering only to God. This duality – the duty to God and the duty to the people, whom God himself appointed the monarch to rule – came to leave a clear mark on the way in which Danish absolutism developed and on the attitude of the people to it. In fact, this dual duty meant that the formal absolute power of the monarch never became pure despotism.

FROM ESTATES OF THE REALM TO HIERARCHY

The king and his aides energetically started to recast the traditional structure of power in the country so that it would conform to the new political reality. A comprehensive reform of the central administration was the most pressing task, as it had shown itself to be inadequate to meet the demands for bureaucratic efficiency required for taxation. It was reorganised on the Swedish model, and the old administrative bodies were divided into specialist departments under the leadership of a group of prominent officials, whose job was to provide the king with the necessary specialist advice and then translate his decisions into everyday practice.

This structure was the forerunner of the modern ministerial system, which has many similarities with the old departmental system under absolutism. The major difference is that now the Danish Ministers and their civil servants are responsible to Parliament, whereas the officials under the absolutist system acted on behalf of the king and were answerable only to him. In so far as was possible, the first decade of absolutism saw the creation of an efficient, bureaucratic central administration with the king as the absolute centre, which extended the royal will to the most distant corners of the realm. Of course the technological limitations of the time set certain practical boundaries to efficiency and scope, but the system proved itself to be so effective that it was preserved in more or less its original form right up to 1848, after which it was converted without any significant major alterations to a democratic ministerial system.

It is interestingly symbolic that the central ministries are still housed in exactly the same buildings at Slotsholmen in central Copenhagen as were used from the first by the absolutist departments. This can well be seen as a concrete expression of the continuity which has characterised Danish central administration for over 300 years.

In parallel to these administrative reforms, the regime started to reshape the medieval society of estates of the realm into a hierarchy in which a large number of ranks tapered up to the absolute monarch at the top of the pyramid. The old Danish nobility, considered by the absolute monarch as the most dangerous opponents in light of the events of 1660, lost most of their privileges, including the exemption from taxation and the monopoly on public office. The nobles were allowed to keep their titles, but as these no longer conferred privileges, they were fairly meaningless. Now the nobles had to pay taxes just like everyone else. This in itself strengthened the national finances. They also had to compete on an equal footing with the clever sons of commoners for public office in the absolutist administration. The commoners very quickly earned more and more of these influential posts and consequently achieved higher ranking in the new system than the members of the old aristocracy. The old oligarchical social order slowly but surely slipped away, replaced by a limited meritocracy in which the talented could reach the top irrespective of their social origins.[6]

An extreme example here was the very able son of a Copenhagen wine merchant, Peder Schumacher (1635–1699). He entered Frederik III's service immediately after the introduction of absolutism, and in the first half of the 1670s advanced to the position of young Christian V's (r. 1670–99) closest adviser, and head of the entire absolutist administration with the title of Chancellor. He was raised to the peerage as Count Griffenfeld, and awarded the highest orders of the country, the Order of the Elephant and the Order of the Dannebrog. It was he who devised most of the initiatives which drove the old nobility down the social and political ladder. These included the establishment of particularly distinguished titled nobility consisting of counts and barons who owed their position exclusively to the king; the new royal favour – the Order of the Dannebrog – whose members enjoyed an elevated position in the hierarchy, and the new system of rank itself, which pushed the old aristocracy way down the social order. Griffenfeld was a shining example of how far the absolute king could elevate even a young man of only modest origin if he showed the right potential. On the other hand, his fate was also a terrifying example of how far the king was ready to let a man fall if he was not absolutely loyal to his royal master. In 1676, Griffenfeld came under suspicion of implementing a foreign policy that did not precisely support the king's interests. He was arrested on the charge of high treason, the punishment for which was death. At the very last moment before the execution, the king granted a pardon to his Chancellor. Nonetheless, the fallen grandee had to spend the remaining 23 years of his life in solitary confinement in a fortress in Trondheim Fjord in Norway, isolated from his family, friends and everything he had held dear.[7]

Although after his fall from grace in 1676 Griffenfeld became a 'non-person' in absolutist Denmark, his brief but hectic social engineering left an enduring trace. The system of rank he introduced has survived until the present day. This can still be observed when the Queen holds her New Year levee at the beginning of January every year for the three highest classes, most of whom occupy posts in the civil service. The titles he created still exist and account for the upper crust of the Danish nobility. Finally, the Order of the Dannebrog, a royal order of chivalry which he conceived, is still a highly regarded honour, awarded to between 300 and 400 people a year, usually with a great deal of public attention. In fact, on close examination, it is astonishing how deeply and enduringly these and other social reforms of the early absolutist period have influenced modern Danish life.

With hindsight, two other large reforms from the period of absolutism can be identified as having left their mark strongly both on the nature of modern Denmark and on the current perception of what it is to be Danish. One is *Danske Lov* (the Danish Law), signed on the birthday of King Christian V in 1683 and followed by *Norske Lov* (the Norwegian Law) in 1687, a comprehensive set of laws for the whole kingdom which created a hitherto unknown legal uniformity in the country and had a long-term influence on the balance between the state and civil society. The other was the agricultural reforms at the end of the eighteenth century, which created a completely new relationship between agrarian groups and between them and the state, and laid an early foundation for the revolution in agricultural production in Denmark which in turn led to efficient modern farming practices.

THE DANISH LAW, 1683–45

Of the numerous extensive reforms which occupied the early absolutist administration, the development of a complete legal code for the whole of Denmark stands out as one of the biggest achievements. After the change of regime in 1660, there was an urgent need for this, if only because the new political reality implied a drastic revision of the mish-mash of laws which governed the dealings between Danes themselves and the relationship between civil society and the state. In addition, Danish legislation had long been a morass of incompatible older and newer laws. Some of the medieval provincial laws from the thirteenth century were still applied in all or parts of the country along with supplements and updates over the years. Earlier, in the seventeenth century, there had been a couple of bold attempts to collate all the existing legislation into a book of statutes for the whole realm. The last was Christian IV's Statute Book of 1643. None of these was successful or satisfactory, simply because the relatively weak and poor dyarchical power was not up to the task. As a result, the state of the law in the realm left much to be desired, as it rested on an inscrutable and incomplete regulatory framework. There was thus a pressing need for a comprehensive reform of the law, which also fitted in with the desire of the much stronger absolutist state to create order, uniformity and transparency throughout the land.

Following many years of preparatory work through various expert commissions, the government was able to issue the Danish Law in 1683. This was a definitive expression of the desire for order and transparency in every aspect of life. The new book of statutes systematically culled the unserviceable parts from the old legislation and added new regulations where considered necessary, resulting in a comprehensive legal code for the whole of Denmark and all its inhabitants excepting the king, who under the terms of the new constitution was above the law. There was no question of any abrupt break with the previous state of the law, rather the code placed the old laws into a system and adjusted them to correspond with the absolutist constitution. This was expressed in a concrete form by the quotation of the central constitutional sections of the otherwise secret Act of Succession which established the king as sovereign and outside the law, thus elevating royal power way above that of the rest of society. Significantly, the first Book was entitled 'The Law and the Personification of the Law', and the first article laid down that the absolute monarch was the source of the law and therefore one with the state and the law. Thus, the king and the state were in themselves the origin of the entire legal code, and all consequent conditions of the individual rights and duties of the citizens were defined on this basis.[8]

To appreciate the extent of this order of priority and the full consequences of this conception of the law, it might be of value to make a comparison to a somewhat later legal code, to wit, the Napoleonic Code of 1804, which had a similarly comprehensive nature. In this, it was not constitutional law, but personal law which initiated the code. In other words, the French revolution made a distinction between the two legislative works. The critical point, however, is that Denmark never experienced such a revolution. The Danish Law – and the concept of the elevated position of the state in relation to the citizens which lay behind it – was decisive for the state of the law and the Danish perception of the relationship between the state and civil society right up to the democratic constitution of 1849 and, with some modifications, up to the present day. The fundamental attitude of modern Danes that the state is a friend and ally, not an adversary, a protector and not an enemy, is very much an unconscious result of the fact that for generations, the Danes have been accustomed to a state of law fashioned by the Danish Law to express an absolutist view of the relationship between the individual, society as a whole and the state.

Yet the Danish Law was in no sense whatsoever an attempt to turn Denmark into a totalitarian state. In fact, given the primitive means available to the state any such project would have been doomed to failure, even if that was the intention. A cursory reading of the legal code will quickly reveal that the law frequently laid down very clear boundaries as to the extent to which the state could interfere in the affairs of its citizens. The fifth Book of the code stated that any promise intended to create obligations of a legal nature should be considered as binding irrespective of the form of the promise and whether it related to commerce or any other contractual circumstance. Even a verbal promise to give a present or to sell a property was considered as binding as if it had been in writing. This allowed the citizens to enter into binding contracts under Danish law with such simplicity and objectivity that it has not proved necessary to add any formal or artificial supplements to this basic law since. This alone makes the Danish legal tradition somewhat unique. It is still true in Denmark that a man is a man, his word is his word and should anyone in public life in modern Denmark fail to deliver on his word or promise, the public will judge him accordingly. The most recent and spectacular example of this was when the previous Prime Minister, Poul Nyrup Rasmussen (b. 1943) made a public promise in the run-up to the 1998 elections not to tamper with the rules for early retirement. When he did so anyway, after forming a government, he was embroiled in a crisis of confidence from which he never recovered. He lost the next election in 2001, not so much because he had chipped away at the system of early retirement benefits, which most people anyway thought was a sensible thing to do, but because he had breached a fundamental principle of Danish law, the binding contract, which dates back to the fifth Book of the Danish Law.

It was a basic principle of Danish Law that citizens are free to deal with disputes and strife without the intervention of the state or the legal institutions. This was already formulated in the first Book of the legal code, which established the right of voluntary agreement either directly between two parties in dispute or through mediation from a third impartial party. The stipulation was that the decision reached either between the two parties themselves or by the impartial third party was final and binding in the future. Such a decision could not be brought before any court, and the law did not lay down any requirements for the nature of the mediation itself. The law thus actually strongly limited its own scope and allowed a great deal of room for popular informal legal institutions of a temporary or permanent nature. In other words, the law deliberately chose not to try to extend its powers to cover the numerous traditional associations and means of interaction through which local societies functioned on a day-to-day basis, and had done so for centuries, be they neighbourhood conventions in villages, or guilds in the cities. Such fraternities could continue to make legal decisions just as they always had.

LEASING OUT THE POWER OF THE STATE

The unequivocal codification of the old legal traditions under the Danish Law was the clear result of a realistic recognition on the part of the authors that despite the formal absolute power of the monarchy, there were narrow limits to the ability of the state to intervene, and areas best left untouched. Nonetheless, absolutism created a state which could act, and act decisively, if vital interests were at stake. The Danish Law shows, however, that the state could also remain in the background when that was appropriate. In effect this meant that there was a great divide between the formal unlimited absolute powers of the monarchy as expressed in the Act of Succession, and the rather more modest daily administrative and legal practice. This gulf continued for as long as absolutism itself, and some historians have used the term 'the leased-out power of the state' to describe the nature of Danish absolutism.[9] This expression alludes to the fact that even such important areas as tax collection and military conscription were farmed out to the private estate owners up to the end of the eighteenth century and were thus outside the direct control of the state. The limits to the scope of the Danish Law described above showed the same tendency, so that despite the ambitious absolutist pretensions of the government, there was always space for independence and freedom for the citizens outside the reach of the state.

Danish society has been clearly formed through this balance between a theoretically strong and effective state and a pragmatic laissez-faire approach in the daily exercise of power. Even the 'Danish social contract' which plays such an important role in modern Danish society is a direct result of this. One of the characteristics of this model is that state legislation over such things as the conditions of the labour market is limited to the minimum, to creating some overall frameworks, while it is left to the players in the labour market themselves to flesh out the framework with concrete agreements about pay and working conditions. If the parties are unable to agree, the issue can be taken to an official arbitrator, just as concrete disputes can be brought before the court of industrial relations, which, despite its name, is not actually a court, but an arbitration institution established by the parties in the labour market themselves. Only if a case reaches genuine deadlock will the state intervene, and then unwillingly. This system has been proven to allow the opportunity for amicable settlements and contributes to a peaceful labour market, precisely because the parties feel constrained to observe agreements they have entered willingly. The patterns of the Danish Law – the freedom of contract and voluntary arbitration with the powerful state as the battleship in the background – are easily identifiable here.

It is often said that it is typical for a Dane that if he encounters a problem or wishes to achieve something, he starts a club. It is undeniable that an uncountable number of clubs exist in Denmark, covering every conceivable aspect of social life and human activity, from the local chess club to the powerful labour market organisations, and the freedom of association is a constitutional right. This particularly Danish way of solving problems outside the influence of the public authorities is a certain modern expression of the tradition for private freedom of negotiation outside the confines of the law established by the Danish Law of 1683.

This law was devised by the relatively new absolutist regime to once and for all create order, transparency and uniformity in the absolutist state. It succeeded, as with its clarity and freedom, it proved to provide a most suitable framework for the development of the powerful state. This was exactly what its many hard-hitting clauses were intended to do. What the architects of the law could hardly have imagined in their wildest dreams, when they set clear and realistic limits to the scope of the law, was that they also unwittingly contributed to creating a formal legal basis for the development of certain patterns of popular behaviour which are still today key elements in the modern Danish social model, as indicated above.

As the extensive civil revolutions swept through Europe at the end of the eighteenth century and the old regimes crumbled in the face of the jubilant commoners, the situation in Denmark was astonishingly calm and stable. Although there were some individual critics of the system, there was no indication of any movement towards revolution in Denmark. This was due not just to the fact that the Danes were a long way away from the epicentre of events in Paris, or that by nature they were more peaceful than others – in fact the long history in which wars and conflicts had played such a prominent role suggested quite the opposite. It was rather that unlike other absolutist regimes during these critical years, the Danish monarchy was seen to be listening to the voice of the people and responding so pragmatically and flexibly that it was possible to ride out the storm fairly easily.

STRUENSEE AND ENLIGHTENED ABSOLUTISM

At an overall level, this can be explained because in the previous hundred years or so there had been a significant shift in the way the regime perceived itself and the way it justified its position. As previously explained, the basis of legitimation was theocratic; the regime considered that it ruled by divine right and was the only legitimate agent of the will of God. This perception held sway until the first half of the eighteenth century, when the divine justification was slowly drawn into the background of a system of natural law based on the concept of a social contract between the king and the people. The ideas of Rousseau about the sovereignty of the people and the general will gained more and more ground in Denmark in the second half of the eighteenth century.

In conformity with this philosophy, Danish absolutism justified itself to an ever-greater degree by emphasising that the king was the only legitimate interpreter and agent of the will of the people. He alone could interpret the will and the needs of the sovereign people, and he alone had the duty to take care of the political and administrative consequences of this special insight. This self-perception was concisely expressed by one of the absolutist kings, Frederik VI (r. 1808–39), himself, when in 1835 he refused to abolish the censorship of printed works with the words:

Just as Our paternal attention has always been directed towards contributing everything within Our royal power to the good of the

State and the people, so can We alone judge what will be to the true benefit of both.[10]

This particular understanding of the position and role of the monarchy in relation to the whole endowed late absolutism with a special sympathy and sense of responsibility. This phase in the history of European absolutism is usually described as enlightened absolutism. There were several similar examples of this special form of absolutism in Europe, for example in Austria, but the sympathy of the regime in Denmark to the voice of the people was so pronounced that some historians have described this late phase as 'absolutism driven by opinion', meaning that the paternal monarch carefully took stock of the wishes and needs of his beloved subjects and adjusted his style of rule accordingly, in so far as possible.[11]

The concrete result of this new sensitivity to 'opinion' in Denmark was that the absolutist regime, formally headed from 1766 to 1808 by the mentally unstable Christian VII, took a range of thorough initiatives for reform. These took the wind out of the sails of the revolutionary critics in the country at a critical moment and modernised Danish society in definitive ways. Taken together, these reforms meant that the state freed itself from its previous dependence on large landowners and thus strengthened its power and freedom of action, and that the principal economic activity of the country, agriculture, was comprehensively reorganised, both in terms of ownership and the methods of working. The reforms put agriculture in a position to adopt the new methods of cultivation and operation which were developed through what is known as the agrarian revolution, which took place earlier in the eighteenth century, especially in Britain and the Netherlands.

One of the pioneers of this extensive process of reform, which continued over 30 years until Denmark became embroiled in the Napoleonic Wars in 1801, was the German-born Johann Friedrich Struensee (1737–1772). Shortly after the change of government in 1766, he was employed as the physician-in-ordinary to the ailing king. Soon afterwards he started an affair with the young, English-born queen, Caroline Mathilde. On the basis of these circumstances, he accumulated so much personal power in the brief hectic period 1770–2, that it would hardly be an exaggeration to describe him as the real ruler of the country.[12]

Before entering the service of the Danish king, Struensee had been part of a group of enlightenment intellectuals, zealous for reform, in Hamburg, who were powerfully influenced by the notion of an enlightened, paternal absolutism inspired by Rousseau's philosophy. He attempted to convert these ideas at a frenetic pace into the political reality of Denmark once he had the chance in 1770. With the stroke of a pen he abolished all censorship, to allow the popular will to be freely expressed, and he replaced the landowner-dominated senior public administration with a body of middle-class bureaucrats, while also centralising the government itself to a cabinet with him at the centre. Through these initiatives, he succeeded in transforming the old feudal central administration into a powerful government by cabinet, which put the absolute monarch or his proxy firmly at the centre of the state. The government, as mentioned, became dominated by middle-class politicians and career civil servants, driving the whole group of traditional power brokers, the landowners, to the periphery. Thus, paradoxically, the first enlightened absolute ruler of Denmark was a German doctor.

However, the end of Struensee's period of power was tragic and gory. In January 1772 he was arrested by a rival faction at Court, who, led by the Queen Dowager, had succeeded in cajoling the ailing king into issuing a warrant. He was then charged with high treason, for which the Act of Succession prescribed only one penalty: death. The sentence was carried out shortly afterwards in a particularly barbaric way. His lifeless corpse was dismembered, and the parts put on display in the central thoroughfares of the capital to serve as a warning to anyone else who might be entertaining the idea of usurping absolute power. The wretched young queen was exiled for life to Celle in Hanover, which had a dynastic union with her homeland, Britain.

The force of the reaction at Court had certainly obliterated Struensee as a person, but the reforms he had carried through could not be so easily removed, and the concepts of enlightenment which had driven him could not be eradicated. His reforms, which gave a voice to the will of the people, had freed the state from the oppressive influence of the landed aristocracy, and so, despite everything, set the scene for a series of agrarian reforms which would ensure the survival of absolutism for a little longer and carry Danish agricultural society into a century of liberalism.

THE GREAT AGRARIAN REFORMS

Seen from a broad perspective, the extensive agrarian reforms at the end of the eighteenth century shifted Danish agriculture from organic or ecologic to commercially based production, that is, from a traditional system based on the conditions of nature, to a business which tried to accommodate the requirements of the market. Another way of looking at it is to say agriculture changed from being subsistence-driven, where the farmers struggled to survive from one harvest to the next, to a system of producing extra produce which could be sold and even exported. From the late eighteenth century, agriculture started to turn its eyes outwards, to the world at large.[13]

This extroversion was triggered by the increased demand for produce to feed the population of Europe, which rapidly increased from the middle of the eighteenth century. Danish agriculture had previously been organised in large, co-operative open-field systems with villages as the basic units of production. This system was quite unable to meet the new levels of demand, and so the need for reform of the very nature of production became increasingly apparent in the later eighteenth century. From the 1780s, the government tried to accommodate the new demands through a series of large-scale reforms which eventually transformed Danish agriculture into a modern, liberal business.

The reforms replaced the old collective open-field system with privatised production, as well as slowly phasing out the compulsory duties of peasants to work on the manor farms and their legal and economic dependence on the landowners. This created an entirely new social class of independent farmers. We will examine the details of the reforms in a subsequent chapter. What is of interest in terms of the current topic is how the government dealt with the process of reform. This provides a good illustration of how the 'opinion-driven' absolutism approached sensitive issues and also gives one explanation for the relative popularity of the regime, which defused any revolutionary urges amongst the population at a time when the rest of Europe was washed over by waves of change.

On 14 April 1784, the 16-year-old Crown Prince Frederik joined the Council of Ministers, the select group of royal advisers. He was the figurehead of a group of landowners hungry for reform, who wrenched control of the apparatus of state from the conservative faction at Court who had been dominant since the demise of Struensee in 1772. The Foreign Minister, Andreas Peter Bernstorff (1735–1797), was the champion of the group, and he exercised decisive influence right up until his death. Two other prominent members of the group were Christian Ditlev Frederik Reventlow (1748–1837) and Heinrich Ernst

Schimmelmann (1747–1831). As the names might suggest, all of these figures were of German origin, and they also all owned extensive property in Denmark, Holstein and northern Germany. The other thing they had in common was that they were eagerly promoting agrarian reform, so that they could exploit the favourable economic circumstances to the fullest extent. They immediately set to work.

They were in absolutely no doubt that they were confronting strong conservative forces both from the ultra-conservative rural peasant communities and the numerous conservative Danish landowners, neither of whom could see any reason for change. The government very wisely chose not to attempt to impose reforms from above, but to encourage them through positive incentives and leading by good example. They introduced the reforms in the places where they had full control, such as the Crown, or state, lands which still accounted for a good deal of the cultivated area of the country, and on the private estates of the members of the government. Here, from the mid-1780s, the government oversaw a systematic exchange of the land of individual farmers from the previous collective structures and a deliberate scattering of farms to achieve a rational distribution of farm buildings over the whole of the arable land. Smallholders were compensated for the loss of grazing rights with small parcels of land. The actual details of exactly where the field boundaries were redrawn and which farms were to be moved were left largely to local communities to decide. The government only intervened in situations where irresolvable conflicts arose.

By 1788 the process was so far advanced that the government was able to present the first copyholds to farmers in north Zealand with great public ceremony. In practice this was a change to independent ownership, turning the former tenants into freeholders in their own right, with full responsibility for their own property. The government established a permanent agricultural commission of civil servants and landowners to ensure the reforms were implemented. In 1790, an official report was issued, to serve as a guideline and an inspiration for anyone involved. The government also adjusted its policies of taxation and subsidy to reward farmers who had introduced the reforms and to penalise those who had not. The government used the same mixture of carrot and stick to gradually remove villeinage, but this process went through several stages before its full realisation in the following century.

By heading up the reform movement by example, the government sent a very clear signal to the private estate owners as to which way the wind was blowing. Through legislation and economic policies, the mix of persuasion and force ensured that the whole Danish agricultural sector fell into step. The result was that the reforms and changes in production, traces of which can still be seen in the Danish landscape, were largely completed before the Napoleonic wars brought things to a halt. Through judicious use of incentives and punishments the government managed to introduce a revolution in just a 20-year period, projecting Danish agriculture from the Middle Ages to modern times, without giving rise to social unrest. This was an extraordinary achievement and a perfect illustration of how a potentially strong and effective state could use persuasive means when there was little doubt as to who was really making the decisions.

THE REFORM OF MILITARY CONSCRIPTION AND THE EMANCIPATION OF THE PEASANTS, 1788

One key point in the reforms of these years was the law which removed adscription, passed on 20 June 1788, which subsequently became a symbol of the emancipation of the peasantry, one of the principal humanitarian aims of the reforms. This was yet another example of the flexibility of the regime to accommodate popular opinion.

Adscription, which forbade the sons of villeins to leave the estate where they were born, became law in 1733, and was a quid pro quo from the government to the landowners for their conscripting soldiers to the military. With the favourable economic circumstances for agriculture, it turned into a valuable scheme to provide landowners with a cheap and reliable workforce, ensuring that the landowners could make the most profit from the advantageous circumstances.

Largely thanks to the reforms that Struensee introduced, the state was strong enough by the end of the eighteenth century to take over full responsibility for conscription, which had always been an issue of critical importance for the security of the country. As the agrarian reforms proceeded, adscription came to appear ever more anachronistic. As the political influence of the landowners had been much reduced by Struensee's reforms, the time was ripe for the government to deal with the problem. With the decree of 20 June 1788, the government took the decisive step of transferring all responsibility for military conscription to the state.

This was in essence what this decree was about. However, this involved a huge reorganisation of the conscription authorities, with the state for the first time taking full control, while the duty of military service was no longer linked to agricultural land, but placed on a particular social group, the male farming population. Thus military service was transformed to a personal, national duty, in conformity with the ideas which held sway in France. In practice this led to an increase in the burden of military service.[14]

Nonetheless, the Danish government succeeded in persuading the Danish people that this was, in fact, a major, liberating reform. This was achieved because the leaders of the government were ingenious in combining the reform of military service with the removal of the detested adscription. The peasants, as well as the liberally inclined elite of the capital, saw this as a social liberation and a decisive victory for liberal ideas.

In reality, the reform of conscription simply made adscription superfluous. The government also had its own interest in removing it, as it involved another weakening of the influence of the conservative feudal landowners. The simultaneous launch of conscription reform and the abolition of adscription in 1788 was not just a real consolidation of power by the absolutist regime. The manner of the launch was a propaganda victory for the regime which subsequently led to a strong increase in the popularity of the government and the monarchy. In the eyes of the population, the king – or rather the Crown Prince – became a popular, caring and well-intentioned paternal figure, who only wanted the best for his beloved subjects.

In this way the monarchy became so popular that only a handful of fantasists even considered starting a revolution in Denmark. Some years later, the grateful population erected an obelisk, called the Liberty Stone, on one of the main approaches to Copenhagen as a tribute to the emancipation of the peasantry and to the monarchy. When, in 1848, the revolution did eventually come, it was peaceful, almost cordial, and the king renounced his absolute power without striking a blow and proclaimed himself to be constitutional king.

By contrast, in France, the Bastille was stormed on 14 July 1789 and a long, bloody revolution followed which swept away both the monarchy and the aristocracy and made long-lasting and profound changes to the structure of French society. In Denmark, the day of the proclamation of the reform of conscription system – 20 June 1788 – was the day when any similar revolution was definitively nipped in the bud, as an enfeebled aristocracy gave the government room to manoeuvre in reacting appropriately to the people's desire for reform, and also because of the masterly political exploitation of the opportunities for propaganda presented by the abolition of adscription. This display of sympathetic flexibility actually prolonged Danish absolutism by 60 years, while the French model of absolutism was swallowed up in revolutionary chaos the next year, in part because of the lack of similar political skills.

The political farsightedness of the absolute monarchy and its administrative abilities through the agrarian and other reforms, introduced in 1784 and lasting up to Denmark's involvement in the Napoleonic Wars in 1801, are attested by the fact that those measures largely came to define the legal and administrative framework for the development of Danish society and mode of production for a very long time. In fact, it was only in the last 50 years that the traces of the great reforms of the late eighteenth century really began to fade away.

4

· · · · · · · ·

Domestic Policy since 1848: Democracy and the Welfare State

CIVIL WAR AND REVOLUTION

The year 1848 was a year of destiny. It was not just the vague spectre of communism which hovered over Europe, but the much more distinct spirit of liberalism which became more widespread than ever and finally unleashed the last of the civil revolutions which had dominated the political stage since the French revolution of 1789. The February Revolution in 1848 toppled the last French king, and in March the revolutionary movement spread throughout the entire area of Germany, where the princes had no choice but to concede to the demands of the subjects for a liberal constitution. Later in the same year, there was a reaction, supported by the more conservatively inclined bourgeoisie, who were alarmed by the ever-more radical demands from the revolutionary left wing. After the eventful months of the summer, the old princes were largely back in control of Germany and Austria.

In March 1848, Denmark also experienced a revolution, provoked directly by the events in Germany.[1] Unlike most of the German revolutions, however, the Danish one was a bloodless change of systems of an enduring nature. The immediate background to the Danish revolution was that the liberal movement in the Duchy of Holstein was impassioned by the revolutionary attitudes of the other German states and so demanded a free constitution, not just for itself, but also for the Danish Duchy of Schleswig. The liberal leaders in Holstein referred to the medieval ruling that the two duchies would always remain together.

Along with their sympathisers in Schleswig, they demanded that both Schleswig and Holstein should join the German Confederation.

Once news of these demands, which in reality would mean the secession of the duchies from Denmark, reached Copenhagen late in March, it created much dismay amongst the nationalist liberal middle class, who also sought a free constitution, but one which included Schleswig. From the point of view of constitutional politics, the liberals of the capital were pretty much in line with the Schleswig-Holstein movement, but the two factions disagreed completely over the nationality of Schleswig. The Copenhagen liberals were also afraid that the conservative ministers in the government would yield to the demands from Schleswig-Holstein. It was a cardinal point for the ministers – as it had always been for the absolutist regime – to preserve the Danish monarch's kingdom and lands under the sovereignty of the king irrespective of any linguistic or cultural differences within the population. There were thus good grounds to fear that the government would bow under pressure and accommodate the demands from Schleswig-Holstein in return for an acknowledgement that the king's sovereignty still extended to the Elbe. Thus, the fear of losing Schleswig and the desire for a combined free constitution for both Denmark and Schleswig goaded the liberal citizens of Copenhagen into action to have the ministers, whom they considered to be untrustworthy, removed.

After a heated mass meeting in one of the large theatres of the city on 20 March 1848, during which one of the main speakers, Orla Lehmann (1810–1870), warned that the nation would take matters into its own hands out of desperation if the king did not meet their demands, the liberal leaders decided to organise a mass procession to the square at Christiansborg Palace the next day to demand the removal of the ministers. When the leaders of the demonstration were granted an audience by the king – Frederik VII (r. 1848–63) – so they could present their demands, they were astonished to be told that their demands had already been accommodated as the entire body of ministers had just resigned. In their place, on 22 March, a completely new interim ministry was created. Naturally, it continued to be dominated by experienced conservative forces, with the previous finance minister A. W. Moltke (1785–1864) at the head as Prime Minister. However, the new government, subsequently referred to as the 'March Government', included some leaders of the middle-class opposition: D. G. Monrad (1811–1887), Orla Lehmann, L. N. Hvidt (1777–1856) and A. F. Tscherning (1795–1874). The most important tasks for the transitional government were to ensure that

Schleswig-Holstein remained under the Danish Crown and to introduce the transition to a free constitution. The latter was essential, as on the adoption of the new government, the king had proclaimed himself as constitutional king. In so doing, he marked the end of 188 years of absolutism and opened the doors to a middle-class, liberal constitution.

This was the culmination of the Danish liberal revolution, which as can be seen was peaceful, indeed almost amiable. The new ministers took up their roles at the centre of power almost imperceptibly, while the previous dignitaries took their leave with an equal lack of sound and fury. This transformation from absolutism to democracy was almost as smooth as that from aristocratic dominance to absolutism itself 188 years before. As then, the changes of 1848 took place in the shadow of war.

The Schleswig-Holstein faction took the change of government as an open declaration of war. They set up their own provisional government in Kiel, charged with ensuring that their demands were accommodated and implemented. As these demands were absolutely incompatible with the programme of the new government, open conflict was inevitable. The result was three years of bitter warfare, when the people of Schleswig-Holstein, supported by Prussia, fought for what they regarded as theirs by right, while the Danish army aligned itself behind the government's desire to include Schleswig in the new Danish constitution which was being drawn up. The final outcome of the war was fairly indecisive, although many Danes chose to hail it as a victory. The great powers intervened to mediate an end to the hostilities in 1850. The Danish government accepted a guaranteed settlement, signed in London in 1852 by the great powers, under which both Schleswig and Holstein remained as Danish Crown territory. In return, Schleswig could not be annexed, just as the previous constitution would remain in force in both duchies. The final upshot was that Holstein remained as a full member of the German Confederation, but with the Danish king as overall duke. The old absolutist constitution was to continue to apply to Schleswig, although the king was a constitutional monarch in Denmark. This extremely complicated situation would give rise to endless problems which heralded the national catastrophe of 1864.

THE 1849 CONSTITUTION – RUPTURE OR CONTINUITY?

In the midst of the First Schleswigian War, on 5 June 1849, the Danish king endorsed the new constitution, the first democratic constitution of Denmark. This was the product of around six months' work by a national assembly of selected representatives of the politically active sections of the population.

The introduction to the new constitution stated that 'the form of government is restricted monarchy'. This entailed the king sharing his previously unlimited power with a parliament elected by universal suffrage of the male population. Women first won the right to vote in 1915. The Parliament, which took over authority for legislation and taxation, was composed of two chambers, the *Landsting* and the *Folketing*, where the *Landsting*, the Upper House, was envisaged as a conservative check on the political decision-making process, to which end its members were chosen on more conservative principles than were the members of the Lower House. Although the new constitution took away many of the king's powers, he was not left without any at all. He still had executive power and was free to appoint his ministers irrespective of the parliamentary majority. However, the new arrangements meant that the king could no longer take action by himself, but required the countersignature of the minister responsible for any governmental decision. The ministers in turn were directly responsible to Parliament for their conduct, whereas under absolutism, they had been exclusively answerable to the king.

In this respect, the new Danish constitution precisely conformed to the principle of tripartite power which Montesquieu had advocated a century before, and which had found expression in the American constitution and a number of later democratic constitutions, most recently that of Belgium of 1831. This meant that power was shared between the executive (the king), the legislature (the parliament) and the judiciary (the courts). The judiciary was endowed with a great deal of independence from the other bodies, and so the three components of state were intended to complement each other through a system of checks and balances.

Compared to the constitutions of many other countries, that of Denmark was very democratic, not least in terms of the extent of franchise. Doubtless this was partly related to the recently introduced duty of universal male military service to ensure a sufficient supply of soldiers for an army at war. Universal military service was enshrined in the constitution, and it would not be unreasonable to interpret universal male suffrage as a quid pro quo. If the state could use the constitution to oblige its citizens to lay down their lives for their country, then it was not unreasonable to grant them a certain political influence.

Once the hostilities were over, the inner political circles immediately regretted that the general rural population, whom they regarded as uneducated peasants, had been allowed a degree of political responsibility which they were incapable of exercising sensibly. The most prominent spokesman for this elitist attitude, the National Liberal minister Orla Lehmann, once expressed the sentiment that in his view power should only be exercised by 'the intelligent, the educated and the rich', in other words, the intellectual elite and the landowners, whereas the great unwashed could simply not be trusted with political responsibility. This meant that one of the most important front lines in Danish politics for the rest of the century was the struggle between the forces that wanted to restrict the concept of democracy in the constitution and the ever-more confident groups of the rural population who wanted to add more political influence to the economic freedom they had already gained through the agrarian reforms.

On first glance, it could appear that the transition from absolutism to democracy took place with the suddenness of a revolution, and that there was a decisive break with the past. However, this in fact was not the case. First, as already mentioned, the absolute monarchy had long considered itself as the interpreter and agent of the popular will, and from the end of the eighteenth century the regime perceived itself as the legitimate and highest expression of the general will of the people, which in turn was the ultimate legitimacy of the regime. The constitution of 1849 created a new institution – the Parliament – which allowed the will of the people to find expression in a formal framework at the same time as the king's freedom to interpret that will was limited. Yet in point of fact, there was no real decisive or fundamental change in the basis of legitimacy of the power of the state. This was still the will of the people, just in different institutional forms – old wine in new bottles. This underlying continuity probably provides a partial explanation as to why what was called a revolution proceeded so painlessly and was not perceived as a clear break, not even by the king, who relinquished his absolute status with no notable resistance. Instead, he earned such great popularity as the 'provider of the constitution' that he went down in history as 'Frederik the Beloved'.

A second point is that democratic forces had long played a role in Danish society. In Denmark, just as in many other places in Europe, national and liberal movements arose in the wake of the upheavals of the French Revolution and the Napoleonic Wars. In the first decades of the nineteenth century, the influence of these two movements for emancipation was hampered because they virtually worked against each other. The liberal circles in Denmark were not nationalist, and the nationalists were not liberal, but rather dyed-in-the-wool conservatives. Up until around 1830, therefore, the two movements each went their own way, and so the regime had very little difficulty in keeping them in check.

After 1830, however, this situation slowly began to change as, following the revolutionary events in France, the regime started to yield to the growing demands of the liberals to be heard. The concession consisted of an acceptance that advisory assemblies of the estates of the realm in the most important provinces be convened. This happened for the first time in 1834, in four places, and even though the government tried to keep these assemblies on a tight rein, they soon became meeting points for the opposition, which could make its voice heard here. So, for the first time, there was an institutional framework for the development of a middle-class public, which was the true prerequisite for growth towards democracy. From that point on, this trend could not be stopped. The last 15–20 years of absolutism were a long rearguard action.

The trend accelerated as the previously internationally oriented liberal movement started to swing towards a more national focus from the start of the 1840s, under pressure from the rapidly growing antagonism between Danes and Germans in the duchies. The trendsetting, liberal middle class became more and more nationalist, leading to a dynamic National Liberal movement which took the form of a real political party with a national programme critical of the system. In the last years of absolutism this became the focus for both the liberals and nationalists of the country. Thus, at last the two strongest and most dynamic ideologies of the nineteenth century united and pulled in the same direction. From the moment this became a reality, which happened in Denmark around 1840, the fate of absolutism was sealed. It was now only a matter of time and, as mentioned, that ran out in 1848.

In other words, this chain of events underlined that in reality there was a great deal of continuity behind what otherwise appeared to be such a pronounced change of the system in 1848. A large number of the changes formally enshrined in the new constitution had been gradually taking place for a long time. Equally, many of the traditions of absolutism remained in place undisturbed after the change. Apart from the sections dealing purely with constitutional law, a large part of the Danish Law of 1683 remained in force; indeed, as mentioned, some of the provisions of this act still apply today. In addition, the central apparatus of power was largely unaltered. It did entail changing the names of the departments to ministries, the heads becoming ministers and so responsible to Parliament, but in essence the central administration remained the same, both in its fundamental structure and its working procedures. And indeed the absolutist pattern of administration can still be clearly seen in the practices of modern Danish government.

Just as under absolutism, the civil servants consider themselves impartial and non-political, totally loyal to the government of the day whatever its colour, as obedient to the government as their predecessors were to the king. This self-perception, shared by every public official from the top of the organisation to the bottom, is clearly inherited from the period of absolutism. It is also the reason why if the government of Denmark changes, the civil servants remain in place. This endows the central administration with a vital stability and continuity which has significant ramifications for the rest of society. One very clear example of this was how the administration doggedly conducted the daily business of state through the last 18 months of the German occupation, 1940–5, even after the government had been forced out of office. This legacy from absolutism is a possible, and perhaps reasonable, explanation for the fact that most Danes today still consider the power of the state as positive, and attribute to it qualities such as honesty, incorruptibility and neutrality.

A final point is that the leaders of the National Liberals in 1848 were no machine-breakers. On the contrary, they were good solid burghers who shied away from social disturbance and anarchy. They were not looking to roll back the power of the state; they simply wanted to be empowered to influence it. Once they achieved this desire through change of the system, they acted as custodians of the status quo with the same assiduity as the absolutist kings. Thus, the political upheaval in Denmark in 1848 only superficially appeared to be a revolution worthy of the name. It certainly set new political agendas and created the framework for a middle-class nation state. Under the surface, the enduring structures of absolutism survived unchanged and so exerted their influence on the nature of modern Danish society just as much as the new concepts of democracy.

THE REVISED CONSTITUTION, 1866

The June Constitution of 1849 was essentially the work of the National Liberals. The extensive concept of democracy enshrined in the constitution particularly reflected the ideas of representative government which were prevalent amongst the intellectuals of the capital at the time. However, these ideas were in one essential regard out of step with the true nature of society. In an ideal world, the provisions of the constitution regarding universal suffrage would have been self-evident, but in reality there were such huge differences within the population and so much political inequality that it proved very difficult to live up to the idealistic requirements therein.

The landowners were the undisputed leaders in the countryside, and they were deeply suspicious of the idea that simple peasants, their former humble tenants, should now be allowed political influence. For so long as the political tone was set by the National Liberals, the majority of landowners did not take an active role in political life, simply because very few of them were willing to take part in elections alongside humble peasants, let alone risk being defeated by them. Yet while the National Liberals securely held the reins of power, there was actually very little the landowners could do to alter the terms of the constitution so that they reflected the prevailing social conditions accurately.

However, the landowners' chance came after the catastrophic war of 1864 when the duchies were lost to Prussia. This marked the end of National Liberalism, as its leaders had led Denmark into disaster. The humiliating peace treaty annihilated the National Liberals as a political movement, and as soon after as 1865, the king appointed a government made up purely of landowners, with one of the biggest landowners, Count C. E. Frijs-Frijsenborg (1817–1896), at the head. From then until 1901, the changing Danish governments were all made up of the landed gentry, and a long, bitter constitutional struggle between the 'large and small farmers' started in 1865. The small farmers finally won in 1901 after 36 years in the political wilderness.

The start was promising enough. Immediately following the appointment of the new government, serious political discussions began between it and I. A. Hansen (1806–1877), the leader of the Small Farmers' Movement, which had a solid majority in the Lower House. The aim of these discussions was to forge a cross-party alliance to unite the whole population behind the government's efforts to steer a course out of the bankruptcy which was the legacy of the National Liberals.

A critical issue in the negotiations was constitutional change in order to incorporate substantial conservative guarantees to guard against any repetition of the adventurism which had led to the catastrophe of 1864. With half-hearted promises of increased influence in the policies of the government, Count Frijs managed to persuade the leader of the Farmers' Movement to support a revision of the 1849 constitution which transformed the *Landsting* into a genuinely conservative political force. Previously all 66 members had been directly elected; now 12 were to be appointed by the king, and the remaining 54 selected through an indirect election where half of the seats were controlled by the largest taxpayers of the constituency. These changes ensured a comfortable dominance for the landowners in the Upper House, allowing them to effectively block any progressive proposals from the *Folketing*.

Parliament accepted the amended constitution, and it was signed by the king on 28 July 1866. However, the farmers' political representatives waited in vain for their promised reward of greater political influence. In fact, the landowners' government, with the support of the remaining right-wing National Liberals, took even less heed of them. In other words, they had simply given away the original wide constitutional definition of democracy and gained nothing in return. This broken promise, as it was seen by the farmers, left deep scars on Danish political life, as it was the basis for an unshakeable mistrust between conservatives and liberals which has to a certain extent survived to the present day.

It was now brutally clear to the farmers that they would gain nothing through negotiation and concession. Their only hope now for advancing their liberal policies was head-on confrontation, and this was the strategy they adopted henceforth. In 1870 they formed a single party, *Det Forenede Venstre* (The United Left), which won an absolute majority in the *Folketing* in 1872. At the same time, the landowners and the remains of the National Liberals, who represented the urban conservatives, formed a common right-wing party. And so the scene was set for the hard confrontation of the following years.

CONSTITUTIONAL STRUGGLE AND PROVISIONAL MEASURES

When the Liberal Party, *Venstre*, achieved a majority in the *Folketing*, its main demand was to form the government, as it represented a majority of the electorate. But neither the king nor the Conservatives were prepared to accept this, as they did not think that the humble commoners were capable of taking responsibility for government. In 1875, the 50-year-old large estate-owner Jacob Brønnum Scavenius

Estrup (1825–1913) became the leader of the Conservatives, and the head of a new government appointed by the king, notwithstanding the liberal majority in the *Folketing*. For the next 19 years he proved to be a powerful adversary of the liberals.[2]

Initially, *Venstre* tried to force Estrup out of office by refusing to vote for the budget. All this achieved was that just before the existing budget expired on 1 April 1877, Estrup prorogued Parliament and on his own responsibility issued a provisional budget, which the constitution formally allowed the government to do. The Prime Minister thus clearly demonstrated that he was ready to give as good as he got, and would not hesitate to use every power the constitution allowed him to fight for the king's right to freely appoint his ministers, just as Bismarck had done 14 years before in Prussia.

From the start of the 1880s, the Liberal Party adopted a new tactic to try to exhaust Estrup's government by a policy of obstruction, voting out every government proposal in the *Folketing* and so paralysing the government. Estrup responded by continuing to govern on the basis of provisional budgets from 1885 to 1894. He also tried to divide *Venstre*, by extensively increasing the Danish armed forces to protect against the superior German neighbour, which most left-wingers also thought to be essential in the light of the humiliating defeat of 1864. The fact was that tax revenues were flooding into the government's coffers under the provisional budgets, while *Venstre's* policy of obstruction prevented any new legislation requiring expenditure from coming into force. In addition, the Liberals were hardly in a position to oppose the build-up of the armed forces for fear of losing the trust of the electorate. As Estrup had succeeded in equating the issue of defence with Copenhagen's fortifications, they reluctantly had to agree to the extensive defensive works. Thus, during these very heated political years, extensive defensive construction work was carried out around the capital to ensure it could withstand any attack until one of the great European powers came to its aid. At least, this was the argument. Quite what would really have happened if there had been such an attack was fortunately never tested. The National Defence Act of 1922 definitively closed down the fortifications. All that can be seen today are the remains of the impressive defences in the west of Copenhagen and a semicircle of sea forts off the harbour entrance, a striking reminder of the masterly gambit by which Prime Minister Estrup managed to split the opposition.

He also succeeded in wearing out *Venstre*. By around 1890 large sections of the moderate factions of the party had simply had enough.

They entered into negotiations with the moderate elements of the Conservatives to seek some form of agreement which would put a stop to the provisional measures. In March 1894 a big compromise was reached between the parties of the Right and the Left. The Liberals had to accept that the defences of Copenhagen were there to stay. In return, the provisional measures would come to an end, and Estrup had to promise to stand down in favour of a more moderate Conservative whom the Liberals could trust.

The result of the agreement was that Estrup, the arch-enemy of *Venstre*, was gone, but the right-wing party *Højre* remained in power in accordance with the express wishes of the king. The Liberals, as mentioned, also had to agree to the defence work – in itself a monument to their abortive attempt to seize political power. The moderates of the liberal side had arguably achieved as much as possible given the circumstances, but under terms which had to be conceded as being somewhat compromising. They had had to give way on both of their main issues in the struggle, the question of the Copenhagen defences and the demand for parliamentary responsibility, meaning that the composition of the government should correspond to the majority in the lower house, the *Folketing*.

Nonetheless, the agreement broke the political deadlock and quietened the almost revolutionary atmosphere which had dominated Danish politics for a dozen years with regular accusations that the government had breached the constitution and the threat that the people would take matters into their own hands. Even though *Venstre* could claim a partial victory, it had split the party and left it in disarray, and they had to admit that to reach the goal of the struggle, to implement the parliamentary principle and gain power, was still a long way off.

As things turned out, it was no further away than 1901, which became the year of *Systemskiftet* (the change of parliamentary system). There were two reasons for this. One was that the right-wing government was ever-more divided internally, the other that *Venstre*, once the advocates of the policy of compromise which had been thrust out into the darkness, finally found a strong and able leader in the person of a staid schoolteacher from west Jutland, I. C. Christensen (1856–1930), who managed to unite the warring party behind him in a determined battle to seize power.

The hard battles of the years of provisional measures had worn down *Højre*. By no means all of the party agreed with Estrup's hard line, as many feared it would drive *Venstre* into the arms of the radical Socialist

Workers who were making their voices heard ever-more clearly and from 1884 were winning ever-more seats in the *Folketing*. The moderate Conservatives saw this as a long-term threat to the entire political system as it existed, and so increasingly advocated a policy of concession to the Liberals, to soften the conflict and keep *Venstre* on a moderate course. This could also be interpreted as an expression that an ever larger number of right-wingers were beginning to lose faith in the birthright of the Conservatives to run the government.

On the other hand, from 1895 the new leader of *Venstre*, I. C. Christensen, succeeded in uniting the steadily growing number of the party members in the *Folketing* into a party of reform, which showed that it could appear united both in election campaigns and in parliamentary politics. With an appropriate mixture of steadfastness and willingness to negotiate, he succeeded in wearing down *Højre* as well as forcing them into a corner by time and time again exposing their powerlessness and lack of energy over even the most trivial political questions. In the election in 1901, the Conservatives won only eight out of 114 seats in the *Folketing*. This catastrophic result triggered such an acute crisis in the party of government that even prominent members of the party near to the king, who had previously resolutely supported his constitutional right to freely appoint his own ministers, were now earnestly urging him to give in and appoint a Liberal government. Abandoned by his most loyal supporters, the ageing Christian IX (r. 1863–1906) eventually conceded. On 24 July 1901 he appointed the first *Venstre* government in the history of Denmark. The long, hard battle of the Danish farmers to convert the economic and legal freedoms they had won through agrarian reform 100 years before into real political influence was finally won.

CHANGE OF SYSTEM AND PARLIAMENTARIANISM

From that point on, parliamentarianism was adopted as political practice in Denmark, and, with one serious exception, it has been respected ever since, even though it was not made formal until the constitutional amendment of 1953. The exception was a challenge to the validity of the principle during what is called the Easter Crisis of 1920, when King Christian X (r. 1912–47) – the grandson of Christian IX – decided on his own initiative to dismiss the government and appoint another without the backing of Parliament. This rash action provoked such widespread political and popular unrest that he immediately had to pull in his horns and put together a government which matched the majority in the Folketing. Since then, the monarchy has very carefully avoided interfering actively in the formation of governments. The change in the political system which was heralded by the appointment of the first Liberal government in 1901 proved to be lasting. From a constitutional point of view, it meant a weakening of the role of the Crown and a significant strengthening of that of Parliament, and especially of the *Folketing*. The Upper House of Parliament, the *Landsting*, was abolished by the constitutional amendment in 1953, and thus the role of the monarchy changed from being an actor in politics to being an institution of mainly symbolic function and a figurehead of state.

But this situation was preceded by 30 years of bitter struggle over the constitution, where at times Denmark was on the brink of becoming a dictatorship, and at times the difference between political confrontation and open revolt was hanging by a thread. At no point in the recent history of the country was Denmark closer to revolution and widespread civil disobedience than in the last quarter of the nineteenth century. The fact that the country never went over the precipice is principally due to the fact that the moderates in both camps were able to assert themselves sufficiently to impose calm, and that, unlike in Germany, the liberal movement had grown to be so powerful, through co-operative and popular educational movements that the right wing had no choice but to concede. In these years, *Venstre*, the party of the Danish farmers, was victorious.

Just how difficult the king and the conservative clique which surrounded him found it to accept the new state of things was immediately evidenced by the formation of the first liberal government itself. It would have been an obvious move to ask the head of *Venstre*, Christensen, to form a government and let him take up the position of Prime Minister. Yet still, neither the king nor his advisers could bring themselves to entrust such a position of responsibility to a simple schoolteacher, who, to compound the problem, spoke a strong west Jutland dialect. So the uncrowned king of Venstre had to settle in the first instance for a position as the Minister for Church Affairs and Education. The king appointed a politically inexperienced lawyer and member of the board of the East Asiatic Company as Prime Minister, Professor J. H. Deuntzer (1845–1918), who as well as being one of the inner circle of the educated citizens of the capital was a regular guest in royal circles. It is reported that it was at such an occasion just before the change of political system that the king asked Deuntzer, 'You are a left-winger, aren't you, Professor?', to which the somewhat nervous response was, 'To some extent, Your Majesty.' The hesitant response convinced the king that he had found the right man to head up the government of commoners he was on the point of forming.[3]

Deuntzer made absolutely no impact of any significance on the policies of the government, and when the government changed in 1905, he disappeared from political history with the same obscurity as he entered it. He was replaced by Christensen, whom the king, to his own surprise, had found he could trust. Christensen had been the de facto leader of the government, and despite the king's misgivings, the government had proved that it could function well. He was astonished that this government consisted of 'terribly nice chaps' with whom he could work very easily. Moreover, unlike the previous incumbents, the new government showed that it was in a position to implement long-needed reform in the areas of education and taxation. Thus, the change of system injected a new dynamic into political life, with a positive impact on commerce and society.

The reason for the change of government in 1905 was that a smouldering division in the *Venstre* party finally caught fire in that year and led to an anti-militarist wing breaking away from the main party and forming its own, which was called *Det radikale Venstre*, which literally means 'the Radical Left', but is generally translated as 'the Social-Liberal Party'. The new party, which recruited 15 of the *Venstre* members of the *Folketing*, appealed especially to the urban intellectual elites and the rural underclass who did not consider that their interests were being served by the policies of *Venstre*, which favoured the independent farmers. The key points of the new party's programme were disarmament, the creation of a new agricultural system of smallholdings by parcelling out the larger estates, and social and taxation policy which would reduce inequality.

Despite its rather limited size, the new party quickly came to play an important role, and continued to hold a key position in Danish politics throughout the twentieth century, precisely because it managed to occupy a position between the larger parties which often battled over forming governments or other major political decisions. The creation of the new party had another critical long-term political effect. As it appealed directly to the rural underclass, it actually forestalled the nascent social democratic movement, unlike, for example, in Sweden and Germany. The effect was that although the social democratic movement had a great deal of support in Denmark, it never achieved an overall parliamentary majority. Just like the other parties throughout the twentieth century, the Social Democrats were obliged to negotiate, accept compromises and co-operate to promote their policies.

In short, the emergence of *Det radikale Venstre* and the effect on the balance of the parties which resulted made cross-party compromises an essential ingredient in Danish politics, and co-operation and consensus across party lines a condition of political survival. The emergence of the new party fashioned the contours of Danish politics right up to 1973: the Social Democrats, *Det radikale Venstre*, *Venstre* and *Højre* (which changed its name in 1915 to *Det konservative Folkeparti*, usually translated as the Danish Conservative Party). Danish politics over the twentieth century has been the history of the tension between these four parties, none of which won an absolute majority, and so all of which were forced to enter into various coalitions, while *Det radikale Venstre*, 'the Social-Liberal Party', was conveniently placed in the centre. Thus, the changes of 1901 and the formation of the Social-Liberal Party in 1905 dictated the terms of politics for the twentieth century – exactly the democracy through negotiation which the former Prime Minister Jens Otto Krag celebrated so warmly in 1973 in the article quoted in the introduction to Chapter 3. This formed the context for the creation of the modern Danish welfare state, with the new workers' party, the Social Democrats, in the driving seat.[4]

THE CENTURY OF SOCIAL DEMOCRACY

It would be fair to describe the twentieth century in Denmark as the century of social democracy as, since the movement took over the government in 1924, it has ruled in one way or another, alone or in coalitions, mainly in the shape of *Det radikale Venstre*, for a total of 50 years. The Social Democratic Party grew up with the modern Danish nation state and, not least because of its social policies, strongly contributed to the particular character of the country – to such an extent that for many outsiders the name 'Denmark' is virtually synonymous with social democracy and the welfare state.

Just like other socialist movements, Danish social democracy started as a branch of the international workers' movement. The International Workers' Association in Denmark was founded in 1871 and from the very start built up its activities on the basis of an international, revolutionary programme which had the ultimate goal of the workers taking over the means of production and the power within society. In its very origin, the Danish movement was even more revolutionarily inclined than the corresponding German organisation on which, in many other respects, it was modelled. The authorities and established middle-class liberal circles thus regarded it as dangerous and socially disruptive and a movement to be fought with all available means.

In 1878 the movement was divided into the trade union movement, which was to take care of the interests of the workers in the workplaces throughout the country, and a political wing, which was to struggle on behalf of the workers at a political level. The latter took the name of the Social Democratic League, but the two branches continued to work very closely together at all levels. In 1965, the party changed its name to the Social Democratic Party of Denmark, a name which underlined the reformist and national path along which it had developed in the meantime. This trend could be said to have reached a logical conclusion when, in 1996, the party decided to break all formal links with the other two branches of the workers' movement, the trade union movement and the Workers' Consumer Co-operative Movement.

The Social Democrats were elected to the *Folketing* for the first time in 1884, winning two seats, and from then on the party took a larger number of seats at each successive election. By the outbreak of the First World War, the party held 32 of the total of 113 seats in the *Folketing*. At this time, *Venstre*, with 43 seats, was still the largest party in the *Folketing* – a situation that continued until the election of 1924 when they were overtaken by the Social Democrats. The Social Democrats remained the largest party in the *Folketing* for the rest of the twentieth century. In 2001, however, the situation changed again, as for the first time since 1924, *Venstre*, now usually called 'the Liberals' in English, overtook the party of the workers and took over the government. The Social Democrats' peak was in the 1960s, when they held 76 of the then total of 175 seats. From then on the number declined, and today they only hold less than 50 seats.

A similar picture emerges from an investigation of the membership of the party. Over the first half of the century, the number of party members steadily rose, reaching a peak of around 300,000 at the end of the 1940s. From the beginning of the 1960s, membership was clearly falling, and by the end of the century it was just 60,000. In part this reflects the general fall in membership of political parties' local organisations, but nonetheless the fall in numbers was particularly marked and, for the Social Democrats, a sign of a party in crisis. This means that it makes sense to talk of the twentieth century, when the party was dominant in many ways, as the century of the Social Democrats. There is nothing to suggest that the party will play a similarly central role in the twenty-first century.

FROM CLASS WARFARE TO NATIONAL CONSENSUS

The first serious confrontation for the young workers' movement came in 1899, when a wave of strikes spread across the country, sparked by a general dissatisfaction with prevailing wages and work conditions. The employers retaliated with a lock-out. Everything suggested that there would be a trial of strength between the Danish Federation of Employers, which had been founded in 1895 by the right-wing government in office, and the Danish Federation of Trade Unions, established in 1898 and backed by the Social Democrats. The conflict was long-drawn-out and painful, and there was no question that it stretched the resources of the workers and the trade union movement to the fullest. Despite the battle of attrition, the conflict was resolved by the September Agreement of 1899, which laid the foundations for the labour market and political developments for the next century.[5]

The two warring parties succeeded in making the agreement without any significant outside political interference. There were some small concessions to the workers, but the key point of the agreement was that the employers would enjoy 'the right to manage and apportion work and to use what they consider to be the most appropriate workforce'. This has ever since been a fundamental principle within the Danish labour market. However, the most important outcome was that the two opposing bodies recognised each other as the only legitimate negotiating organs in any future collective bargaining. This was the starting point for the highly organised labour market of the twentieth century, where, in total accordance with the old Danish Law of 1683, they were themselves enabled to form necessary agreements without any political interference, and administer the conditions of the labour market on their own. The union-run unemployment insurance system was recognised by the state in 1907, and in 1910 a permanent court of arbitration was created to broker any conflicts arising from the system of collective bargaining. In other words, the September Agreement of 1899 paved the way for the workers to improve their wages and working conditions through negotiation rather than bruising conflicts. Thus, the conditions were in place for the non-revolutionary reformist approach which has ever since characterised the Danish workers' movement.

The agreement also had an important effect on the political branch of the movement, the Social Democrats, as in response they gradually moved away from their Marxist, revolutionary standpoint and took a reformist direction, accepting that socialism could be introduced through incremental reforms rather than a revolution. The underlying philosophy was that the working class could use the ballot box to win power, step by step, and once they had control of the apparatus of state, they could introduce comprehensive reforms to the benefit of the workers. Thus, the party decided to take a pragmatic approach of negotiation, fully respecting the rules of parliamentary democracy. At the same time they abandoned their original international orientation and became an ever-more purely Danish party, in step with the other parliamentary parties. Typically, the arch-enemy of the Social Democrats through the twentieth century was not the bourgeoisie in Denmark, but international communism, which was committed to revolutionary Marxist-Leninism. Perhaps the clearest expression of this was during the German occupation of Denmark from 1940 to 1945, when the leadership of the Social Democrats, in close agreement with Liberal and Conservative politicians, distanced themselves from armed resistance, particularly because they feared it could result in the communists seizing power.

The transformation of Social Democracy from a movement focused on the international class struggle to the guardian of the Danish nation state and its values was cemented when in 1916, in the middle of the First World War, the party agreed to join the national coalition government and contribute to resolving the current crises. This was despite a previous resolution of congress not to enter the government before obtaining an absolute majority. Through this act, the leader of the Social Democrats at that time, Thorvald Stauning (1873–1942), unambiguously declared his colours. The Social Democrats from then on were willing to conduct their policies on the premises of the nation state and to observe the rules of parliamentary democracy. Once the party took office in 1924, these two perspectives – that of the national state and social democracy – slowly merged, ending in the Danish Project, which the Social Democrats increasingly saw as synonymous with the social democratic project.

Typically, the leader of the Social Democrats, Thorvald Stauning, managed in his last long period as Prime Minister between 1929 and 1942 to achieve virtually cult status as the father of the country, not just in the eyes of the Social Democrats, but in those of the entire population. He himself was a symbol of the fact that the Danish Project and the Social Democratic Project were identical. This exact identification perhaps also serves to explain the crisis of the Social Democrats in the last quarter of the twentieth century briefly described above. The timing of this crisis corresponded exactly to the moment the Danish Project, or the Danish Model, for which the Social Democrats were principally responsible, came under strong pressure from internationalisation, increased immigration of people from very different cultures, and joining the European Union.

THE DANISH MODEL OF THE WELFARE STATE

The particularly Danish manifestation of the welfare state, which as mentioned was principally the achievement of the Social Democrats, although it won broad political acceptance, is in more ways than one a Danish project. It rested strongly on the underlying historically conditioned concept of freedom of negotiation, and the strong but not aggressive state formally created by the Danish Law in 1683. In addition the welfare state was established at a time when Danish society was still homogenous and comparatively uniform in terms of culture and traditions. None of these circumstances exists any more. Modern Danish society has become multicultural and multiethnic, and the power of the Danish state is waning in step with the increasing influence of the EU institutions and the growing demands from below for decentralisation and subsidiarity. So, under these pressures from several directions, the model is currently facing a serious crisis.

Although in essence the Danish model which was developed during the twentieth century is a system of welfare and social security, it is in fact much more than that. It actually permeates the whole of society in all its aspects, from the system of taxation to the way in which the citizens conduct themselves. It would not be an exaggeration to talk of a whole philosophy of life, tightly linked to being Danish and a particular Danish way of doing things. One factor, in common with the welfare systems in the other Nordic countries, is that the system is universal, meaning that it includes all the inhabitants of the country. It is also based on a legal principle that every citizen who meets the criteria for receiving help is legally entitled to benefit from the welfare services. In addition, the system is financed through taxation rather than insurance payments, as for example in Germany. Since the all-encompassing system of 'free services' has to be made available to all citizens from cradle to grave, the implementation of the model has required one of the highest tax burdens in the world. On this point alone, the model has profound socio-economic effects which impact on all aspect of society.

Historically, the earlier Danish welfare legislation was inspired by the Social Laws that Bismarck passed in the 1880s, which were based on an insurance principle. The conservative-dominated Danish Parliament copied the system. In 1891 a law on old-age pensions was passed, followed a year later by legislation on health insurance, and in 1898 by a law on accident insurance. A number of smaller laws followed, which together made big improvements in the social security net. The Social Democratic–Social Liberal government implemented a huge social reform in 1933, assembling a mass of previous legislation in one simple, transparent legal code which laid the foundation for the modern Danish welfare state, not just with the greatly extended insurance system, but especially because the law stated clearly that financial support under the terms of the law would no longer entail a reduction of the civil rights of the recipient. Thus the legal principle was introduced into Danish social legislation.

The political reality behind this social reform was the world economic crisis, to which Denmark was not immune, and which led to mass unemployment and a growing threat from the totalitarian movements of Communism, Fascism and Nazism that had taken control in the Soviet Union, Italy and Germany, and were also active in Denmark in the 1930s.

The warning signs were very clear. In the parliamentary elections in November 1932, the Danish Communist Party (DKP), whose loyalty was to Moscow, obtained 16,000 votes and thereby won two seats. The newly established Danish National Socialist Workers Party (DNSAP), which was closely associated with Hitler's National Socialist Party in Germany, received less than 1000 votes at that election and won no seats; but throughout the 1930s it was a bellicose and vociferous voice of dissent that rejected democracy and advocated a *Führer* concept on the German model. However, the party only became a serious threat to the parliamentary system after the German occupation of Denmark in 1940. Even the Liberal Party, *Venstre*, had to contend with right-wing extremists in its own ranks in the form of the Agrarian Revival Movement, *Landbrugernes Sammenslutning*, which was founded in 1930 as a reaction to the agricultural crisis. This strongly dissident opposition, whose ideas were akin to Mussolini's fascist movement in Italy, won increasing support among the hard-hit farmers that were *Venstre's* electoral stronghold, and they sought from within the party to steer it in an undemocratic direction. Finally, the Conservatives, *Det Konservative Folkeparti*, had to deal with a rapidly growing youth movement within the party that adopted a uniform which was clearly inspired by the *Hitlerjugend* and whose behaviour and ideology were not dissimilar.

All these warnings that the parliamentary democratic system was under threat and that the coalition government under the leadership of the Social Democrats could be overturned prompted the party's leading ideologist, the classicist Professor Hartvig Frisch (1893–1950), to write a book that was published as a *festschrift* on the occasion of the sixtieth birthday of the party leader and Prime Minister, Thorvald Stauning in 1933. The title of the book was *Plague over Europe: Bolshevism – Fascism – Nazism*. It contained a critical analysis of the dangers posed by these totalitarian movements, and it also suggested how best these threats could be responded to by a small country such as Denmark. The book strongly influenced political thinking and actions at that time and afterwards, not only within the Social Democratic Party but also within the other democratic parties. Its careful analysis of Danish society was instrumental in shaping the eventual welfare-state model, and it could therefore be said that it became one of Denmark's most important political works of reference.

The basis of this analysis by Frisch was that all totalitarian movements are directly opposed to democracy and, inevitably, lead to repression, the destruction of life, and ruin. For a democracy, such as Denmark, which is based on freedom and peaceful co-operation, not only could there be no question of alignment with any of these movements – regardless of the reason – but they should be opposed, both internally and externally. The question was, how? Because of Denmark's military weakness, Frisch dismissed any thought of armed force and, in its place, he advocated the adoption of a policy that closely linked concepts such as democracy, personal values and social responsibility in a comprehensive political – or, more precisely, Social Democrat – programme of action.

Referring to the great mistake by the Social Democrats in Germany which, so far as Frisch was concerned, was that the party had allowed Hitler to hijack the German national agenda – the recovery of Germany after the humiliation of the Treaty of Versailles – he emphasised that nothing like that should be allowed to happen in Denmark. As the largest political party in the country, the Social Democrats should ensure that anything of fundamental national importance would be included in the party's agenda, and should actively develop an awareness of the essential link between being Danish and being a democrat. At the same time, the party should oppose the totalitarian plague on a broad front, ranging from an ideological defence of the basic principles of democracy to the implementation of a strong social programme that, amongst other things, would ensure that the disadvantaged would also be able to have a decent life and a sense of belonging within the Danish community. And most importantly, the parliamentary parties should show the country that, through constructive co-operation within a democratic framework, they were in a position to bring the country safely through the economic crisis without compromising any fundamental democratic principles or values.

Frisch's penetrating analysis was studied with close interest, not only by the Social Democrats but by all politicians. His carefully considered advice struck a chord within the ranks of the centre-right parties, and his ideas thereby formed the ideological basis for the cross-party consensus that brought Danish democracy through the totalitarian storms of the 1930s. Those ideas were also at the heart of the new Social Democrat manifesto in 1934, *Danmark for Folket*, 'Denmark for the People', which firmly established the Social Democrats as the foremost party at the centre of Danish politics, and they laid the foundations for the political consensus on matters of social security that characterized Danish politics for the remainder of the century.[6]

The welfare model first took its final form after the Second World War, just as the political influence of the Social Democrats reached its zenith. The basic elements were a law on retirement and invalidity pensions in 1956 which gave all Danes the right to receive an old-age pension, and a law on public welfare in 1961 which added a much finer mesh to the previous social law of 1933. In 1973 a compulsory public system of health insurance was introduced, which abolished the old health insurance societies and so finally terminated the original principle of insurance. All of this was collated in the Social Security Act of 1976, which streamlined and unified the whole of the welfare legislation. The results achieved precisely the ideas of an all-inclusive welfare state, which the Social Democrats had been advocating and fighting for systematically for most of the twentieth century. It is this very system, along with the Social Democrats and the Danish nation state – actually three aspects of the same thing – which is now in serious crisis. The threats are both internal and external.

THE CRISIS OF THE DANISH WELFARE STATE

The social democratic Danish welfare model is in a certain way a beautiful utopia, testifying to a genuine concern on the part of the state for the citizens for whom it is responsible. It also created an outstanding social and economic security for the descendants of the poor Danish agricultural population of not so long ago, who literally lived from hand to mouth on the edge of starvation. Because of its all-encompassing nature, it was built upon three important assumptions, each of which has to be maintained if the system is to continue.

The first is that society continues to grow economically. In principle the social, health and educational requirements of the welfare society are infinite. Interest groups and well-intentioned politicians constantly present new demands. However, the means to finance these requirements are finite. After all, there are limits on how tight the screw of taxation can be turned before it has a negative impact on the very economic activities which ultimately pay for the system.

These harsh but unavoidable facts could easily be blurred in the 1960s, when it seemed that there were no limits to economic growth. The cake of the total production of society to be divided up was very big in these years, and so the burden of the ever-increasing taxes was not felt so painfully as to make the population react in an undesirable way. However, this situation changed abruptly with the oil crisis and the subsequent recession in the 1970s. Complaints about the very high taxation and the apparent inability of the politicians to set limits to the growth of the welfare state were expressed strongly in parliamentary life. In what is called the 'landslide election' of 1973, the four old parties – the Social Democrats, the Social Liberals (*Det radikale Venstre*), the Liberals (*Venstre*) and the Danish Conservative Party – who were jointly responsible for the edifice of the welfare state all lost votes, and with them their control over developments. Until this fateful election, together the parties could show the support of around 84 per cent of the electorate. Afterwards, this had fallen to 58 per cent. The disappointed and frustrated electors voted a number of protest parties into the *Folketing* instead. The key issues included lower taxes and better conditions for house owners. The 'tax evasion party', Fremskridtspartiet (the Progress Party), under the leadership of the charismatic tax lawyer Mogens Glistrup (1926–2008), became the second biggest party after the Social Democrats. This political earthquake completely changed the nature of the Danish Parliament, throwing the model of the welfare state which the four old parties had built up step by step after the Second World War, with the Social Democrats as the chief architect, to the winds of fate. It is still impossible to be certain of the route it is taking or its destination.

The second assumption which the Danish welfare state needed to be able to function is that the citizens of the country are fairly homogenous in economic circumstances and culture, that the social divides are narrow, and that the population as a whole share inherent feelings of solidarity and ideals of equality which are the real foundation of the whole welfare system. These conditions largely prevailed in the middle of the twentieth century, when the system was seriously implemented. However, the large-scale immigration of recent decades, including the influx of refugees from the Third World, has radically changed the situation. These new citizens in principle have the right to the same welfare services as native Danes, but they also bring with them their experience and traditions which are inevitably not the same as those on which the Danish welfare system is based. Many of them are also alien to the entire political consensus and tradition of agreement which is an essential historical condition for the welfare system to function. As a result of this immigration, the Danish population is slowly becoming multicultural and multiethnic, and the Danish, tax-financed, universal welfare system is poorly designed to accommodate such social changes. So a new, unforeseen factor has become a part of Danish political life.

The third assumption behind the welfare state is a general popular trust in the state and its strength and ability to conduct a style of politics which provides the greatest security for as many as possible. As already explained, this trust is deeply anchored in Danish tradition, as far back as early absolutism, and is one of the explanations as to why, since the Second World War, the Danish people have accepted one of the highest levels of taxation in the world without a murmur. This trust has been seriously shaken over the last 25 years. First, this is because of the domestic internal politics mentioned above, but it is also because the state has limited its power and independent freedom of action through joining the EU, as well as the increasing internationalisation of business, which has given companies a previously unknown mobility, and thus new opportunities to move work and capital to regions with less restrictive policies, more sympathetic to business than Denmark. The result of this political weakening has been that Danish parliamentary life had become less stable by the end of the twentieth century, and more oriented towards spectacular individual issues than before, while voters feel freer to change their party allegiances. This in itself could in the long term undermine the ability of the welfare state to operate, as it is essentially based on a reciprocal trust between the state and the people. This is being eroded by both internal and external factors.

GOODBYE TO WELFARE DEMOCRACY?

The Danish welfare model, which is in many ways very similar to that of the other Scandinavian countries, is the result of a broad political consensus between the four old parties which dominated politics for several decades after the Second World War. It is thus not just a social democratic project, but an expression of broad political agreement about ends and means. It could even be said that the very prerequisite for the implementation of the project was the existence of a broad political consensus and a political culture which celebrated negotiated democracy and avoided confrontation, again just as described by Jens Otto Krag in the quotation which introduced the previous chapter.[7]

This dominant fundamental agreement about ends and means disappeared with the 'landslide election' of 1973 and the resulting dissolution of the classic nature of Parliament. The old style of negotiation was replaced with more confrontational and narrowly sectional lines of battle in Danish politics, which, when all is said and done, threw the welfare model into a risky course and may well end in its shipwreck. The new situation in Parliament has created a growing asymmetry between those pushing for greater state intervention and the continuation of the provision of the welfare state, and those who wish to keep the tax burden within limits. With the help of numerous interest groups and well-intentioned voices in the comprehensive public system and the mass media, politicians keen to earn a prominent profile are constantly pressed from all sides to patch the leaks in the system without concerning themselves about the costs, which anyhow have to be shared amongst the taxpayers and are thus felt only marginally. Such issues can win a lot of votes in an election. There are not so many votes in saying no to new expensive proposals. In the new confrontational political environment where political survival often depends on taking a prominent stance on a single issue, it seems almost impossible to stop the welfare state, and so the tax burden, from spinning out of control. The situation is even more critical because the age structure of the population, in line with that of most European countries, is changing, with more and more elderly people requiring care, while the economically active section is becoming smaller and smaller because of the low birth rates of the 1970s and 1980s. Then there is the increased immigration of people from the Third World, whose workforce in many ways is necessary for sustaining the welfare society because of the ageing population, but, due to often insufficient integration, also place an extra burden on the system.

Despite several courageous political attempts in recent years to set limits to the unrestrained growth of the welfare state and so prevent taxes from soaring even higher, at the turn of the millennium there is no sign that the development will ever be brought under control as it was in the 1960s. The situation in Parliament is not right for that. Quite how things will develop in the long term is extremely difficult to predict.

The alternative to the unhampered expansion of welfare services and the consequent tax bill can hardly be to completely abandon the welfare model which has produced outstanding social stability in Denmark for most of the twentieth century. One possibility is a gradual move towards the insurance model used in continental Europe, which does not encourage people in the same way as the Danish system to think that 'free services' are actually free, but to realise that just like everything else, they come at a price. A move in this direction is supported by the country's growing integration into the EU system. Common monetary, financial and labour policies could be used by the weakened Danish state as an excuse to modify the system and re-create the necessary symmetry between the demand for welfare and the ability to find the means to finance it.

Thus the Danish political model and the Danish utopia, which this book argues has grown out of an absolutist society and conception of law to fully flower as the modern Danish welfare system, can hardly be said to have yet reached the end of the road, but it has, nonetheless, reached a point where the way ahead is deeper into a European community created by the EU and the ideas on which it is based. To manoeuvre correctly and carefully into this large and largely unexplored territory will be perhaps the greatest challenge lying ahead for Danish politics in the twenty-first century. The late Prime Minister Jens Otto Krag, previously quoted, saw this very clearly. It was he who was mainly responsible for the fact that Denmark was the first Nordic country to join the European Community, and so throw its lot in with Europe rather than pursue a utopian dream of an isolated Nordic community, the very limited capacity of which is illustrated by the long histories of the Nordic countries.

5

The Church and Culture from Luther to Postmodernism

THE REMOTE CHURCH

In a book published in 1995, the theological historian Jørgen I. Jensen maintained that modern Danes belong to the *Distant Church*.[1] By this he meant that the Church is seen as a white building on the distant horizon, just as depicted in many of the superb landscape paintings of the Danish Golden Age in the early nineteenth century, by no means a dominant motif. For the modern, secular Dane, the Church is a barely discernible humble location, but it is nonetheless still there.

Modern Danes do not attend church regularly, and are far from fanatical in their religious observance, but very few actually renounce their faith or deny the existence of God. When questioned closely, most people would say that they carry within them a sense of the existence of something divine, although it is often very difficult to explain exactly what that consists of, just as the more violent nature paintings of the Golden Age reflect a dark intimation of an invisible higher power at work, the precise nature of which is never really shown.

The role of the Church in its very loose modern form is mainly to provide a relatively fixed framework of ritual for the various phases of life. It is quite normal to go to church on Christmas Eve, and many people like to celebrate a christening or wedding in church. The Church is especially important at the end of a life; by far the majority of funerals are still conducted in a church by a minister. Yet on ordinary Sundays, the churches are normally deserted. In other words, regular church attendance does not form part of an average normal Dane's existence. Despite this, the Church helps to define Danish culture, and remains as a living symbol of a centuries-old spiritual tradition. No one wants to abandon this age-old common cultural inheritance, and this reluctance is perhaps most clearly expressed when the Church is challenged by the fundamentalist factions amongst the rapidly growing number of Muslim immigrants.

Yet the Church is still today not just a ritual stage and a cultural symbol – it still has a religious meaning. Danes still need somewhere to crystallise their religious feelings, and the Church is the very place to do so. The Church is, in other words, a symbol of religious sentiment in modern society. Certainly, it is far away from the centre of most people's vision, but there is no doubt that it has to exist. For that reason most Danes continue to pay their Church taxes, even though doing so is voluntary, without seeming to gain much in return as they so rarely go to church. To opt out of the Church would be the same as to sever the link with the religious sentiment itself – the mysteries of existence – and to cut off the religious nerve which exists in most Danes, however well hidden.

In many respects the modern Danish Church is a strange phenomenon. It is not, as in many other Protestant countries, a national Church. It is a Popular Church which operates independently of the state. Yet it is funded by the state, and a great deal of its business is conducted by the Ministry for Religious Affairs, a secular governmental body.[2] This exceptional position has arisen because the constitution of 1849 simply stated that the situation of the Church would be regulated by special legislation. This never actually happened, and so the Church was free to develop without any particular legal framework. Thus, there is no true head of the Danish Church, either spiritual or political. It really is a Popular Church in the true sense of the word. No individual or group has the authority to speak on its behalf on either political or religious matters. The ministers of the churches are appointed by the parish councils elected by the people, the composition of which reflects the differing perceptions of the evangelical-Lutheran Christianity on which the Church is based. The ministers are only answerable to the parish council and to God for their preaching and spiritual work, not in any sense to any public authority or church hierarchy.

A visitor to Denmark may well form the impression that it is one of the most secular societies in the Western world, just as many Danes will, if asked, say that the Church and Christianity play no significant part in their lives. Many of them hardly know when they should stand up or remain seated during a service, but nonetheless most still clearly feel that the Church is something special which should not be tampered with.

This is also true for the workers' movement and its political branch, the Social Democrats, which was certainly originally anticlerical. Yet strangely enough, the workers' movement later adopted more and more of evangelical-Lutheran Christianity in a secularised version. It could even be said that the mission of the Church and the political programme of the Social Democrats grew closer and closer together through the twentieth century as the party's ideas of a welfare state became a reality. A key issue for the Church is to care for the weakest in society, which was exactly what the workers' movement considered important in its practical policies. Here socially committed citizens and church circles met, and the message of the Sermon on the Mount about loving thy neighbour had perhaps as much importance as the Marxist theories of which very few contemporary Social Democrats can be said to have experienced at first hand.

The practical implementation of the policies of the workers' movement in Denmark was principally an ethical project, which could very easily be incorporated into Christianity. The pillar of the evangelical-Lutheran Danish Popular Church was Martin Luther's concept of the ministry, that individuals could address God directly without any intervention, assistance or apology. This concept lies deep at the heart of the Danish mentality, and can also be seen in the attitude the Danes have to the law, which in a secular society takes the place of God. Danes consider the law as a general system of moral guidance for decent behaviour in matters great and small. The workers' movement succeeded in building on this throughout the twentieth century to establish a practical duty of care towards the weakest members of society.

In this way, the view that Denmark is very secular and a long way away from the preceding Christian society is actually superficial. Christian values and evangelical-Lutheran attitudes can, on closer examination, be seen to have permeated Danish mentality and actually to be the ethical foundation of the modern Danish welfare state. So, to fully describe and understand Denmark and the Danes, we also need to look at the development of Christian morality in this broader sense from when it first truly took root in Danish soil – the Reformation of 1536 – to the present day.

THE REFORMATION, 1536

Just as in other places in Northern Europe, the Catholic Church in Denmark began to show obvious signs of weakness and started to collapse at the beginning of the sixteenth century. Many of the bishops were more concerned with their role as secular dignitaries and storing up wealth and land than their proper business as leaders of Christian society and spiritual advisers to the congregation. Many monasteries fell into disrepair, and the essential charitable role of the Church – *caritas* – the provision of spiritual and earthly help to the poor and the needy, was ever-more neglected. The Church came under increasingly vocal criticism from popular religious movements, who, inspired by Martin Luther and other German reformation movements, demanded that the Church and its earthly servants return to a Christian way of life and once more take their Christian duties seriously. This increasing popular dissatisfaction created fertile ground for reformatory movements. Luther's open revolt in 1517 added fuel to the fires of dissent in Denmark.[3]

The secular powers, in the shape of King Christian II (r.1513–23), certainly tried to remedy the failures of the Church by passing legislation to limit its authority and transfer some of the responsibility for dealing with social problems to the temporal government, on the basis of the Dutch model. Yet the courageous attempt by the king to carry out the tasks which the Church had failed to perform did not have the desired effect. Instead, it provoked a revolt against him from the aristocracy, which included the bishops, and finally ended with his dethronement in 1523.

The Catholic aristocracy won a temporary victory when Christian II's paternal uncle took to the throne, taking the name of Frederik I (r.1523–33). At the start, the new king was just a puppet for the aristocracy. As it still owned around a third of all the cultivated land in the country, the Catholic Church was still formidably powerful, and would not be toppled by some popular protests.

However, the victory soon proved to have been hollow. Frederik I soon showed himself to be a skilled politician who was not prepared to dance to the tunes of the Catholic aristocracy. Without ceremony, the king appointed bishops of his own accord. The head of the college of bishops, the Archbishop of Lund, was not ordained by the pope, as was traditional, and so was not able to ensure the apostolic succession by ordaining new bishops on behalf of the pope, which meant that the bishops rapidly lost their spiritual authority in the eyes of the faithful. In 1526 a national assembly headed by the king made it official that it was no longer necessary for bishops to receive papal approval, and that the monies which were previously paid to the pope should be used for defence of the realm instead. It was also prescribed that the bishops should obey the king, in direct contradiction of canonical law. These measures turned the Catholic Church in Denmark into a national Church under the de facto leadership of the king, even though the articles of faith continued to be Catholic.

However, before many years had passed, this too changed. This was mainly because the evangelical teachings of Luther were quickly taken up by the wider population, who had long felt under the heel of the hierarchy of ecclesiastical power, and saw in Luther's concept of the generality of the priesthood and the equality of all Christians in the eyes of God a liberation from centuries of suppression. Luther's ideas spread across the country like wildfire, and evangelists drew huge audiences. Despite strong pressure from the Catholic leaders, especially the erudite monk Povl Helgesen (c. 1485–1535), who was a devoted follower of Erasmus of Rotterdam and his ideas of a gradual reform of the Catholic Church from the inside, the king refused to intervene, simply saying that he had no mastery over men's souls. Alongside these developments, the form of services became more evangelical, and were said in Danish and German rather than Latin.

In a determined attempt to bring order to the chaos, a national assembly was convened in Copenhagen in 1530, where there was a real disputation between the conflicting clerics. A group of 21 evangelical priests defended the evangelical creed against the Catholic prelates. They were so persuasive that the assembly decided that the Danish Church could in future only preach specifically what was stated in holy scripture. In itself this was hardly a crystal-clear statement, but it did open up the way for the expansion of evangelical-Lutheran teachings. The Catholic Church in Denmark was rapidly disintegrating, mainly because of the king's equivocal behaviour in avoiding conflict in the long ecclesiastical controversy. In the event, the Danish Reformation extended over 10–15 years, and there was no particular point which can be identified as being decisive. Instead, it was a slow process of change which was completed with Christian III's coup in 1536, when after emerging victoriously from the civil war he arrested and defrocked the Catholic bishops and officially proclaimed evangelical Lutheranism as the national religion.

The exact details of the course of the Reformation are of somewhat lesser interest. It is worth noting, however, that the monarchy at the same time confiscated the lands of the Church and dissolved the monasteries, with the result that at a single stroke the monarchy became the largest landowner in the country. This huge increase of funds left the king in a position to pay off the huge debts remaining from the civil war without any difficulty, and helped to create a solid economic foundation for the powerful state which emerged.

THE NEW CHURCH

With this move, the king had, in practice, taken over the full responsibility for the continuation of the Church – he had, in a manner of speaking, taken on the responsibility for the project of the Church in its evangelical-Lutheran form. He lived up to this responsibility by issuing a completely new structure for the Church, in Latin, in 1537. This was followed by a Danish version in 1539, and a number of amplifications in 1542. All of the new organising principles had been drawn up in close collaboration with Lutheran theologians and had also been sent to Wittenberg for the approval of Luther himself and of his inner circle of advisers. In this way Danish church organisation followed the smallest details of the Lutheran reformers' ideas, which had already been tried out in practice in various places in northern Germany.

The new church organisation transformed the Danish Church into a Lutheran princely Church on the pattern of what had happened in northern Germany. In accordance with Luther's teaching about the two regiments and the sanctity of all authority, the king took over full responsibility for the administration of the Church, the community of Christians and the introduction of the Kingdom of God. The king thus took over the position of the steward of the entire Christian community in Denmark from the pope. To clearly underline this shift, the official title of the bishops was changed from *biskop* to *superintendent*. However, the old title came back into usage after just a few years. To put this more accurately, it could be said that the Church as an organisation was dissolved by the Reformation and brought under the monarchy, which in return accepted full responsibility for the Christian role which the Church had shown itself to be unable to play.

It fell to the king to ensure that only true doctrine was preached from the pulpits of Denmark, to oversee the appointment of the clergy and make sure they were paid and to look after the physical maintenance of the churches. Thus, he also took over all the Church's property and income. While previously the Danish clergy had been an independent and powerful group on equal footing with the aristocracy, the Reformation reduced them to the position of civil servants, directly answerable for their conduct to the state. As a result of this subordinated role, the Danish clergy became ever-more instruments of the state over the following centuries. In fact, they became the most significant mouthpieces of the state to address the wider public. On Sunday after Sunday, Lutheran dogma about the sanctity of authority and unconditional obedience to the king and the state was impressed upon the congregations – and attendance at services was compulsory. Thus, the clergy became the most important tool for the state in the comprehensive religious and social regimenting of the people, so that they not only all became faithful Lutherans, but also useful and loyal subjects of the state.

As the pastors were in constant contact with their flocks, they became the front line of the new powerful state being built, and the ever-present local representatives of secular authority. A natural extension of this was that they were expected to carry out various tasks regarding control and surveillance, which had very little indeed to do with their spiritual role, but could be entrusted to faithful civil servants with good local knowledge. In fact, until the end of the eighteenth century, the Church was the only organisation which could reach out to the most remote corners of the kingdom. It covered every single square inch of the land, and this meant that the parish priests were very well-placed to act as the eyes, ears and even the voice of the king in even the most isolated communities. It was in this role that, in 1646, the clergy was required to keep systematic records of the most important church rituals – baptism, marriage and burial – thus providing the authorities a previously unknown view of the size of the population, its composition and demographic distribution. They also played a key role in conducting the censuses, which a hundred years or so later became fixed regular events. Even today, Danish citizens are obliged to register births and deaths at the local church office, whether or not they are members of the church. The only exception is the inhabitants of southern Jutland, who follow a secular system imported from Prussia during the period of German rule between 1864 and 1920.

Very soon after the Reformation, the clergy also started to play a central role in poor relief, health care and education, both in providing them and ensuring on behalf of the state that everything was run correctly. To some extent this function continued until after the Second World War.

In this way, the Lutheran Reformation led to a thorough and lasting change in the position of the Church within Danish society and corresponding transformation of the role and function of the clergy. The clergy then became a central instrument for the long-lasting process of imposing orthodoxy and discipline, which over several centuries turned the Danes into one of the most controlled and disciplined nations in Europe. On the other hand, the Reformation meant that the king and his successors had to take their duties as Christian princes seriously in quite a different way to before. As the highest authority of both Church and State, they were now not only the sword of God on earth, but also the spiritual leaders, a role they wrenched from the hands of the Church. The new dual role of the king as the defender of the faith as well as the highest secular authority was expressed very clearly in the constitution itself.

As early as the Middle Ages, the coronation charters, which were effectively contracts determining the distribution of power within society, always included a clause stating that the king was obliged to love God and the Holy Church and support and protect the rights and privileges of the clergy. In the charter which Christian III signed in 1536, there was indeed the usual clause about the faith, indeed the first paragraph of the entire document. However, the actual content of the paragraph had been significantly changed. The king now promised to love and worship God and to support and protect his holy scriptures and teachings. Remarkably, there is not a word about the Church as an institution; this had simply been removed from the text. The only possible explanation for this is that the king now perceived himself as the proper head of the Church, and so the institution itself had been subsumed into the apparatus of state. Thus, the Church was turned into a true princely church and the entire medieval ecclesiastical organisation with its rights and privileges had simply disappeared. The successive coronation charters, including that signed by Frederik III, the last of its kind, followed a similar formula.

The unlimited power of the king, including in the ecclesiastical domain, was very strongly underlined in the Act of Succession of 1665 – the constitution of absolutism. The very first article stated that the most important duty of the king was to worship God according to the letter of the Bible and the *Confessio Augustana* of 1530, and it is emphasised that his paramount task was to ensure that his subjects remained in the true faith, and that he should protect them against all 'heretics, fanatics and blasphemers'. Thus, as an absolute Christian prince, the Danish king was the real guarantor of Christian society and the true faith on Danish soil. There is still an echo of this in the current Danish constitution, which, in Section 6, states that 'the monarch shall belong to the evangelical-Lutheran church'. This presents a paradox, as the self-same constitution lays down freedom of religious observance as a principle (§67) while compelling only the monarch to be a member of the Danish Church. This is doubtless a reflection of the redefinition of the role of the monarchy in regard to the Church as a result of the Reformation, even though today the monarchy has no influence on the Danish Church.

THE PARISH PRIEST AS CIVIL SERVANT

The radical redefinition the Reformation wrought of the relationship between Church and State led to a significant increase in the state's duties and powers. In harness with military responsibility, this perhaps in itself created the foundations for the growth in the exercise of authority and power which is distinctive in the early modern development of nation states. As well as the religious responsibility, other very important new responsibilities emerged, such as poor relief and education, which in the Middle Ages were the province of the Church.

Christian III introduced fairly comprehensive legislation regarding these social and health-related areas in 1539, laying down overall guidelines for how poor relief and nursing care were to be organised. The fundamental philosophy was that everyone who needed help should be helped. There was, however, a distinction between the deserving and undeserving poor. The first were those in distress through no fault of their own. They were entitled to receive assistance. The latter were those who were in difficulties because of criminality, drunkenness or indolence, and they were not entitled to receive help. With this exception, though, the principle of the law was universal as it applied to all, irrespective of condition or social rank. In practice, a great deal of the work of implementing the law fell to the parish priests, who represented the state externally. This introduced two important principles into Danish law, which still exist in the legislation of the modern welfare state.[4] One is that the right to social services is universal, the other that concrete decisions about the law should be taken as close to the citizens as possible. Over the following centuries, there were many other provisions, and in 1708 the entire rambling body of law was collated into a large poor law which attempted to set up a fixed, uniform framework for social assistance while also ensuring an adequate financial basis for it.

This legislation determined that public assistance should in principle be based on voluntary contributions, although when it came to the point the contributions were a little less than purely voluntary. Alms boxes were placed in all the churches and inns of the land, and the congregation were to sign up for particular contributions to parish poor relief, under the supervision of the priest. Anyone who omitted to contribute risked having their names read out from the pulpit, and in extreme cases the public authorities could levy the contributions. There was also a regular, assessed tax of one per cent on all clergy and royal officials in the towns. This scheme relied heavily on the administration and control of the parish priests in order to function. This statutory order from 1708 is often identified as the start of modern public assistance in Denmark, as for the first time it abandoned a system of permitted and regulated begging as the main element and replaced it with an organised system of relief, which was regulated and supported by public finance. This in turn was the precursor of another of the key principles of the modern Danish welfare state: that social services are financed through taxation.

The entire educational system, which in Catholic times had been the province of the Church, also came under the state after the Reformation. The University of Copenhagen, which was founded in 1479 with papal authority, was languishing quietly during the Reformation. It was reopened by the king himself in the very year of the Reformation, 1536, and significantly made effectively into a college for the clergy with the principal aim of training priests for the new Church. Theology continued to be the most important subject at the university well into the nineteenth century.

Because of Luther's thesis about the direct relationship of the individual Christian to God and that God's kingdom found expression only in the Bible, it was essential that the Christian laymen could read the Bible rather than just hearing about it through the words of a learned theologian. There were two necessary conditions for this. One was that the Bible be not just available in Latin, but also in vernacular translation. The other was that the people in general were sufficiently literate to be able to read it. Neither of these were the case at the time of the Reformation.

The king first of all organised the translation of the Bible into Danish. It was natural to take Luther's German Bible as the source, as it was considered to be more faithful to scripture than the Vulgate version. The first Danish Bible was completed in 1550 and called the Christian III Bible after its commissioner. There have been many subsequent versions. Luther's catechism was also translated into Danish. This came to be widely used for domestic prayers and formed the basis of Christian teaching in schools, where its contents, the Lord's Prayer, the Creed, the sacraments and the Ten Commandments, were learned by rote.

From 1537 a number of schools for small children were founded by the monarchy, often housed in the old Catholic monasteries. The idea was to bring up children in the true Christian faith and impart sufficient reading skills for them to be able to learn Luther's catechism and read the Bible. This rather flimsy educational system was developed with the introduction of more schools with different levels of instruction, all supervised by the priests. Initially, these schools were set up in the towns. A significant breakthrough for the educational system in rural areas did not happen until 1721, when Frederik IV (r. 1699–1730) allowed the organisation of 240 board schools in the royal cavalry areas, that is, those parts of the Crown estates across the country which served to support the household cavalry. The teaching in these schools was mainly in religion and reading, but students who paid could also learn writing and arithmetic. At the same time the king invited private landowners to follow his example, although there was only a limited response.

The state was involved in setting up a form of compulsory education for all the children of the country in 1736, when the ceremony of confirmation was introduced. For their confirmation at the age of 14, the children had to take a test in elementary evangelical knowledge, and it was compulsory that they were prepared through teaching from the parish priest or his proxy. To some degree this marked the beginning of the general compulsory basic schooling introduced by the Board School Act of 1814 – the first of its kind in the world.

Thus, a general educational system, mainly with a religious intention, developed early in Denmark. At least in its ambitions, it was intended for all the children of the country regardless of social status. The educational legislation of 1814 also formally made Danish primary schools universal as it made it compulsory for all children to receive elementary teaching. In comparison with neighbouring countries, this was very early. Norway first introduced compulsory education in 1827, and Sweden in 1842. The result in Denmark was that widespread illiteracy was eradicated long before most other European countries. Thus, a steadily increasing section of the population learnt the skills of reading and writing which were a prerequisite for becoming good evangelical Christians and useful members of society. This in turn laid the foundations for the farming classes to participate in public life, and thus in the longer term the necessary educational basis for popular support of the democratic welfare state of the twentieth century.

Once again, the priesthood played a central role, both as evangelical spiritual advisers to their flocks and the local embodiment of the state. It was the priest who ensured that the ambitions of the government regarding education were put into daily practice, who guaranteed that the teaching stayed within the prescribed religious confines and so achieved the educational and social effect that the government wanted. It was the parish priest who, under the Board School Act of 1814, was the chairman of the local education committee intended to supervise the activities of the schools. In addition, after 1814 a large number of priests were involved in training teachers, and this was gradually institutionalised through specialised teacher training colleges. The vast majority of the first generation of these colleges were founded by priests. All in all it is hard to imagine how quickly compulsory schooling throughout the country could have been implemented so early without the active involvement of the priests.

In education too, there were the first signs of the model that subsequently became typical of the modern Danish welfare state, in particular the attempt to create a universal model of teaching and the desire to place the administration and inspection of the practice as locally as possible.

THE CHURCH'S PROJECT – THE STATE'S PROJECT

Given the importance of the role of the clergy and the Church in the process of spreading religion and social discipline after the Reformation, the question could well be asked as to whether it really was the state which took over the role of the Church, or the Church which took over the aims of the state. Good arguments can be made for both views.

Whichever interpretation is preferred, there is no doubt that the projects of Church and State in the centuries following the Reformation did not just run in parallel, but virtually merged into a combined effort to turn the Danish people into good evangelical Christians and useful members of society. After the Reformation, the kings assumed the overall responsibility for this project, and the clergy willingly accepted their leadership for so long as there was nothing incompatible about being both a good Christian and a useful member of society. The schism first really came during the Enlightenment, when the influence of the Church started to wane in favour of secular thinking. But that is a different story, which will be told a little later on.

In the meantime, there can hardly be any doubt that the merging of Church and State for several centuries after the Reformation had a profound and long-lasting influence on the nature of Danish society and its relationship with the state. The willingness of the reformist clergy to act as civil servants created entirely new opportunities to reach out into the most remote local communities. With the priests in the heart of the communities, acting as the eyes, ears and voice of the central state, there was little room indeed for civil disobedience. Conversely, the active role of the clergy in alleviating poverty, education and health care meant that precisely the issues which most directly affected people's everyday life and were essential for social well-being were resolved and decided on the spot, by those who knew the local circumstances best. There are reasons to think that the fact that the controlling power of the state was not seen as remote and impersonal, but near at hand and appropriate, had a beneficial effect on social peace and stability, and that this had a great deal to do with the active role of the local clergy. This is partially supported by the fact that after the Reformation, Denmark never experienced a single peasants' revolt of the kind which ravaged various other European countries during the period.

Another factor is that the Danish state enjoyed greatly increased power and administrative opportunities with the clergy as part of the apparatus of power. The unity of the power of Church and State created a hitherto unseen capacity for the state and a decentralised structure. This pattern of a powerful yet decentralised state continued in the twentieth-century Danish welfare state, which can thus be said to have had its roots in the post-Reformation social structure. It was in the same society that the still prevalent fundamental universal principle started.

Caritas – care for the sick and the poor, traditionally the responsibility of the Church – was transferred as part of the Reformation from the Catholic Church to the king, and thus to the secular state. The practical management of these 'soft' areas which came under the state was to a large extent delegated to the parish clergy. This endowed the state with a human, Christian face in the eyes of the people. Sunday after Sunday, the message from the pulpit was that all authority was sacred and originated directly from God. The fact that the most obvious representative of the state was an ordained cleric working on behalf of the state to alleviate social need, promote health and provide education for the children only served to confirm the message. As well as carrying out these tasks, the priest was also a spiritual guide for the parishioners through the harder moments of life. As a tiller of the lands of the manse, he was a part of the local community as well, and often a pioneer of new agricultural methods. As a result, the priest was normally regarded with sympathy and respect, and, as he administered the charitable offices of the state, this sympathy and respect often extended to embrace the distant central power that the priests represented.

This is probably the reason why in the recent history of Denmark, there has been no especial disparity between the government and society in general as often experienced in countries where Church and State have existed as separate entities. Danes still see the state as fundamentally good and trustworthy. This is a necessary condition for the welfare state to function efficiently. The unshakeable conviction that the state truly has the interests of its citizens at heart is deeply anchored in Lutheran Protestantism and the finely meshed system of power and administration which it built hand in hand with the monarchy over the centuries after the Reformation.

Even though, as shown, the organisation of the Danish national Church, one of the most powerful Lutheran princely churches, gave rise to some of the fundamental and enduring attitudes and patterns of Danish mentality, the trend was slowly seasoned by other religious and ideological movements which have also left a significant mark on Danish history and mentality. Two such are Pietism and the philosophy of Enlightenment.

PIETISM

At the end of the seventeenth century, there was still an established dogma that the power of the state – as personified by the absolutist king – carried the ultimate responsibility that the subjects recognised and practised the correct Christian faith. This concept came under pressure from the start of the eighteenth century from Pietism, a movement which started in the German town of Halle before spreading to Denmark, where it found favour especially amongst the more prosperous citizens and made a marked impact on the royal Court during the rule of Christian VI (r. 1730–46). (In some ways Pietism resembles Evangelicalism in other countries, and so it is sometimes translated thus.)

Pietism – a name taken from the Latin *pietas*, or piety, had its roots in Luther's theology, especially the doctrine of salvation by faith alone. This concept was somewhat pushed into the background over the course of time within the larger Lutheran state churches, including the strong Danish state Church governed by the king, where the ecclesiastical hierarchy came to overshadow the personal, intimate relationship of the individual to God. The Pietists reacted to this by asserting that in the final instance, religion was a private matter with which the state had no right to interfere. Instead, they preached a new, intimate and personal relationship to God based on the individual's personal experience of God and the conscious faith in Jesus as the saviour of all. A sign of entering this condition was normally a personal religious experience in the form of a regeneration or awakening. The Pietists considered formal membership of the authorised state Church as of minor importance. What was of primary importance was the personal religious experience of regeneration.

In Denmark, this form of personal piety is usually referred to as 'convention Pietism', as it mainly developed in closed religious assemblies, or conventions, consisting of prosperous citizens, first of all in the towns of southern Jutland, where a central figure was the hymnodist Hans Adolph Brorson (1694–1764), who later became Bishop of Ribe, but later also amongst the bourgeoisie in the capital, from where it spread to the Court and the higher circles throughout the country. Under Christian VI, who as mentioned was an ardent Pietist, the movement gradually took on the form of a kind of state Pietism in that the state tried to force the entire Church in a Pietist direction through various means. Such means included stricter legislation about the observance of the Lord's Day, punishments for not attending church and the introduction of confirmation in 1736. According to the law, the confirmand was to be examined in the official catechism and answer 759 questions satisfactorily before being confirmed.

The early Pietist movement did not spread very widely amongst the general population, but nonetheless it was an expression of the fact that the complete unity between the ambitions of Church and State which had existed since the Reformation was beginning to crumble. Just 100 years later, this schism became even clearer when a popular religious regeneration movement swept across the land in the first half of the nineteenth century. A particular characteristic of this mass movement, clearly inspired by the earlier Pietism, was the abandonment of the idea that the Christian community had to include everyone. In fact, the belief was that a true Christian community should be achieved in small, select groups rather like the original Christianity had been. Thus, the movement formed small exclusive groups of the 'awakened', which actively attempted to separate themselves from the surrounding 'dead' society of conventional Christians and atheists.

This Pietist concept of the gulf between the saved and the damned, between 'us' and 'them', was in obvious contradiction to the basis of the universal state Church. In the decades around 1800, the official Church, with the backing of the secular authorities, fought a fierce battle against the revivalist movement, using as weapons fines, imprisonment and even threats of forcibly removing children. Nonetheless, this did not succeed in exorcising the movement – its dynamism and the belief behind it were simply too strong. Unlike early Pietism, this was a mass movement which caught the imagination of the ordinary people – perhaps the first true grass-roots movement in more recent Danish history.

It was hardly a coincidence that the revivalist movement flourished strongly just after the break-up of the ancient agricultural communities at the end of the eighteenth century described in Chapter 3. The revivalist movement can perhaps be interpreted as an attempt by the rural population to re-create the old close-knit communities which had been dissolved by agrarian reform. Yet, it cannot be ruled out that the difficulties arising from the Napoleonic Wars, in which Denmark was embroiled in 1807–14, were also a factor. The tough economic times and deep national sense of crisis could well have pushed people to band together in religious groups to try to find a meaning for existence which was on a higher plane than the daily struggle and offered more security than the familiar institutions – from village communities to the Danish government – which all seemed to be collapsing in the face of change.

Religious revivalism was in origin almost exclusively a movement amongst the laity which developed outside the ecclesiastical system and slowly attracted adherents from the humbler levels of rural society. Both the absolutist state and the official Church were thus very concerned, and as described tried to fight the movement. Later in the nineteenth century a large number of revivalists were integrated into the Grundtvigian movement, which was seen as less threatening to the established order. A great deal of their passion was absorbed in what was to become some of the hallmarks of that movement – the Folk High Schools, meeting houses, elective congregations and nonconformism – all places where the living word and popular gatherings could provide inspiration and lift the spirit without threatening the system. The farmers' co-operative movement, which experienced a sharp upturn at the end of the nineteenth century, was also to some extent the product of the immense energy released by popular revivalism.

However, some revivalists did not allow themselves to be drawn into the Grundtvigian movement. These were the congregations which arose around a number of lay preachers connected to religious assemblies of the poorest rural classes: smallholders, agricultural labourers and fishermen. These deprived social groups found it difficult to feel comfortable amongst the more prosperous Grundtvigian farm-owners and High School enthusiasts. The social differences and distances were simply too great, despite everything. These congregations formed the core of what is known as the 'Home Mission', an evangelical branch of the Church.

This sect later became a very powerful movement. It was formally established in 1853, and, having started as a movement amongst lay preachers, it was at first very uncertain where it would position itself in regard to the official Church and clergy. The unanswered question was quite simply whether the movement would develop in line with or in opposition to the established clergy, who in the meantime waited cautiously to see which way the wind was blowing, even though a trickle of ministers joined. The doubts were dispelled when, in 1861, three priests from the official Church, under the leadership of the charismatic clergyman Wilhelm Beck, who was to remain the unchallenged leader of the movement up to his death in 1901, took over the leadership of the mission under circumstances resembling a coup, and turned the mission in a new direction.

Under their leadership, the mission started to collaborate closely with the established ecclesiastical authorities, and so developed into what it has since remained – a powerful faction in Danish church life acting within the framework of the official Church and trying to persuade the Church from the inside to adopt its views of what constitutes true Lutheran Christianity. The Danish name of the movement, literally, 'Inner Mission', is itself an expression of its policy of promoting its views through working within the framework of the established Church. This work continues today through membership of the parish councils which elect priests, running schools and teacher training colleges, and through its influence in the Scout movement and certain mass media.

These developments meant that the original revivalist movement, originally outside the system and at times hostile to it, moved closer and closer to the official Church and the established culture, to the point where it was integrated into the establishment – in the case of the Home Mission completely, for the Grundtvigian movement, slightly less so. So, after some decades of disunity around the 1800s because of the revivalist movement, State and Church once again found themselves in harmony. After this, the ambitions of Church and State were once again the same, just as they had been since the Reformation. And so the situation remained until the end of the twentieth century, when internal tensions once again arose because of the large-scale immigration of people from foreign cultures and without a Christian background.

THE ENLIGHTENMENT

The European philosophy of Enlightenment also helped to chip away at the post-Reformation symbiosis of Church and State, as its secularised nature pushed the state in a direction which the Church, and especially the Pietists, found hard to accept. Perhaps the briefest way to explain this is as follows. The aim of the medieval Church was to turn people into good Christians, while the medieval kings attempted to create loyal and useful subjects. After the Reformation, the state took over the role of the collapsed Catholic Church and so the overall responsibility for both of these tasks. The triumphal progress of Enlightenment philosophy in the eighteenth century meant that the secular powers increasingly placed the emphasis on creating loyal and useful citizens at the expense of their religious aims. This set the scene for renewed separation of Church and State. The Pietist movement was one of the symptoms of this.

The European Age of Enlightenment, with its productive mixture of English empiricism and French rationalism, corresponded roughly to the eighteenth century, which has sometimes therefore been called the Age of Reason. The concept of rationalism – the belief in the unbounded possibilities of human reason – was a key ingredient in Enlightenment philosophy. A fundamental element of this concept was the faith that humankind could themselves, through disciplined thought, make the world a better place and forge progress through reforms. In this, there was an implicit rejection of God and the fixed belief in his constant intervention and omnipresence which had under-pinned the medieval Church. In other words, Europe was becoming secularised, and divine worship was becoming a matter of private conscience. Consequently, the state increasingly redefined its duty as creating useful citizens. Whether they also happened to be good Christians was largely their own affair.

The assimilation of this philosophy in Denmark in the first half of the eighteenth century was largely due to one man, the Norwegian-born writer and historian, Professor Ludvig Holberg (1684–1754). As a young man, he undertook extensive study tours in England, France, the Netherlands, Italy and Germany, where he came into contact with the new schools of critical enquiry based on rational thought which, at that time, were sweeping Europe and questioning traditional values such as the dominant role of the Church and the belief in divine provi-dence. In Paris he was fascinated by the thoughts of the philosopher Pierre Bayle and the French *Encyclopédistes*. whose audacious views on religion sowed doubt in many minds. This led him to develop a fundamental, secular philosophy that placed importance on rational thinking and was critical of blind faith in God and the authority of the Church on all issues.

During the 1720s, Holberg wrote a long series of comedies in the French and Italian style for the newly established national theatre in Copenhagen, in which he poked fun at the Establishment and inherited prejudices, and placed emphasis on sound common sense and civil enterprise as cornerstones in the evolution of society. These comedies enjoyed enormous popularity amongst the growing middle class at the time, and many of them eventually became part of the Danish cultural heritage and are still performed today. Holberg thereby contributed to an increase in the self-esteem of the bourgeoisie and opened its eyes to many absurdities in a social order dominated by the Church.

Although Holberg was strongly critical of the Church and resolutely advocated common sense as a better guide in moral and political issues, like his French contemporary, Voltaire, he was not a social revolutionary.

In the numerous historical and ethical works that flowed from his pen after 1730 he ardently defended the concept of absolute monarchy which, like the English philosopher Thomas Hobbes, he regarded as the best protection against a return to a natural state of anarchy and, shortly before his death, he published a response to Montesquieu's well-known treatise on political theory, *l'Esprit des Lois*, because he found that the concept of absolute monarchy had been wrongly presented. On the other hand, he was totally dismissive of the belief that had prevailed until that time in the divine right of kings and, in conformity with the views of the Enlightenment, he portrayed the monarchy in terms of natural law with its legitimacy based on a contract – a social pact – between a ruler and the nation.

Through his popular comedies and a wealth of influential historical and philosophical works that he wrote from 1720 to 1750, almost invariably in straightforward and easily understandable Danish, Holberg brought the ideas of the European Age of Enlightenment to Denmark and thereby sowed the seeds of a critical middle class that, towards the end of the century, became a significant driving force in a redefinition of the relationship between the state and the people. It is due to Holberg, and the political philosophy which he endorsed, that a civic awareness and a critical middle-class society began to emerge which eventually became the most important force for change in Denmark at the time of the French Revolution.

Perhaps the clearest symbolic manifestation of this change in the perception of the role of the state in Denmark was how the royal motto was changed through the eighteenth century. Custom and practice dictated that on accession to the throne, the king choose a motto to encapsulate his intentions in government and express the underlying values by which he intended to rule. The motto was carefully chosen and so could be considered to make an important statement about the way in which the king, and thus the state, perceived himself and the role of government.[5]

An examination of the royal mottoes shows that up until 1660, the post-Reformation kings chose mottoes which centred on God, and which strongly emphasised the position of the monarch as the agent of divine will. Thus, Christian III (r. 1534–59), the king at the time of the Reformation, chose 'May the Lord's will be done'. His son and successor, Frederik II (r. 1559–88), took 'Without God – nothing'. His son and successor, Christian IV (r. 1588–1648), decided on 'The fear of God makes the kingdom strong', his son and successor, Frederik III

(r. 1648–70), who became the first absolutist king of Denmark, picked 'The Lord is my providence'. These mottoes serve as evidence that the complete unity of State and Church established by the Reformation continued unaltered until the end of the seventeenth century.

However, things then began to change. When Christian V (r. 1670–99) took the throne as absolute monarch, he chose for his motto 'Fear of God and justice'. His son, Frederik IV (r. 1699–1730), opted for 'The Lord is my helper', and his son, Christian VI (r. 1730–46), who favoured Pietism, took 'For God and the people'. Thus, we can see that in the early Enlightenment, God had been moved slowly to the background in favour of secular notions such as justice and the people, and instead of being the main purpose of the activities of government, He was slowly reduced to the rank of an assistant. This change fitted in well with the contemporary deist idea of a remote deity – God as the big watchmaker who had set the world in motion in the mists of time, but then withdrawn from his creation and left the rest to mankind itself.

The last two kings of the century of Enlightenment, Frederik V (r. 1746–66) and Christian VII (r. 1766–1808), chose mottoes in accordance with the secular spirit of the age. Frederik V's was 'With care and constancy', and his son's 'Love of the Fatherland is my glory'. Neither of these includes God, but instead important concepts of the Enlightenment such as care, constancy and the Fatherland, thus symbolically clearly demonstrating that the paths of Church and State were dividing under the influence of the secularisation of society, and so the aims and ambitions of the two were also moving in different directions.

With the exception of Frederik VII (r. 1848–63), who was the king who presided over the transition from absolutism to democracy in 1848 and so chose the motto 'The love of the people is my strength', all subsequent Danish monarchs have returned to the custom of mentioning God or the Lord in their mottoes along with various designations of Denmark. This can probably be taken as a symbolic expression of the fact that during the nineteenth century, the purposes of Church and State once again began to approach each other under the impact of the revivalist movement, the effect of Romanticism and the rising tide of popular nationalism, although with an increased weight on the secular role of the state compared to the religious duties.

The extensive and influential writings from the 1840s by the theologian and philosopher Søren Kierkegaard (1813–1855) also contributed to extending the clarification of the relationship between general existential conditions and the claims of religion. Kierkegaard's harsh critique of the Danish state Church system was based on classical Greek philosophy, but also included a deep respect for the religious dimension of existence. Thus, he helped to unify the two great interpretations of life – the secular and the religious – into a coherent existentialist world-view. Kierkegaard's prolific writings have since been translated into countless languages and so have exercised a decisive influence on the general existentialist philosophy of the twentieth century.

Viewed over a very long time span, the picture that emerges is of such a close partnership between Church and State in post-Reformation Denmark that it makes sense to say that although the balance between them has varied, they have been closely linked participants in one and the same project – to turn the Danes into useful citizens and good Christians. Nonetheless it is important to add that the secular aspect – creating good citizens – has gradually become the more dominant as the religious aspect has slipped further and further into the background. However, one and the same project it has clearly been. The only deviation in this long-term trend was during the late Enlightenment period in the second half of the eighteenth century when the conflicting pressures of Enlightenment thinking and the Pietist movement threatened for a time to pull in different directions and so sunder the unity of Church and State. This point was never in fact quite reached, largely due to one man, whose initiative and philosophy has set an indelible stamp, not just on the Danish Church, but on the whole way in which Danes perceive themselves and their ideas of what being a Danish citizen means. That man was a priest, a hymn-writer and social commentator – N. F. S. Grundtvig.

GRUNDTVIG

Nicolai Frederik Severin Grundtvig was born in 1783, and so was a child during the later period of the Enlightenment, a young man when the waves of Romanticism swept over Denmark at the beginning of the nineteenth century, and in his old age when Realism and *Realpolitik* superseded the mystical world of Romantic ideas. He lived until 1872, and so saw his country defeated and humiliated in 1864 by the harsh demonstration of *Realpolitik* by the Prussian Chancellor, Bismarck. All of these strong philosophical currents contributed in their own way to his thinking, and so to the creation of a particularly Danish 'ism' – Grundtvigianism – which probably affected Denmark far more than other European political or ideological movement.[6]

In his youth, which coincided with the Napoleonic Wars, Grundtvig produced an extensive body of historical works. Probably in response to the numerous calamities the war brought for Denmark, he took his material from a distant, heroic past. His pen brought the pagan Norse myths, with their gods, demi-gods and giants, to vivid life for his fellow countrymen. In the following years, as a trained theologian, he opened up controversial theological and ecclesiastical issues to public debate – he thundered equally against the narrow Lutheran orthodoxy which governed much of the Church and the rampant revivalist movement which was flourishing outside it. His trenchant views and vehemence quickly made him a controversial figure not just within ecclesiastical circles, but also in the wider social debate which was gathering steam during the 1830s.

Between 1829 and 1831, he made three extended study visits to England, which had a great influence on his future development and his opinions as a whole. The actual purpose of the trips was to study medieval English scripts, but the deepest and most enduring impressions he came back with were of the pragmatic outlook of the English and their respect for independent thinking, whether religious or temporal. Life in the here and now, and freedom of thought and deed, became key elements in his thinking. His encounter with the undogmatic English encouraged him to formulate one of his most quoted maxims, from 1832: 'First a human – then a Christian' – an aphorism which expressed his fundamental attitude to the relationship between faith and life, between the Church and the State. The statement clearly shows both his rejection of the primacy of religion and his perception of the Church as a concrete historical phenomenon to be understood and judged in its exact chronological context rather than as an eternal and immutable institution of salvation.

This pragmatic and terse statement was also the expression of a very clear position on the debate about the relationship between Church and State then raging, in favour of secular society. For Grundtvig secular aims were more important than religious aims, and he continued to express this clearly in his numerous prose works and the innumerable hymns with which he enriched the Danish hymnals. It says a great deal about his lack of dogmatism that the Catholic Church in Denmark has since included some of his hymns in its hymnbook.

The insight contained in the aphorism 'First a human – then a Christian' was one of what came to be called Grundtvig's 'unique discoveries'. Another was his recognition of 'the living word from the mouth of the Lord', which he later developed into a particularly religious view, according to which the Christian faith and the interpretation of existence came not from long sermons by learned theologians, but from conversations between equals, where the living word formed the basis of reality and the understanding of it. This idea was the foundation of the religious and educational philosophy he slowly developed during the 1830s. He attracted an increasing following of liberal thinkers.

THE FOLK HIGH SCHOOL AND THE DANISH CHURCH

His fundamental idea in the area of education was to establish a 'school for life', where the living word could stimulate and enlighten people, in contrast to the traditional grammar school, which Grundtvig called 'school for death' and which was the preserve of a small, carefully selected elite. This idea was the first seed of the 'Folk High School' movement in Denmark, which in a few decades became the biggest popular educational project of the century, aimed especially at rural youth, who had always been deprived in educational terms. The goal was to offer young people the chance to stay in a school during the winter, where inspirational teachers and the living word could awaken their dormant spirit and sharpen their perceptions. In short the intent was no less than to transform the inarticulate masses into responsible and articulate citizens in the new democratic society which was slowly taking shape.[7]

These new ideas about education sounded a chord within the population and bore fruit in 1844 with the opening of the first Folk High School in the southern Jutland village of Rødding. One such school after another opened, especially in rural areas, and immediately before the war of 1864 there were no fewer than 14 across the country. Just ten years later, the number had grown to 50, and around 1900 there were no fewer than 75. Students arrived in droves, especially young people from the countryside and, for many of them, their lives were changed as a result. At the same time, there was an even greater number of independent ('free') primary schools, inspired by Christen Kold (1816–1870), a teacher and a disciple of Grundtvig. They had no formal affiliation to the official education system and taught the pupils on the basis of Grundtvig's philosophy. So, the Folk High Schools for the youth and the Free Schools for the children formed a completely separate alternative educational system, and the public were free to use this instead of the official schools. Grundtvig and his pioneering followers thus founded the tradition of liberal education in Denmark which is still flourishing. In complete congruence with this, there is no legal compulsion for children in Denmark to attend any particular type of school. Instead, there is an obligation to provide an education, in the sense that children have a right and a duty to be taught according to a defined curriculum. How and in what form this teaching takes place is not a matter for the public authorities to decide for so long as the final results match the prescribed norms. This distinction between compulsory attendance and compulsory teaching, which has been and still is of critical importance in the liberal education tradition in Denmark, was the result of Grundtvig's extensive influence on legislation in the first decades after the introduction of democracy in 1848.

Grundtvig, with his high public profile and strong social commitment, was an obvious choice as a member of the national constitutional assembly in 1848–9, and then as a member of parliament, where he also made a deep mark. It was not least because of his determined opposition to fixed forms and compulsory frameworks that the Danish Church was not, as mentioned previously, accorded any particular status in the constitution of 1849, but had to be satisfied with some vague comments that their position would be dealt with by later legislation. Similarly, Grundtvig was the principal force behind two of these later laws. These were an 1855 law repealing the obligation to attend the local parish church exclusively and thus allowing people to choose which church they attended, and another in 1868 allowing people to form their own congregations and select their own ministers if for any reason they were dissatisfied with the traditional structure of their church. Neither of these measures necessarily required breaking links with the national Church.

Through these initiatives, Grundtvig and his followers, who had always been critical of the way in which priests could be used as the long arm of the state, created an effective breach between the two, but, notably, without breaking the numerous traditional links between them. The Danish Church was no longer a state Church in the old sense, but precisely a popular Church broad enough to accommodate all the varieties of Lutheranism, from the traditional High Church, through the Grundtvigian to the Pietist Home Mission.

This breadth is the probable reason that the Danish Church did not fragment during the turbulent nineteenth century under the pressure of the many revivalist movements, but in fact managed to include most of them and so preserve an external unity despite its internal diversity. This was similar to the way in which the deliberately vague formulations in the constitution concerning the relationship between Church and State ensured that the traditional bond was not severed in the transition from absolutism to democracy, even if the form in which they remained was somewhat diluted and ambiguous. Thus the ambitions and aims of Church and State were once more on a parallel course after diverging for a few decades at the start of the nineteenth century. In no small part this was due to Grundtvig and the latitude of the popular tradition of freedom of which he became the exponent.

In essence, the church organisation which Grundtvig and his comrades created 150 years ago still stands. This also serves to explain from a historical perspective the vagueness and ambiguity of the current church organisation outlined at the very start of this chapter. This applies equally to the modern educational system, where the name 'Folk School' deliberately echoes the name of the Danish Popular Church (*Folkekirken*) to emphasise that these institutions belong to the people and not to the state, and enshrine the freedom of the citizens to choose the type of schooling which suits their needs and beliefs. This tradition is also both a legacy and extension of Grundtvig's philosophy.

GRUNDTVIG'S CONCEPT OF POPULAR DEMOCRACY

The impact of Grundtvig was so great during his life and after that his name and the eponymous movement he began have earned an almost religious status in the Danish consciousness. The overriding reason for this is that he, in perfect keeping with the predominant spirit of the times and the democratic revolutions, based his philosophy on the people – ordinary people and their needs – and built everything on this cornerstone. He was the first Dane to use the term 'popular' as an exclusively positive concept which had to permeate everything – laws, rules and regulations, institutions, behaviour – if they were to be genuine and of value.

This Danish word for 'popular' – *folkelig* – and all its connotations is virtually untranslatable, as it has a very specific Danish context and includes so many overtones and secondary meanings that only

Danish ears can fully apprehend. As touched on before, the English word 'popular' is often used with pejorative or dismissive connotations which simply do not attach to the Danish word. The German cognate *völkisch* was used to describe ethnically pure people and to justify dictatorship, the Nuremberg Laws and the Holocaust, and so is very far indeed from the Danish word. In fact, German has a not dissimilar word, *volkstümlich*, but although this has some overlap with *folkelig*, it also has undertones quite different to those of the Danish concept of *folkelighed* – which means a sort of mixture of popularity, popular democracy, folksiness, simplicity, unassuming warmth and ease, and so on! The word can also be read in another way, *folke-lighed*, 'the equality of the people'. It is therefore essential to try to describe the diversity of this Grundtvigian concept, not least as it continues to play a very important role in the way in which Danes perceive themselves.

The concept was first coined in a series of lectures which Grundtvig delivered at Borch's College, Copenhagen, from 1838. They have since been published, entitled *Mands Minde* ('The Memory of Man'). The lectures took the form of a number of commentaries on contemporary problems in society. In the face of the ever stronger forces pushing to replace the absolutist regime with democratic government reform, Grundtvig was particularly concerned with the question of how to transform the hitherto inarticulate general public into responsible citizens in the coming democracy – in other words, to turn the humble subjects of the king into good democrats. It was in this context that he created the word *folkelighed* to represent a central concept.

Grundtvig thought that this project could only be carried out by reaching out to the groups previously marginalised or considered incapable of managing their affairs where they actually were, taking them seriously and striving to draw them into a national community through broadly targeted education and enlightenment. He thought this was the only way to forge these separate groups of society into what was the essential prerequisite for the success of democracy – a people, a nation. In 1848 he wrote a poem called *Folkeligheden*, where he encapsulated this idea:

> To one nation they belong
> If that's their chosen fashion
> They share a common tongue
> And love their Fatherland with passion.[8]

As expressed here, belonging to a nation was a matter of free choice. One could choose to join or to remain outside. Choosing to join the popular, that is, national, community meant accepting certain duties towards that community as a whole, not just linguistic, but also in the form of taking responsibility for the whole and an obligation to include those who wanted to be members in a *folkelig*, a mutually committed community. The core of Grundtvig's concept of *folkelighed* was precisely this mutual obligation and the desire to actively share it with others who wished to join. This also became the guiding principle for his ideas on liberal education and the Church, as described above.

The Grundtvigian movement was a colossal popular success, not least amongst the least well-off rural populations, who saw in it an ideology which enabled them to turn the economic freedom they had obtained through agrarian reform into political power and influence. Grundtvig's strong emphasis that the 'popular' was not just a means, but an end in itself – his clear signal that anyone who chose the 'popular' route therefore themselves belonged to the elite – gave the politicians of the farming communities sufficient courage and self-confidence to talk directly to the old elite in the new democracy. It empowered them to speak on behalf of the whole as true representatives of the *folkelighed* that they had learnt during their stay at the Grundtvigian high schools, the very essence of a democratic nation.

Even though the Grundtvigian outlook naturally took root most strongly amongst liberal factions, it was not attached to any particular political party. Grundtvigian ideas could be found amongst all political camps. The social democratic labour leader, Frederik Borgbjerg (1866–1936), described himself as a Grundtvigian, and the intellectual left took in a great deal of his philosophy between the wars, although not the religious aspects. It is even the case that most of the leaders of the Danish factions in the student revolts of 1968 were mainly inspired by Grundtvigianism, which brought a high degree of verbose tolerance to the revolt, which very seldom erupted into real violence.

The spiritual legacy of Grundtvig probably also explains why the Danish Social Democrats moved fairly rapidly from being an internationally minded, class-based party to a broad Danish movement. This was because Grundtvig's concept of obligation to the whole permeated the ranks of the party, while their political opponents also showed the Grundtvigian mentality in seeing their role not as to marginalise the party, but to draw it into the *folkelig* community through dialogue. Correspondingly, the Grundtvigian duty of *folkelighed* prevented the *Venstre* Party which, for most of the twentieth century, was essentially the party of the independent farmers, from turning into a purely agrarian party, as happened, for example, in Sweden. The unilateral promotion of narrow class interests at the expense of other members of society would have been in flagrant contradiction to the party's roots in Grundtvig's notion of the spiritual obligation to the whole. It is interesting in this regard that when the party did succeed in taking over office from the Social Democrat Party in 2001, it was after the leadership had convinced the voters that the party would continue to defend and extend the welfare state, which in its universal solidarity can well be seen as the concrete manifestation of Grundtvig's concept of *folkelighed*.

GRUNDTVIG'S LEGACY AND THE DANISH MODEL

In virtually every area imaginable, the ideas developed by Grundtvig and his circle at a particular historical point in the middle of the nineteenth century have left a deep and long-lasting impression on the Danish psyche and on the way in which Danish society operates today. This is not necessarily because any of these ideas were in themselves especially original, but because at a critical crossroads in the history of Denmark, he was able to formulate his thoughts in such ways as to create a great impact and a comprehensive programme of action able to change the humble subjects of an absolute monarch into mature members of a democratic society and at the same time unite the inhabitants of the remains of the Oldenborg state as one people, a Danish nation. The key concepts in this were *folkelighed*, tolerance, openness and liberal-mindedness; the means were enlightenment and committed dialogue.

It may well be that one particular reason for the outstanding success of the Grundtvigian model was that in many respects it was an extension of a culture of agreements and negotiations, which, as discussed earlier, characterised the social conventions of the old agricultural communities. Indeed, it could be seen as the raising of village culture to a national level. In this respect it was tailor-made to support the new powerful group in the emergent democracy: the liberally minded independent farmers. Another explanatory factor in this success was that it came to fruition in a geographically small area – Denmark (i.e. Jutland and the islands) – where, as a result of the loss of the Norwegian and German parts of the old kingdom, the inhabitants were fairly homogenous in terms of language and culture. In short, the Denmark of the nineteenth century could be reasonably accurately described as a gigantic village, where uniformity predominated and social distances were modest. In such an environment, a modernised model of agreement and dialogue such as Grundtvig's had a good chance of succeeding, whereas it is far from sure that it could work in larger multiethnic and multicultural European societies. This is perhaps the precise reason why the model has become so specifically Danish and not suitable for export.

At the same time, though, it should be pointed out that the grip of Grundtvigianism on Danish cultural and spiritual life was not so constricting as to deny room to a number of influential artists and scientists who did not restrict themselves to the concept of Danish popular equality, but earned international renown. One such was the composer Carl Nielsen (1865–1931), a son of the soil of Fyn, who, with his symphonies, from around 1900 revolutionised the dominant Romantic movement in music in a way that resonated throughout the world, while at the same time preserving a particularly Nordic expression of his geographical origins. Nor did the aristocratic author Karen Blixen (1885–1962) pander to *folkelighed* in her seminal work, placing the life of modern women firmly on the agenda of international literature while also earning international acclaim. Another towering example is the physicist Niels Bohr (1885–1962), whose epoch-making theories of quantum mechanics earned him a place amongst the fathers of modern nuclear physics alongside Albert Einstein. For many years after the Second World War his institute at Copenhagen University attracted the best nuclear physicists from around the world. None of these figures could be described as *folkelig* in the Grundtvigian sense, yet they were undeniably important to Danish spiritual and cultural life in the twentieth century. While this was certainly characterised by the Grundtvigian consensual approach, it had broadened and deepened to allow room for powerful innovators who were not willing to sacrifice their work to the levelling traditions and ideals of popular equality.

This open, tolerant model of consensus – where the essential and implicit prerequisite is a fundamental agreement about the common framework of values linked with the concept of *folkelighed* within which differences are allowed – meant that after some decades where schism threatened, the Church developed into a broad popular institution with room for theological diversity, yet with a common responsibility for the entirety. With such an absence of dogmatism, the Church could be easily brought round to pull together with the secular authorities.

Both were now parts of the same Grundtvigian popular consensual project. Therefore, the remarks at the beginning of this chapter concerning the ostensibly superficial attitude to the Church that Danes exhibit should not be taken to mean that Danes are on the whole any less religious or more anticlerical than other nations. They are not, for the simple reason that the Church and religious observance are essential elements in the Grundtvigian – and thus the Danish – model.

Should anyone doubt that the Church still plays a central role, it is only necessary to point out the violent reactions to the apparent challenge from Islam in recent years. These reactions can hardly be attributed to Danes feeling threatened in their own faith, but relate to the perception that any attack on the Church is an attack on the entire basis on which Danish society is built. To this extent the model, the Grundtvigian model, is on the whole religious – or rather would be inconceivable without the Lutheran Christian foundation on which it heavily rests.

The Danish educational system, with all its strengths and weaknesses, is also a product of Grundtvig's ideas. The strength is that it offers a wide freedom of choice, and just like the commitment to popular democracy – embraces a wide range of ideas. The Danish national schools seek to include everyone – including the least able – in an educational community. Thus, a great emphasis is placed on bringing up children to be independent, critical members of society who can take responsibility for themselves and for the community as a whole. These are praiseworthy and useful values, essential for fully-fledged inhabitants of Grundtvig's country.

However, there is another side to the coin. The educational commitment to the *folkelige* in Grundtvig's sense has had the unfortunate consequence that the level of ambition is relatively lower than in the educational systems of many other Western European countries. This is true throughout the entire system from primary school to university. At one point in the 1970s, a Minister of Education unintentionally expressed the fundamental ideology of the educational system with crystal clarity: 'Unless everybody can learn it, nobody should be taught it!' This was a somewhat radical interpretation of the Grundtvigian principle of equality, and to be fair, it must be added that this statement was met with vehement protests from both teachers and the wider public.

Nonetheless, in all its laconic cynicism, the statement does expose the Achilles' heel of the Grundtvigian educational system: its enormous focus on mediocrity, which certainly means that no one falls out at the bottom, but also ensures that no one excels. The disheartening result has been that Danish education has fared poorly in a number of comparative studies of children's literacy and numeracy which the OECD has conducted in recent years. Danish children perform less well in a number of critical areas than those in the countries with which Danes normally compare themselves. The results of these studies have several times created huge shock waves in the Danish educational system and provoked concrete political initiatives to try to improve the basic skills. The politicians responsible clearly appreciate that this is not a sustainable situation in a globalised world, where later on Danish children will have to compete with people from other countries. Yet the difficulty lies in how to achieve better levels of performance and a more elitist system of teaching without compromising the very core values of the Danish model of equality. In reality this is probably an insoluble dilemma, not made any easier because it bears on a central element of the way in which Danes perceive themselves.

In conclusion, there are several clear signs that in the areas of both education and religion the particularly Danish model, which originated in the Lutheran church organisation and the old village communities and took a definite programmatic form in the hands of Grundtvig, is currently in crisis. This can be attributed in the final instance to the fact that Denmark is no longer a tiny, cloistered nation state, but part of a global society which is developing at breakneck speed. Whether the model, and the particularly Danish way of implementing it, can survive is an open question.

6

Economic Conditions: The Old Denmark, 1500–1800

WAY OF LIFE AND THE ECONOMY

In Sir James Mellon's book about Denmark and the Danes mentioned earlier, the former British Ambassador to Denmark made some general observations about the economic system and its wider functions.[1] One of these was that the economics of a country, in addition to the obvious goal of providing goods and services to ensure the highest possible standard of living through co-operation, was also generally geared to take into account the traditional lifestyle of the people and the common aims and values which society prized most highly. The examples he quoted were the Soviet economy, created in accordance with the ideology of the Communist Party; the German economy between 1870 and 1945, in which the most important task was to transfer resources from civilian production to munitions; and the Iraqi economy, geared to support Saddam Hussein's dream of glory. Most Western economies, in accordance with the tradition of freedom, operate according to market conditions and so underpin the dominant liberal ideology.

In his opinion the modern Danish economy is constructed not just to create a high standard of living for the entire population, but also with the important goal of consolidating 'Danishness', by which he meant the particular Danish tribal mentality which he identified as a key element of the way in which Danes perceive themselves, founded in the limited size of the country and the relatively small population. In this regard, he identified two factors which were decisive in shaping the modern Danish economy. The first was the desire for 'justice' in the distribution of wealth, in the sense that everyone, even those unable to contribute to economic growth, should share equally in the high standard of living. He thus thought that the redistribution of wealth was considered a critical economic mission. The second factor he identified was supporting and strengthening Danish institutions in their competition with other countries as a means of promoting 'Danishness'.

His perception of the modern Danish economy was that it is not just a matter of diligence and industry in an area with few natural resources, but that it is also a crusade for uniformity and economic equality, where foreign influence, which constitutes a threat to the struggle for equality, must be excluded.

In many ways this is a just and accurate description of the Danish welfare economy as it was shaped in the lee of the international boom from around 1960, when the dramatic increase in prosperity made it possible to convert the growing surplus into vastly better living standards, not just for the working population, but also for the destitute, poor and excluded. This was definitely a growth-oriented economy, where the politicians did everything in their power to increase production, using slogans such as 'make the good times even better' to ensure that there was a bigger cake to share, while, using slogans such as 'better welfare for all', they underlined the fundamental philosophy of equality which underpinned the welfare state.

So, Sir James Mellon interpreted this extreme effort to achieve equality and uniformity in the Danish economy as a product of the particularly Danish welfare state, but also as a special attempt by a tiny nation – a tribe – to maintain an independent identity despite the challenges of the wider world. This view could well have much to recommend it, but it can hardly in itself explain the full nature of the modern Danish economy. In part, this is because Sir James limited his analysis to the latter half of the twentieth century. A more sophisticated explanation, not just of the dominance of the ideal of equality, but also of the truly remarkable fact that in the twentieth century the Danes managed to turn their country from an impoverished sandbank into one of the richest countries in the world in terms of production per head in just two generations, requires a little more background and a longer historical perspective. A good place to start would be Danish agrarian society in the sixteenth and seventeenth centuries.

THE SOUND DUES, DENMARK AND THE WORLD ECONOMY

The geographical position of Denmark, on the fringes of the European mainland, meant that it was also on the periphery of the world economy during the sixteenth and seventeenth centuries. At the beginning of the early modern period, the fulcrum of world trade had shifted from the Mediterranean to the area around the English Channel, bordered and driven by the populous Netherlands, northern France and south-east England. The commerce of this region dictated the pace and strength of the world economy and created waves which rippled through Europe and on to the colonies. The Baltic region was important in the wider configuration, as the extensive fertile steppes of Eastern Europe became the breadbasket for the densely populated areas of Western Europe which could no longer produce enough food to support themselves. More and more ships, especially from the Netherlands and England, made the harbours of Poland and the eastern Baltic regular ports of call to collect cargoes of grain and shipbuilding materials. Previously, most of the transportation of these goods had been over land or along the wide German rivers. This was expensive, slow and difficult. New marine technology made it possible to dispatch fleets of large ships around Skagen, the northern tip of Denmark, down through the *Øresund* and into the Baltic. This trade route rapidly became the busiest and most important in Europe. As it ran through Danish waters, it naturally had a significant effect on the long-term developments within Denmark.[2]

The increased shipping traffic linked the country more closely than before to the international commercial system – and so also to Europe – with all the advantages that brought in terms of the exchange of goods and culture. However, it also brought a number of disadvantages as the large trading nations took more notice of relations with Denmark, and especially the relations between Denmark and neighbouring Sweden. At times this severely restricted the freedom of action of the Danish government, and for an extended period in the seventeenth century virtually made the country an economic vassal of the mighty Netherlands. This, however, was the price of economic integration, which also brought a clear economic gain through the vastly increased customs receipts. As early as 1429 the Danish King Erik of Pomerania forced foreign commercial vessels to pay dues for sailing through the *Øresund*, which was part of Danish domestic waters until the cession of Skåne to Sweden in 1658. Ever since, the masters of foreign ships dutifully paid their dues at the customs house in Helsingør – directly under the threatening cannons of Kronborg – every time they passed through the Sound. Thus, the large increase in shipping turned the *Øresund* into a veritable gold mine for the Danish king. The income almost exploded and actually became the state's biggest source of revenue. For a long time, the money raised financed the state's payments to the royal household and the construction of royal castles and fortresses.

For various inscrutable reasons, the Danish government managed to continue to extract the Sound Dues even after the border between Denmark and Sweden moved in 1658 to the middle of the Sound, actually making it an international waterway. Although some countries were periodically exempted, the Sound Dues continued unassailably right up to 1855, when the US Congress decided that from 1856 American ships would no longer pay. The dominant international climate of free trade meant that in the long term it was impossible to maintain the Sound Dues, and they were definitively terminated in 1857 as a result of international negotiations. Denmark received a one-time payment of 33.5 million *rigsdaler* from a number of seafaring nations as compensation.

For more than 400 years the Sound Dues had filled the royal coffers and put the Danish Crown in a position to maintain the armed forces, the royal household and a civilian administration on a much greater scale than would have been possible with just the relatively modest resources of the country itself. They also, though, came at a political price in the form of the ill-will of the seafaring nations. Their intervention in the conflict between Denmark and Sweden in the sixteenth and seventeenth centuries which resulted in the *Øresund* becoming the boundary between the two countries can largely be attributed to the Sound Dues, which were seen as an impediment to the desire of the maritime nations for free navigation. It could also be said that it was because of the effortless customs income that the Danish government was relatively late, at least when compared to Sweden, in implementing the process of modernisation which changed Denmark from a medieval monarchy to a modern state relying on taxation. This rich stream of customs income meant that the Danish Crown was exceptionally rich compared to the impoverished Swedish government, and able itself to finance the activities of state right up until the middle of the seventeenth century, while Sweden had been obliged to rationalise the apparatus of state

100 years earlier, in the process changing the country into a very effective military state. This meant that at a critical point in the history of the country there was a structural asynchronism between Denmark and Sweden, to the detriment of Denmark, which goes some way to explaining why Denmark ended up by losing the long conflict with Sweden over Nordic hegemony.

Despite the indisputable short-term economic gains produced for the country, the Sound Dues also thus had unfortunate longer-term political implications and also eliminated any incentive for reform and modernisation – a situation which can well be compared to that of many of today's oil-producing countries. Just like Denmark in the heyday of the Sound Dues, the dependence of these countries on a single large source of income prevents them from investing in the infrastructure which could raise their economies up to a par with those of the modern industrial countries. From this perspective, the Sound Dues were a short-term blessing but a long-term curse.

THE OLD AGRARIAN SOCIETY

From the point of view of the climate and the soil, Denmark enjoys the best conditions in Scandinavia for agriculture. Accordingly, this was the country's most important economic activity long into the twentieth century. Indeed in the sixteenth and seventeenth centuries it was virtually the only primary economic activity.

More than 75 per cent of the country's 800,000 inhabitants were peasants, running just about 60,000 farms. The urban population thus only accounted for 12–13 per cent of the total, and around a third of these were concentrated in Copenhagen, the capital, which with its 30,000 inhabitants was far and away the biggest city. The remainder lived in the 70–80 market towns, all of which were very small. Only a small handful of regional towns approached a population of 5000. The others just boasted a few hundred. The rest of the population consisted of landed nobility, clergymen and a significant number of people with no means of support.

To put this in perspective, the total population of Europe at that time was 110 million in round figures. With its 19 million inhabitants, France was by far the most populous European country. Next were Russia and the area of Germany, each with approximately 15 million, Spain and Portugal with a dozen or so million, and the Italian peninsula with more or less 13 million. A long way down the list came the British Isles, with 7 million, Poland with around 5 million and the Netherlands with roughly 3 million. Denmark had one of the lowest populations in Europe; even the mountainous Switzerland, which could claim around 1 million inhabitants, had more. The population density was also very low compared to Europe as a whole. In the sixteenth and seventeenth centuries the density of population in Denmark was 14–15 inhabitants per km^2, which was very low in comparison with the Netherlands or northern Italy, where the corresponding figure was 100. This in turn was only a little lower than the population density of twentieth-century Denmark, which is approximately 120 per km^2.

These figures demonstrate clearly that early modern Denmark was a sparsely populated agricultural country. Although agriculture was the absolutely dominant economic activity, the very largest part of this was subsistence-based, with by far the most production being used for simple survival. The limited extra production consisted most importantly of grain and meat, especially beef. The agrarian production system was exclusively based on the landed estates of the Crown and the nobility. The social structure and other commercial activities were organised around this system.

The ownership structure remained relatively unchanged until the end of the seventeenth century. Around 94 per cent of agricultural land was owned by the Crown and the very few, but highly privileged, nobles. This aristocracy consisted of fewer than 2000 people – counting men, women and children, in other words, less than a quarter of a per cent of the population as a whole. As previously mentioned, after the Reformation in 1536, the Crown owned approximately half of the culti-vated area of the country, the nobles around 44 per cent and the remaining 6 per cent belonged to the dwindling minority of freeholders. The reason for the stability of the structure of ownership was that the property of the nobles was in effect immunised, as it was built into their legal privileges up to 1660, when the system changed. This quite simply prohibited the transfer of aristocratic land to anyone other than other nobles. The national laws were precisely tuned to support and preserve this structure of production, with the estates of the Crown and the nobility as the fulcrum.[3]

Nonetheless, remarkably enough, this feudal system in Denmark did not really lead to the large-scale operation of estates based on villeinage like those in, for example, the areas east of the Elbe and in Eastern Europe. One possible explanation is the undulating moraine landscape which, unlike the plains of Eastern Europe, did not lend itself to extensive agriculture. The structure of the Danish landed estates followed a basic pattern of tenancy, where the manors were relatively small, while most of the agricultural production was carried out on the subsidiary tenancies. Around 1650, for example, only 5–6 per cent of agricultural land was run as manorial estates. This decentralised structure no doubt to some extent explains why Danish peasants, despite everything, never really suffered legal and social oppression to the same extent as their counterparts in Eastern Europe.

Even though a single poor harvest or an outbreak of cattle disease could dramatically tip the balance over the delicate line between surplus and famine, Danish agricultural production under normal circumstances was adequate for the country to feed itself and even achieve a small surplus for export. In the middle of the seventeenth century, around 5 per cent of the total grain production of between 6 and 6.5 million barrels went to export, especially to the Netherlands, where Denmark was a secondary supplier after the large-scale producers of Central Europe. From the second half of the seventeenth century, however, a growing volume of Danish corn was directed to Norway to address the problems the Norwegians were having in producing enough to feed themselves. This trend continued to grow over the following centuries until Norway separated from the Danish Crown in 1814.

It is difficult to quantify the other main product, beef. It would seem that in the middle of the sixteenth century the total Danish export of bullocks to the critical Dutch market amounted to 40,000–45,000 live cattle, which were driven in huge herds down through Jutland and the duchies to their destination in the Netherlands. However, except for a brief boom at the start of the seventeenth century related to the truce between Spain and the Netherlands, the long-term export trend was downwards. At the beginning of the eighteenth century, the exports only amounted to half of those in the heyday of the mid-sixteenth century. This was in part due to increased competition from other European countries, but probably also because the agrarian revolution was finally changing Dutch farming and thus reducing the reliance on imported foodstuffs.[4]

As a result of its proximity to the main markets of Northern Europe, Denmark was able to take maximum advantage of the general prosperity of the sixteenth century, even though, as noted, the Danish exporters took second place to huge Eastern European exporters. However, with the exception of cattle, which were at least periodically in great demand in the Netherlands because of their relatively high quality, Danish agricultural exports were essentially a niche phenomenon.

Nonetheless, both the Crown and the nobles showed that they were in a position to take the best possible advantage of the growing demand and rising prices from the middle of the sixteenth century. For the next few decades, Denmark was able to record a handsome export surplus and thus a positive balance of trade. The estate owners as a whole enjoyed a number of golden years, which effectively lasted until the 1620s, when the Thirty Years War provoked a lengthy crisis in the traditional markets. Around 1610, exports of grain reached a formidable volume of around half a million barrels, and cattle exports peaked at the same time, with more than 50,000 bullocks a year driven south past the Danish customs houses.

Taking everything into account, this represented a temporary high-water mark in the history of Danish export. Except for a short-lived, price-led boom in grain exports in the 1630s, when the extensive European war created propitious conditions for the big exporters, the exports gradually declined. Danish agriculture, although still the primary economic activity, slipped into a deep long-term crisis from which it only started to recover around 1740.

One significant reason why the crisis affected Denmark so deeply and for so long in the seventeenth century lies in the country's weak and uncertain position on the foreign markets, which made it very sensitive to changes in the international economic situation. In addition, in the middle of the century there was major change in the climate – a 'mini-ice age' – which made the conditions for production much tougher. However, yet another factor was the rigid system of production with the manors and *landsbyfællesska-berne* (village co-operatives) as the main units. The collectivist structure in itself was not particularly open to innovation and actually encouraged the tendency to continue with the traditional production – grain and beef – even at times when changes in the export markets could have rewarded initiatives for reorganisation and new methods.

The considerable profits which accrued not least to the aristocratic landowners during the boom times of the sixteenth century were used only to a very limited extent to introduce operating improvements on the model of the agrarian revolution which was advancing at full steam in the Netherlands and England. Proper dairy production was a virtually unknown phenomenon in Denmark before the end of the seventeenth century. By far the majority of estate owners, including the Crown, preferred to spend their large profits on building ostentatious stately homes, luxury goods and expensive foreign travel for their sons. Thus, large volumes of money were diverted from the production itself and used for investments which from an operational point of view were unproductive. This very limited ability to introduce reform and rationalisation, as well as the reluctance to invest in the operation itself, resulted in locking agricultural – and thus the whole of Danish – society in an iron grip, which only started to loosen when the international economic situation in the middle of the eighteenth century finally once more turned in favour of Danish agricultural exports. This in turn was the trigger for the extensive agrarian reforms at the end of the eighteenth century, which, as briefly touched on before, turned the fundamental structures of the principal economic activity of the country on their heads.

In the early modern period there was effectively no industrial production in Denmark whatsoever. Certainly, at the beginning of the seventeenth century, Christian IV, influenced by the state mercantilism of the time, attempted to encourage the establishment of some manufacturing industry, principally in the immediate vicinity of Copenhagen. He also took the initiative in setting up a number of trading companies on the model of those in England and the Netherlands. The vast majority of these met a dismal fate. After just a few years they were either languishing or had been forced to shut down. This failure can be especially attributed to factors such as lack of natural resources, absence of adequate expertise and, not least, chronic shortage of capital. Most free capital at that time, as mentioned above, was channelled into land and property – the only things which brought prestige and status in a country dominated by landowners.

The first signs of any growth in international trading companies came towards the end of the seventeenth century when, in the shelter of the European conflicts, a small group of German and Dutch merchants based themselves in Copenhagen. Still, any non-agricultural production or international shipping trade worthy of mention definitely lay a long way in the future. Denmark was, and remained in the sixteenth and seventeenth centuries, a specifically agricultural area on the periphery of Northern Europe.

THE STRUCTURE OF THE LANDED ESTATES UNDER ABSOLUTISM

Ignoring the provinces of Skåne, which were lost to Sweden in 1658, there were just about 60,000 farms of various sizes in Denmark in 1650. This number did not change to any great extent over the ensuing centuries. However, around this time there were some important changes resulting from the comprehensive sale of Crown lands to private hands to pay off the national debt and the disposal of the large aristocratic estates to cover the debts of the war years. It is estimated that around half of all property had changed hands by 1680, often several times. This naturally meant very significant changes of ownership of the agricultural land.[5]

Before the change of regime in 1660, as stated, around half of the arable land of the country belonged to the Crown. The huge sell-off during 1660–75 reduced this holding by half, and even if the lands belonging to the Church and the university are included, by 1700 the Crown still controlled only a third of the land. In turn this reduced the income of the Crown considerably. Ignoring for the moment the fact that the actual composition of the nobility changed dramatically in the latter half of the seventeenth century, the amount of land they held remained roughly the same, at about 45 per cent of the total. This apparent continuity disguises the large loss incurred by the old, pre-absolutist nobles to the benefit of the new absolutist aristocracy, mainly consisting of newly ennobled civil servants and middle-class business-men. With this, a whole new class of estate owners was born: the middle-class capitalists, who now owned around a seventh of all the land. In particular, these were those who had given credit to the state during the years of war, and been repaid in this way, and so some indebted landed estates had fallen into their hands. There were other losers in this great redistribution, namely the small group of freeholders. This group was virtually made extinct by the unfavourable economic circumstances and the growing demands for tax from the absolutist state.

The period from 1630 to 1700 is often described as the time when large-scale landed estate operations really started in Denmark. The increased taxation of the peasantry which began in 1630 in contrast to the exemption of the aristocrats in the last decades of aristocratic government also contributed to the expansion of the manor farms and the subsequent dissolution of peasant tenancies. It is also certain that the rapidly growing problem of derelict farms after the Swedish wars pushed in the same direction. Finally, the tax policies of early absolutism, based entirely on land, provided an incentive as well, and this was further underlined by a decree in 1682.

This decree meant that only 'complete' manor farms could enjoy exemption from taxation. Such a 'complete' manor farm was defined as one which had at least 200 *tønder hartkorn* within a radius of two miles, which corresponded to 30 or 40 ordinary tenancies.[6] This was a clear incentive by the state to create and assemble aggregated estates with the manor house as the centre of production and the subsidiary tenancies as providers of labour, in the form of villeinage. This development was further stimulated by the privileges Christian V gave to counts and barons in 1671, and the Danish Law of 1683, which allowed the establishment of entailed estates for the first time in Denmark. All of these factors worked towards large-scale operation and a standardised system of production involving all the extensive demesnes, with the manors at the core and equalised peasant tenancies in the immediate vicinity.

However, as previously stated, the importance of this development should not be overstated. Despite this tentative initiative, the Danish system of estates never became anything which could approach the extensive nature of farming in Eastern Europe, supported by serfs and labourers who owned no land. It remained based on a system of tenancy as in the late medieval period, with relatively small manor farms and a large number of tenancies of uniform size, each with just enough land to support the tenant and his family.

It is very unclear as to how many farms were suborned in these centuries as part of the creation of large manor farms. For the entire period 1525–1700, this number can be estimated as being around 2000, of which a half ceased to exist around 1650. In other words, the attempts to create large-scale estate operations after 1650 absorbed at most 2 per cent of the farms in the entire country. Given the high rate of dereliction following the Swedish wars, this can hardly have created any great problems for the agricultural population.

In fact, it is surprising that the total number of farms, despite local variations, remained fairly constant, albeit with a small decrease. In all probability this was in the first instance due to the tax system applied by the aristocratic government, which took a single farm as a unit for taxation. In itself, this made the government reluctant to authorise dissolution. After the introduction of absolutism in 1660, there was a change to taxation on the basis of area, and so the reasons to preserve farms as separate units disappeared. However, a quite different mechanism came into force because of the new private landed estates, consolidated by legislation from the early period of absolutism relating to the new role of estate owners as tax collectors and the dramatic increase in villeinage which started from the end of the seventeenth century.

The limited apparatus of power at the disposal of the state during the period of early absolutism meant that the burden of tax collection was in reality placed on the shoulders of the private estate owners, who in fact became responsible for raising the taxes levied on the peasants of their estates. This became known as the 'leasing out of state power'. This gave the estate owners an easily understandable interest in keeping the tax base of the estates intact, and thus ensuring that the tenancies were of a sufficient size to allow the peasants to meet the tax payments from their own production. To make this system as manageable as possible, many estate owners made their tenant farms of equal size, to ensure an equal distribution of the taxation and to simplify its collection.

The increased villeinage – the duty of ordinary peasants to work on the manor farm for one or more days according to detailed rules – which quickly became the method through which the manor farms were run, pushed in the same direction. The tenants were normally obliged to use their own tools and resources to carry out this compulsory work, and so it was necessary that the tenants themselves ran farms big enough to allow them to do this. Villeinage also played an ever greater role from the point of view of the estate owners, as the increasing demands from the state for taxes from peasants limited the extent to which they could compel them to put their money and work at the service of the estate. This was yet another incentive to keep the medium-sized tenant farms of 50–60 acres as the basic units of production.

THE AGRICULTURAL CLASSES

Thus, all these factors, which demonstrate a certain symmetry between the interests of the state and that of the estate owners and the ordinary peasants, combined to create and consolidate the structure of ownership under absolutism. Typically, this consisted of a number of smaller manor farms surrounded by a relatively unchanging number of reasonably large peasant tenancies. These tenant farms tended to be of standardised sizes to facilitate just distribution of taxes and efficient administration.

In essence, this system was allowed to continue unaltered until the period of agrarian reforms at the end of the eighteenth century. As such, it formed the basis for the class of independent farmers with roughly equal holdings of land which grew out of these reforms and became politically articulate in the nineteenth century.

This structure was strongly supported by the conservative state, which saw the creation of uniformity and transparency in its areas of influence as goals in themselves, although they resulted in a lack of flexibility and were totally incapable of coping with a growth in the population. As the population began to increase at the end of the seventeenth century, the number of farms could not increase correspondingly through division, for example, except in the most sparsely populated parts of Jutland. Thus, the pressure of growth expressed itself in another way, in a huge increase in the numbers of smallholders with either no land to speak of or very little. Around 1500, these crofters accounted for only 5–10 per cent of the total number of farms, by the end of the seventeenth century this had increased to between 30 per cent and 40 per cent, and 100 years later, at the start of the period of agrarian reform, the proportion had nearly doubled. This rise was a clear indication of the strong pressure from the increase in population on the land and striking proof of the stability and rigidity of the structure of landed estates under absolutism.

Although the actual social conditions of these smallholders varied greatly, from prosperous artisans through agricultural jobbing labourers to the impoverished elderly, together they constituted a rural underclass. The explosive growth in their numbers from the middle of the seventeenth century was in itself an expression of the stratification of rural society and evidence of the increasing poverty and social degradation of the most exposed groups amongst agricultural communities at the same time. The trend also reflected the eruptive growth of the tax-based absolutist state and the limited efforts of the landowners to use their money to improve farm productivity in competition with the growing power of government.

The unfavourable economic climate in the latter part of the seventeenth century thus, just as the absolutist state wanted, created an aristocratic land-owning system in Denmark which was primarily geared to the needs and interests of the state and the estate owners. This, in turn, laid the foundations for the solid and often very prosperous middle class of tenant farmers, who with the security of their virtually equally sized farms formed the backbone of agricultural production. This fuelled the development of a rapidly growing rural underclass, the heterogeneous group of crofters which included a large number of the indigent. They often eked out a wretched existence on or around the starvation line.

In short, Danish rural society from the end of the seventeenth century became very divided, and the social differences continued to widen. The poor economic circumstances of the time were not alone to blame. The absolutist system of power with its tax policies and lack of administrative capacity was even more aristocratic than the previous regime. This pattern did not change until the end of the nineteenth century when industries in the towns started to absorb workers from the lowest stratum of rural society, and when, in 1899, the state started introducing measures to allow a greater number of smallholders enough land to provide a rudimentary living for a family.

The absolutist legislation in the areas of tax and agriculture were also responsible for two other characteristic traits of rural society, which were not only of critical importance to Danish agriculture right into the twentieth century, but also to what it meant to be Danish. The first of these was the conspicuous uniformity which came to be the hallmark of the key element of Danish agriculture, the peasant farms. Under the encouragement of the tax system, these came to have a standard size of 50 acres virtually throughout the country. Thus, absolutism unwittingly created the typical Danish system of family-run agriculture which distinguished agricultural society and the Danish landscape itself right up until the second half of the twentieth century.

The other characteristic is related to the fact that the solid middle-ranking peasant population created by the structure of land-ownership under absolutism were not just the mainstay of the national economy as a whole, but came to set the political tone for a large part of the twentieth century. Their strength and impact was due to the high level of solidarity and cohesion they managed to maintain, precisely because their material circumstances and lifestyles were so similar. This gave them a powerful sense of equality when they met in the old village communities, for so long as they existed, and had the necessary basis to continue to act collectively and pull together when the open-field system vanished in the wake of the agrarian reforms at the end of the eighteenth century.

GOOD TIMES AND FLOURISHING TRADE

Around 1740, the protracted slump which had locked the Danish economy in an iron grip for nearly a hundred years finally lifted.

Not least because of the large-scale clashes between the naval powers seeking hegemony in Europe which started with the War of the Austrian Succession, 1740–8, and lasted until the final defeat of Napoleon at Waterloo in 1815, there were excellent opportunities for neutral shipping to grasp a large share of the international transport market, at the same time as both the prices of and the demand for agricultural produce were rising. Both these factors worked in Denmark's favour.

The neutrality of the country during the great power confrontations created previously unknown opportunities for Danish ships. Sailing under a neutral flag, they could carry cargoes for the warring nations, who were prevented from doing so precisely because they were at war. In the second half of the eighteenth century the Danish commercial fleet expanded rapidly under cover of neutrality. Danish freight ships sailed regularly to ports in Europe and the Far East, and the docks at Copenhagen became a hub for goods passing to and from the ports of the belligerent powers. Warehouse after warehouse shot up along the waterfront in Copenhagen to support this frenzied activity, a physical representation of the undreamed-of wealth that was flooding into the country, and especially into the capital. A veritable fairy tale for seafaring, which had begun hesitantly during the earlier conflicts of the great powers with Louis XIV at the end of the seventeenth century, but then receded again, now came true, and within a short period in the second half of the eighteenth century brought riches to the impoverished agricultural country of Denmark on a scale that no one would have dared even to dream about just a few years before. The description of this golden period is often referred to as the halcyon days of Danish trade, and not without reason.[7]

For the first time in history, the Danish economy was not exclusively reliant on agriculture, but was now also supported by merchant shipping, an ideal trade for a country with such long coastlines and so many harbours. However, the opportunity really came only once the de facto monopoly on sea transport that the Netherlands had exercised was smashed by Britain, and Britain herself became totally occupied by the business of war. This spectacular commercial boom changed Denmark in just a few years into a seafaring nation with links around the globe. Quite what this would have meant for the Danes and Denmark had the situation continued is very hard to imagine.

However, it was not, in fact, allowed to continue. Once Denmark was forced into entering the Napoleonic Wars on the side of France in 1807, the good times came to an abrupt end. The neutrality which was the true basis of the fairy tale was lost. The Danish navy, which had afforded the merchant vessels protection, was confiscated by the British and the ships were left to rot in British harbours. Denmark's position as a significant seafaring nation suffered a similar fate. After the defeat in the Napoleonic Wars, Denmark and the Danish economy returned to its familiar agricultural basis. After a few years of eagerly setting their sights on distant lands, the country and its people closed themselves off again and slowly began to concentrate once more on tilling the land, just as they had for centuries before. Danish large-scale shipping only became possible again during the First World War, when Denmark once again enjoyed a position of neutrality. One enduring result of this second endeavour to turn Denmark into a seafaring nation on an international scale is the shipping company of A. P. Møller, which today, from its head offices in Copenhagen, runs what is not only far and away the biggest company in the country, but one of the largest in the world.

THE AGRARIAN REVOLUTION ARRIVES IN DENMARK

The years of plenty around 1740 also brought large-scale change to agriculture. In fact, this was the start of a long process which led to the agrarian reforms at the end of the eighteenth century. The improved outlets, especially to the British market, and the favourable prices encouraged the agricultural sector to find ways to increase production and so reap the maximum gain from the propitious circumstances. However, this was easier said than done, as the traditional three-field system, the dominant method for both the manor farms and the village collectives, was too inflexible to allow widespread changes and not suited to experimentation.

Naturally, the estate owners had the greatest freedom, as they themselves could decide how to run their manorial land. They could speedily introduce new and more efficient methods without violating the ancient rules of the collectives. Such innovations had already been introduced in the Netherlands and Britain, pioneering countries in terms of agriculture, where the old three-field system had been replaced with the more efficient method of crop rotation. This involved dividing up the land into several bounded and drained fields, allowing a more flexible rotation of crops and the introduction of new rotation crops such as clover and root vegetables. This meant that the soil was less exhausted and supported larger herds of cattle, which in turn significantly improved the manuring of the land. In brief, this new system turned the vicious circle of the old methods, where the natural fertilisers in the soil were slowly exhausted as the same crops were grown year after year, to advantage, where rotation of crops and better fertilisation of the land with animal manure not only preserved the soil, but actually made it more productive.

In Holstein, where agricultural practices were advanced, the estate owners reacted quickly to increased demand by adopting crop rotation. It was from here that the Danish landowners drew their inspiration to convert their methods, a process which gained momentum in the 1750s. This resulted in greatly increased productivity on the manor farms, but in itself this did not really mean a great deal, as the manor farms accounted for only around a tenth of the entire cultivated land in the country. The other nine-tenths were run by the tenants on collective methods, and here it was much more difficult to adopt the new ideas because they conflicted with the conservatism of rural society and the tangled regulations of the collectives.

Initially, the ordinary peasants treated the new methods with distrust and obstinately refused to become involved in anything similar within the framework of the village collectives. There were two main reasons for this. One was that at first the peasants could see only the negative impacts of the reforms being introduced on the manor farms. The new way of farming was considerably more labour-intensive than the old methods, and the landowners met the demand for more labour by increasing the duty of villeinage. As we have mentioned, from ancient times the peasants were obliged to make themselves available for some of the time to work on the manor farms. How much of their time they were to give was very often unclear since there were no written rules. As the need for labour on the manor farms exploded in the 1750s, so the peasants found they were having to work more and more for the manor, gaining nothing in return. As this change was attributable to the new operating methods, the peasants perceived the innovations themselves as a bad development.

The second reason behind the distrust was that as far as the peasants were concerned, there was nothing much to be gained from the new methods, and a great deal to lose in terms of security and predictability. The old three-field collective system, as we have seen, represented a subsistence economy; it was designed principally to ensure survival and so not aimed at maximising production. The focus was on the greatest degree of security and the widest possible spread of risk, to a much greater level than could be expected from experimentation and outweighing what increased productivity could offer. In order to maintain the fairness of the system and to reduce the risk for each individual as much as possible, village farms were normally divided into dozens of strips scattered over the open-field system of the village. This ensured the greatest possible solidarity in times of both feast and famine, spreading the very real risk of starvation as broadly as possible. While this system was very practical in circumstances where hunger was never far away, it came at the price of a remarkable lack of flexibility or capacity for change. This collective and mutually supportive nature entailed that all decisions about farming and crops were taken jointly, and if no agreement could be reached to introduce change, then things simply went on as they always had. Such a means of arriving at decisions was in practice a virtually insurmountable impediment to any great technological progress.

It was by no means a straightforward undertaking to explain to an ordinary peasant quite why he should relinquish his trust in the old collective and introduce similar reforms to those at the manor farm. Apart from anything else, if the innovations did improve his own farm, this would not be to the benefit of his descendants, but to the advantage of the real owner of the land. Even if he should succeed in increasing productivity as a result of introducing new methods and working harder, this would probably just mean that the estate owner would demand higher rents, so in the end there would be no gain. From the point of view of the ordinary peasant, there was simply no incentive to take the risk of adopting the same experimental methods as were being used up at the home farm. As the estate owners were ever more dependent on the labour from compulsory duty, they had no special interest in making their tenants more productive, as they needed them to be out on their land. This deadlock could only be resolved by outside influence.

THE GREAT AGRARIAN REFORMS

In 1755 the government promoted an open debate as to how agriculture could be improved and productivity increased. Over the next years a great deal was written on this, especially by civil servants and progressive estate owners. One clear conclusion of the many contributions was that the only way to expand production for ordinary peasants was to redistribute the village land so that it was aggregated into a few large plots that would be suitable for the new method of crop rotation. In parallel, some of the village farms would have to be moved to the outlying plots of land to reduce the need for transport between the fields and the farm buildings. In addition, the peasants needed to be given incentives, whether through owning land themselves, or at the very least a reduction of the terms of tenancy to take their interests much more into consideration than previously. Finally, there should be very clear limits to villeinage, either to abolish it completely or replace it by regular paid work.

Taken together, these proposals presented a blueprint for a sweeping revolution of the fundamental economic and social institutional structures in the country and incorporated the potential for a conclusive alteration of the balance of power between the two dominant groups of rural society, the estate owners and the tenants.[8] They were thus political dynamite, putting the very stability of society in jeopardy. However, the government had little choice but to side with them. In point of fact, the state finances were in a wretched condition because of the heavy expenditure on armaments necessitated by the recurrent conflicts between the great powers in the eighteenth century, most recently the Prussian Seven Years War and the American War of Independence. The only way out of the economic crisis was to attempt to increase agricultural production and so raise the tax base. So, even though the interests of the estate owners traditionally had weighed heavily in government policy, now the state backed the proposed reforms wholeheartedly, and the leading political figures, themselves large landowners, took the lead in implementing the reallocation of village lands and the scattering of farms on their own initiative.

The really big breakthrough for the reforms came when Christian Ditlev Reventlow, a progressive large estate owner, took over the state's finances in 1784 and so became one of the most prominent figures in the government. In 1786, the government established the 'Great Land Commission' to turn the proposals into reality. Under the authoritative chairmanship of Reventlow, aided by his dynamic secretary, the Norwegian-born Christian Colbiørnsen, the commission immediately set about creating the necessary legal framework for implementing the reforms and encouraging the continuation of the scheme in local areas.

The first law was issued as early as 1787, giving the tenants a stronger legal position. On 20 June 1788, the law which has since been treated as the crowning glory of the reform movement was promulgated. This was the previously mentioned statutory instrument which abolished adscription, the system which forced the tenants to stay on the estates where they were born and raised. Naturally enough, this liberation did not take place at a single stroke, as the law allowed for a period of transition which stretched right up to 1800. Nevertheless, it had an immediate epoch-making effect because it rocked the balance of power between the estate owners and the tenants.

Once adscription was abolished it was very difficult for an estate owner to force the young son of a tenant to take tenure exclusively on the landowner's conditions. As the estate owners lost their coercive power, so it suddenly became in their interests, unlike before, to define the duty of villeinage precisely. In practice, this put an end to the vague duty to work on the manor farm which had previously haunted the tenants. In many cases the changes went even further, as in many places landowners and tenants agreed to remove this duty completely and replace it with a defined annual payment in money or grain. Under the pressure of the legislation, the landowners and tenants really had a mutual interest in such arrangements. Seeing the way things were developing, the landowners foresaw that it would be increasingly difficult to make the old system effective, and so a system of fixed payment which could be used in return for work was, despite everything, to be preferred. The tenants could use all their labour on their own farms, and with the prices for agricultural produce rising could easily pay the compensation.

Once the operation of the manor farms no longer relied on the villeinage of the tenants, the landowners slowly began to appreciate the advantage of abandoning the tenant farms and the obligations that tenure brought. Thus, the idea of letting the tenants own the farms themselves ripened, in so far as the tenants were willing to pay a reasonable amount. The state passed legislation in 1792 precisely to ensure a reasonable financial basis for the capital-intensive shift from tenancy to self-ownership. Thus encouraged, and discreetly supported by the state at critical stages, the estate owners and the tenants united in implementing one of the biggest economic and social upheavals in the history of Denmark. Over the course of the next 30 years, more than 60 per cent of the tenant farmers in the country took over ownership of their own land, and in the same period virtually all of the land in the 5000 villages was exchanged to form compact holdings, and farms were moved accordingly. Nonetheless, this was a slow and difficult process and by no means free from conflict or human cost. The last village collective was abolished only in 1861.

The duty of villeinage for the remaining tenancies was set at a relatively high level by a law of 1799. This put a definite end to the vague duty, but the high level and the corresponding high cost of compensation meant that the phenomenon, and its equivalent compensatory mechanisms in the form of payments to the landowners, continued for a long time. It was well into the twentieth century before the final feudal remnants of the duty to work finally disappeared.

This was, though, the price that the government and the tenants had to pay for the compliance of the estate owners and the transformation of tenancies to independent farms, which reduced the power of the landowners over their subordinates. Another reason why the landowners were willing to accept the new terms without striking a blow was the rapid increase in the population of the country, which ensured a plentiful supply of labour even when much of the previous compulsory work was disappearing. This population expansion created a new, extensive underclass in eighteenth-century rural society. This was the group of smallholders who were unable to run a tenant farm and so obliged to live by working for others. Sometimes they could supplement their modest income by rearing a cow or a couple of sheep which could graze on the commons and uncultivated land of the villages. This rapidly growing group, which was more numerous around 1800 than the tenant farmers, were available to offer their labour to the estate owners, often for a pittance, just as the obligation on the tenants to work for the estates was disappearing. For the next hundred years the landowners ran their farms almost exclusively with the labour of these smallholders.

Thus this group of people with either no land or very little were the real losers from the agrarian reforms. While the landowners and the previous tenants, who were the future independent farmers, either coped with or significantly benefited from the reforms, the smallholders slowly but surely were deprived of most of their ancient rights, such as grazing rights and limited access to the common resources of the area, which had helped them to survive under the old system of village collectives. As the strips were enclosed and more and more common land came under the plough, the smallholders were marginalised and reduced to being a true rural proletariat, offering such a large and cheap workforce that it was many generations before it was economically advantageous to introduce new labour-saving technology into the operation of agriculture. It was not for a hundred years after the agrarian reforms that there were any serious political efforts to improve the lot of this rural proletariat.

THE NEW RURAL SOCIETY

The agrarian reforms marked a final farewell to ancient subsistence agriculture and the relative social security of the agricultural collectives. It also meant the end of the old open Danish landscape as it had existed for centuries. The tightly packed villages surrounded by extensive open land and commons soon became history. The enclosure of the land and the shifting out of farmhouses also removed the dense villages in favour of dispersed buildings and field hedges which still characterise the Danish countryside today, even though the landscape is slowly changing once again with the advent of new extensive modern methods. Now independent farmers did not live in the cosy safety of villages, but rather in the many new isolated farms which were shooting up everywhere. They could no longer rely on the community or the protection of the manor, but had to survive on their own and, through their own skill, provide for their needs and sell their produce. Thus, the new situation and economic climate gave rise to the self-reliant and independent class of farmers of the nineteenth century. In the new conditions, feelings of independence and self-awareness germinated, which, helped by better schooling and enlivening stays at the Folk High Schools, slowly turned the submissive tenant farmers of the past into the most dominant political force in the country over the next hundred years.

The process of change which Danish agriculture underwent during the hectic period of agrarian reform could be described in a nutshell as a large-scale transformation from organic to economic farming methods. The ancient system under the village collectives was organically based in the sense that most of the operation followed the conditions of nature itself and was intended not to increase production, but to ensure survival through the spreading of risk. The new methods resulting from the reforms were economically based, in that they responded to the pressures of the market, and through intensive use of labour, fertilisers and systematic crop rotation were intended to maximise the yield and so allow an increasing surplus to be taken to market. The old system was dictated by the whims of nature, while that which replaced it was driven by market forces – supply, demand and pricing.

In complete accordance with the liberal economic theories of the time about the free market and the right of private ownership, as formulated by the Scottish economist and philosopher Adam Smith in 1776, the main idea behind the reforms was to give market forces the freest possible play by privatising the right of ownership of productive land and strengthening private initiative. In this way, agrarian reform was a mammoth process of privatisation. It slowly transformed Danish agriculture from a feudal, collectivist system of production into a network of private producers, operating on their own account and shouldering the risks of the market. As such, it was a successful initiative to adapt the ownership structure and production methods to meet the new economic reality which emerged from the triumphal progress of liberal philosophy from the end of the eighteenth century. From a human and social point of view, there were naturally both winners and losers in this process of change. The biggest gains fell to middle-ranking peasants, the more prosperous peasantry, who now enjoyed unprecedented legal and economic freedom. The previous owners of the land escaped relatively unscathed because of the handsome compensation they received for losing the tenant farms and their increased freedom to expand the operational improvements on the manor farms which they had already started to introduce. As stated, the losers were the large group of smallholders and labourers. Virtually at a stroke, they lost their mutual safety net in the form of the village collectives. After the tidal wave of privatisation and reform, there was no room left for them. On the contrary, they were brutally forced out of communities and ended up as an impoverished proletariat, a rural underclass. Nobody else really cared about their miserable lot until, around a hundred years later, they finally became of interest once again in the nascent industrialisation and growth of socially committed policies from left-wing parties.

The boom which started at the beginning of the eighteenth century and lasted for some 50 years completely changed the fundamentals of the Danish economy and, in its wake, left a transformed society with different, and significantly more, people: from 1750–1800 the population grew from around 750,000 to just about one million. Inevitably, Denmark was still an essentially agricultural country, with 80 per cent of the inhabitants living in rural areas, 10 per cent in the market towns and 10 per cent in Copenhagen, but the deep changes heralded the new society of the nineteenth century.

As late as 1780, around 80 per cent of Danish agricultural land was owned and controlled by a few hundred families. Just 25 years later, two-thirds of the 60,000 former tenants owned their land. The old system of village collectives had been broken up once and for all, and each farmer decided how to run his own farm. At the same time, agricultural productivity grew to its highest level ever. The new economy, with its focus on money and markets, had replaced the old agrarian reliance on benefits in kind and subsistence farming. These huge changes had other effects long into the next century. The new independent farmers' self-sufficiency accorded well with liberal economic individualism and so laid the foundations for a popular breakthrough and the establishment of a system of agriculture in Denmark which proved itself to be competitive at an international level.

These gains came at the cost of a rural class system with divisions wider than had previously been seen. Certainly, the old agrarian society had contained marked social differences, but the divisions within any individual village had not been especially pronounced. The economic changes created a new gulf between the classes, between those who owned property and those who did not, between employers and workers. This division cut through the heart of rural society and the state actively contributed to making the divisions insurmountable through its differential treatment of the classes.

The old feudal structure was another victim of the economic changes. The old tenant farming system collapsed as the estate owners sold off the land which had been the very basis of their power. The government accelerated the process by taking on all the tasks relating to raising taxes, conscription and administering justice which it had previously delegated to the estate owners, simply because it had not had the capacity to carry them out. The stronger government of the late eighteenth century could manage to perform these essential tasks, and so the role of the landowners in carrying out a significant part of the business of state became a thing of the past. The remaining status which the estate owner enjoyed was in fact only due to his being the largest property owner in the area. The old-fashioned position of being a kind of local viceroy was swallowed up by the agrarian reforms, which at least formally created direct contact between the citizen and the state.

In the towns, and especially in the capital, the boom also created a similarly new social structure with a new mentality and a capacity to cope with change. During the upturn of the golden age of trade, the earlier type of industrial production, in the form of small arts and crafts businesses, won a foothold, and Copenhagen developed to being a European marketplace and an international seafaring centre of reasonable importance with the help of the comprehensive customs reform of 1797, which was constructed on liberal free-trade principles rather than the previous numerous protectionist measures. Even then, however, there were few industrial ventures, and these were rather fragile. Once the Napoleonic Wars started, this boom was mercilessly exposed as a temporary phenomenon. The most striking expression of it – the sudden prosperity – evaporated like dew in the morning sunshine in the wars with Britain and the subsequent peacetime crisis due to the chronic and chaotic condition of government finances. However, the short-lived enterprise and prosperity did leave a legacy of commercial skill and an international outlook which proved useful and was revived when conditions once again improved in the nineteenth century, or, in the words of the historian Marcus Rubin about this period of riches: 'It was built on sand, but there was gold in the sand.'

From a longer perspective, the political effects of the wave of prosperity in the late eighteenth century should not be underestimated. It laid the foundations for a new self-confidence amongst the middle classes. The citizens of the Romantic period were not slow in expressing their views of both the state and society with all the weight that their new economic status afforded them. In other words, one product of this extended boom was the creation of an urban middle class which would continue subsequently to take an important role in society and social debates. It was during this self-same period that Danish absolutism changed into what has been called 'opinion-driven absolutism'. This meant that the absolutist state not only recognised the powerful political shifts within society and so listened to public opinion, but also that often this opinion led its policies. At root, the Danish urban middle class was very loyal and conservative. The fact that the absolutist government became increasingly sympathetic to the ideas about intellectual freedom, equality of the citizens and a fixed national identity which flourished amongst that group, along with the new-found prosperity, help to explain why Denmark was never sundered by the revolutionary waves that, from 1789, washed away the very foundations of so many other European absolutist regimes.

7

Economic Conditions: The New Denmark since 1800

DENMARK AND THE DUAL REVOLUTION

In an international context, there was a very clear watershed in economic history in 1815, the year which saw the end of the Napoleonic Wars, and the Congress of Vienna established a new order for Europe after the preceding decades of chaos and warfare. In subsequent years, the Industrial Revolution crossed the English Channel and, in combination with the widespread civil revolts on the Continent, created what the historian Eric Hobsbawm has appositely called 'the dual revolution'.[1] This became the dynamo of the process of modernisation which, over a few decades, created the European nation states and transformed them from agricultural to industrial societies.

Denmark was only peripherally involved in these developments. One of the reasons for this was that in many respects Denmark ended up as the biggest loser from the Napoleonic Wars, in terms of the economy, territory and population. From an economic point of view, the rapid growth of prosperity at the end of the eighteenth century reversed into a profound economic crisis which affected the whole of Danish society. Territorially, the Danish Crown had to cede Norway to Sweden – although significantly not the Norwegian dependencies of Greenland, Iceland and the Faroe Islands – which represented a considerable amputation of the extent of the monarchy. In terms of population, the loss of Norway meant a large and ominous change in the composition of the people. What had been a multinational monarchy was now effectively binational, and the German proportion of the overall population rose at a stroke from 25 per cent to 40 per cent, with all the problems of nationality that that caused.

Thus, it was a shaken and threatened absolutist state that had to agree to the treaty in Kiel in 1814 which definitively marked the end of the 400-year history of the double monarchy with Norway. The effects were particularly felt in Copenhagen – the previous centre of the entire kingdom – which was now left as the oversized capital of a truncated state, whose economy had to attempt to cope in the new post-war world order, where free trade dominated.

The commercial life of the capital in particular had thrived in the boom years of the first phase of the Napoleonic Wars. The huge commercial fleet based in Copenhagen had exploited Danish neutrality to the full and flown the flag on the seven seas, and riches had accrued to the shipping companies and traders of the capital. In 1807, this all ended. In that year, Britain, fearing that the large Danish fleet would fall into the hands of Napoleon and be used to cut off the Baltic trade essential for the war, launched an amphibious attack on Copenhagen, which was very quickly surrounded by British troops. After three nights of bombardment intended to terrify the inhabitants, large areas of the city were ablaze and the city had to capitulate. One of the terms of surrender was that the government was forced to hand over the entire Danish navy and its provisions to the invaders. At the same time the British broke up Danish trading vessels, both in Danish harbours and abroad. This destroyed the very basis of the flourishing trade of the capital in one fell stroke. The subsequent years of free trade on the open markets brought the once prosperous commercial metropolis to its knees and put it out of the running. The result was a long period of stagnation which lasted right up to the first real wave of industrialisation in Denmark at the end of the century.

To make matters worse, the finances of the government, indeed of the whole country, lay in ruins as a result of the war. In part this was due to the heavy increase in military expenditure, but it also reflected the government's failure to use the rewards of the boom to create order in the country's finances. Instead, the government had allowed public debt to rise to irresponsible levels in an attempt to buy popularity by offering increased state support for the costly agrarian reforms without balancing the expenditure with corresponding increases in tax revenues.

This neglect was now rebounding with a vengeance. In the final phase of the wars with the British, the economy actually collapsed, inflation was rampant, and one bankruptcy followed another while the government was reduced to watching helplessly. In 1813, the government had to declare itself bankrupt, which took the official form of a statutory instrument 'concerning changes in finances', but which was later more accurately called 'national bankruptcy'. The order declared that the state was unable to honour its own banknotes. Out of the ruins of the previous financial system, a new national bank, the Rigsbank, grew. Its purpose was to issue new reliable notes based on a lien on all the landowners of the country, who were obliged to pay 6 per cent of the value of their property into a government fund which backed this banking liability. Significantly, this payment was to be made in silver, a stable currency.

Even this aggressive measure, which itself led to another chain of bankruptcies, did not succeed. People had little more confidence in the new notes than in the old, and so the rate fell to catastrophic lows. In 1818 the state had to throw in the towel once again and let the Rigsbank founder. It was replaced by the first-ever independent national bank, with full responsibility for managing the monetary system. In this, Denmark was finally following the example of the large trading nations of Britain, the Netherlands and France, all of whom had had independent national banks of issue for a long time. By rigorously withdrawing worthless notes from circulation, the new National Bank finally succeeded in raising the value of its own notes to the point where, in 1830, they achieved parity. This had, however, been a long, painful and costly process, and the damage inflicted by inflation and national bankruptcy was inevitably remembered for a long time to come. Nor did the people fail to notice that faith in the financial system was only truly restored once the government relinquished any influence in issuing notes. In other words, this represented a serious defeat for the absolutist government, and the resulting loss of confidence in this and other areas weakened the authority of the government. This interlude in fact marked the beginning of the end for the Danish absolutist regime.

At the same time, commerce as a whole was running into deep difficulties. The end of the big war, as often in such a situation, produced a huge fall in prices on the world markets. Grain prices were not least affected, and fell drastically through the 1820s. Denmark was especially hard hit, as Norway, previously a safe domestic market for Danish grain, was now a foreign country. The British Corn Laws also greatly reduced their imports of grain. In addition, Danish grain was generally of poor quality, and for this reason alone was hard to sell. This slump meant that many farmers found it extremely difficult to meet their tax obligations and debts, which in turn threw them back into an economy based on self-sufficiency. Thus, the crisis and the poverty it brought spread to the towns, as rural poverty reduced the hinterland markets which were the lifeblood of their existence.

The entire budding commercial life of the country, based on independence and enterprise, which had been created by agrarian reform and supported by the golden years of boom, was on the verge of disintegration. There was a huge temptation to abandon the uncertainties of independence and retreat into the safety of community, and the old protective feudal system of landed estates. However, the rural population demonstrated that despite everything, they valued their newly won freedoms more highly than collective security. The vast majority of farmers struggled with diligence and thrift to survive the crisis of the 1820s without relinquishing their independence, and were so in a position to reap the rewards of their privations and fighting spirit once the economic climate started to swing upwards again around 1830.

The government also showed that in these critical times it was resolved to back the agrarian reforms by alleviating in various ways the conditions of the beleaguered farmers. To prevent a general impoverishment of rural society, in 1819 a statutory instrument was issued forbidding the creation of farms with less than 20 acres of fertile land. The intention here was to preserve a size of farm adequate to provide for a family and which could afford the payments to the public authorities. This legally enshrined the typical middle-sized family agricultural system which, as explained, had its origins in early absolutism and continued to put its mark on the landscape of Denmark for the next 150 years. This also became an important factor in the competitiveness of market-oriented agriculture later in the century and for the success and endurance of the co-operative movement from the end of the century.

'A SMALL, POOR COUNTRY'

In the first half of the nineteenth century, Danish society underwent rapid change. This was not just because the population grew at a rate previously unseen – from less than one million around 1800 to 1.3 million in 1850 – but also because the period itself saw rapid and comprehensive changes. It started with a boom, agrarian reform and flourishing trade, continued through the war, 1807–14, when those who already had a lot gained more, while the poor suffered hardships. Then this changed again into a protracted crisis when the peace came, which left a wide section of society impoverished. Hope was only once again restored towards the middle of the century, when economic circumstances improved and progress once again gained pace.[2]

Measured in purely economic terms, though, the recession was perhaps not as serious as many statements from the period suggest. In real terms, the value of Danish production overall increased by more than a third from the end of the war to the middle of the century. Over the same period, the population increased by roughly a fifth, and so in fact there was genuine economic growth measured per head.

However, the picture is somewhat different when calculated in actual prices, that is, if the fluctuations in the exchange rate are included, which in fact provides a truer representation of the purchasing power resulting from production. In 1818 – the year when the National Bank was founded – the total value of the country's production was 230 million *rigsdaler*. Four years later it reached a dramatic trough of just 153 million, representing a fall of a third in terms of actual prices in this short period. After this low point, it slowly started to rise again, but it was not until 1840 that it rose above the level of 1818, with a value of 236 million. Naturally enough, the producers and consumers of the country had to consider what they earned for their efforts and what they could buy for their money. From this point of view, the period between 1818 and 1840 represented a long, hard struggle just to keep their heads above water through a prolonged recession.

This extended crisis was a real test of the new structure of agriculture which the reforms had created. Despite this acid test, imposed by the direct confrontation with free competition on the world market, agriculture survived the crisis through extra efforts and cheeseparing as well as the introduction of new crops. During the years of adversity, the nature of the whole society and the people who constituted it slowly changed. The new, independent system of agriculture fostered a completely new class of resourceful and self-sufficient farmers who no longer perceived themselves as nonentities with neither responsibility nor influence, but as an active part of society with just demands for political participation. This class ever-more clearly demarcated itself from the big landowners above them in the hierarchy and even more clearly still from the rapidly growing group of impoverished smallholders and agricultural labourers below them. These decades laid the basis for the development of a rigid class system within the rural population. This, in turn, set the tone for the long social and political struggle which eventually brought victory to the middle-ranking farmers through the changes in the political system in 1901 and the final demise of the big landowners with the forced dissolution and partial fragmentation of the old, previously sacrosanct, large estates through the abolition of entailment in 1919.

In the years of poverty after the end of the Napoleonic Wars, while the 'dual revolution' was taking wing in transforming European society, battered Denmark found itself in a virtually permanent state of crisis. At times this threatened to roll back the tide of modernisation which the agrarian reforms had launched, but the crisis also involved elements which pointed forward to the continued modernisation of the backward Danish society so that it could, from a material point of view, keep up with the rest of Europe. Danish society teetered precariously through these decades between profound despair on the one hand and an optimistic faith in the future and determination to battle through adversity on the other.

The contradictions of this mentality, awareness of being an insignificant poor country yet maintaining hope for the future and faith in the country's own abilities, were expressed very accurately in a poem written in 1820 by one of the leading poets of the time, Poul Martin Møller (1794–1838). During extensive travels in the Far East, and in response to the inconceivable wealth and splendour of the East, he wrote a homage to his tiny, poor fatherland, which could not begin to match such magnificence. The following verse exemplifies his view:

> In Manila's shacks, the clerks exclaim:
> 'The land of Denmark is small and poor'
> The wealthy sons of Java claim,
> Batavia's ailing traders too complain:
> 'The land of Denmark is small and poor'.

Nonetheless, he entitled his poem 'The Joy of Denmark'.[3] Thus, he captures the particularly Danish self-image, which was born in the years of adversity but has since become a standard trope of the Danish mentality. Even though Denmark is tiny and poor, this is not a reason to give in and wallow in despair. On the contrary, it is a cause for celebration that when we work together, things work out well. This dogged attitude became in itself the true force driving the process of modernisation which, in due course, created modern Denmark.

Paradoxically, it was during these years of war that Denmark produced a storyteller, Hans Christian Andersen (1805–1875), who was to put Denmark definitively on the map of world literature. His numerous fairy tales, related in a 'childlike' manner, rapidly spread beyond the borders of the country. Their durability is shown by the fact that today they have been translated into no fewer than 125 languages and are still favourite reading for children and adults alike all over the world. One possible explanation for their popularity is their underlying optimism and the message that despite all manner of adversities and setbacks, the world still turns. Andersen's own fairy-tale life, the son of an impoverished cobbler in Odense going on to achieve international fame and recognition, was in itself a vivid illustration that such optimism was well-founded. His life and writings provided a much-needed boost for his fellow countrymen during the difficult years of the first half of the nineteenth century.[4]

GRAIN SALES AND MODERNISATION

The deep crisis which dominated the Danish economy in the decades immediately after the Napoleonic Wars slowly began to lift, as in 1828 Britain gradually started to ease the restrictive Corn Laws which had effectively put a halt to Danish grain exports. In 1846 the British Parliament finally decided to remove the remaining import duties levied on foreign corn and this heralded the start of a long, prosperous grain trade for Denmark, which lasted for around 30 years. Rising volumes of grain at favourable prices could now be sold on the important British market, and this growing export revived initiative and prosperity for Danish agriculture. New land was taken under the plough, and that which was already under cultivation was improved through drainage and marling. Grain production rose to heights previously unseen. The new prosperity was gradually reflected in the very farm buildings themselves. Brick replaced the classic half-timbering, floorboards replaced trampled clay in the living room, proper bedrooms replaced the old recesses, and visitors were received in parlours, decorated with tapestries and furniture. During this period, the independent farmers took on the role of the rural upper-middle class, while servants had to be satisfied with humble quarters in the stables.

The new affluence in the countryside affected the whole of Danish society. Right up until 1870, agriculture accounted for over half of the total commercial production of the country, and 95 per cent of that in the primary sector, that is, agriculture, forestry, horticulture, fur farming and fishery. It was not until the last decades of the nineteenth century that the share of the total value of production derived from agriculture fell to around a third. This was not because of any decrease in agricultural productivity, but because of the ever-more rapidly growing industrial activity. Thus, farming continued to totally dominate the economy of the country, and when the farmers did well, so did the rest of society.

This could be clearly seen in the towns as well, as the purchasing power of the country dwellers increased. There was a brisk trade in building materials, tools and luxury goods such as tobacco, sugar and coffee as well as ordinary consumer goods. The new affluence meant that the villagers were abandoning their old self-sufficiency and buying more and more from the towns, and so finally creating the broad basis for the growth of Danish industry which had hitherto been lacking. Iron foundries, which manufactured agricultural tools and the popular new stoves for domestic heating, mushroomed in towns all over the country; sugar factories and breweries geared for mass production were set up. This was the beginning of a process which would in time fundamentally alter the structure of society. The population of the towns began to grow much faster than that of the countryside.

At the same time, the revolution in transport, which had started in Britain in 1825 with the first railway, reached Denmark. The first stretch of railway in the kingdom was opened in 1844. It ran from Altona to Kiel, thus linking a North Sea port with a Baltic port. The first line in Denmark itself came into use in 1847, and ran between Copenhagen and Roskilde, but was soon extended to Korsør on the Great Belt. Just 30 years later, the framework of the Danish railway network as we know it today had been built and was in use. In 1874 it was possible to take a train from Copenhagen to Frederikshavn in the very north of Jutland, or to the new port of Esbjerg in the west. The trains travelled at the awesome speed of 30 km an hour. The road network was also greatly expanded, and the main roads were converted to highways which could support heavy traffic. At least as important for a country of islands such as Denmark was the introduction of scheduled passenger steamboats uniting the main areas of the country through an integrated transport system. The first steamboat route was introduced between

Copenhagen and Kiel in 1819. In 1828 a fixed route over the Great Belt between Korsør and Nyborg followed. In 1834 this was supplemented with a direct route from Zealand to the main city of Jutland, Aarhus, and within a few decades the whole country was connected by a web of steam crossings.

This revolutionary improvement in transport did not just unite the many islands of Denmark from a geographical point of view. It also opened up entirely new economic perspectives. Commerce and the exchange of goods were now much faster and cheaper than before, and so the market itself changed radically. A factory in Copenhagen could use the new means of transport to sell its wares all over the country without prohibitive costs and delays. The new communications also meant that the towns could finally shake off their medieval designs and expand by locating residential and industrial buildings in the surrounding areas. The boom times for grain trade allowed Denmark for the first time to shake off its medieval topography and change to mirror the enormous European revolution in energy, transport and communications which had finally reached the country. Thus, the Danes were well on their way to modernity, even though there was still some way to go before industrialisation reached the same levels as in other European countries.

THE CO-OPERATIVE MOVEMENT – THE SECOND AGRICULTURAL REVOLUTION

Precisely these same innovations in transport caused the golden age of grain sales to peter out from around 1870, as the price of the country's most important exports fell. This forced a new set of changes on to the agricultural sector of a scope and impact comparable with the earlier agrarian reforms.

The reason for the drop in prices was a glut on the European grain market. The railways in both North America and Russia were expanding so extensively that it became possible to transport cheap grain from the Russian steppes and the prairies of middle America to the marketplaces of Europe at relatively low cost. The result was that these markets were literally drowning in corn, and prices tumbled.

Naturally, the European grain producers were hit very hard. Many larger countries, such as Germany and France, chose to defend their own farmers by introducing protectionist measures in the form of duties and state subsidies. A country such as Denmark did not have this option, as it was an exporter and so dependent on free trade. The response here was an extensive conversion from grain production to livestock. The prices of animal produce such as milk, butter and meat were not falling anywhere near as quickly as those of grain, and indeed started to rise around 1890, whereas the price of corn continued to fall for another decade or so.

A measure of the extent of the conversion and change of structure is that Danish arable production, principally grain, amounted to around half of all agricultural production in 1850. This had fallen to a third by around 1900. On the other hand, dairy products – milk, butter and cheese – rose as a proportion of the total over the same period from almost 18 per cent to over 42 per cent, and the direct production of livestock – pork, veal and beef – rose from a third to half of the total. The vigour of this conversion is underlined further by the fact that the total agricultural production in 1900 was worth over four times as much as in 1850. In effect, Danish agriculture was turning itself into a colossal factory which processed primary crops into refined animal-based foodstuffs. The Danish co-operative movement was a child of this huge reorganisation.

Producing good-quality cheese and butter competitively and profitably naturally requires a continuous supply of relatively large volumes of fresh milk. In turn, equally naturally, this requires reasonably large dairy herds. These only existed on the bigger estates, and so it was precisely here where dairy production was first introduced with sales in mind. Ordinary farmers found it much more difficult. They had few cows, and so not enough milk to supply enough dairy produce to take to market, let alone to export markets, where the home-churned butter had to compete with the much better and more consistent produce of the manor farms. Thus, it was impossible for them to compete on an individual basis.

Ordinary farmers with tiny dairy herds could, however, sell any surplus milk to a neighbouring manor-farm dairy, or to any other wealthy individual who had the means to operate a commercially viable dairy. Indeed, some did. In most areas of the country, however, the farmers chose to band together and build their own dairies in a central location within their parish. These new collective dairies were nearly all set up as co-operatives. This meant that the members of the co-operative society were obliged to deliver their surplus milk to the dairy, and to be paid at the going rate. Any annual profit was then shared amongst the members in proportion to the amount of milk that they had supplied over the year, rather than the amount of money they had originally injected into the dairy. The idea behind this system was to give an incentive for the members to supply as much milk as possible. Democracy was ensured because each member had an equal vote at the annual meeting, irrespective of the amount of milk he had delivered and whether he was a smallholder or an independent farmer. This strengthened solidarity and prevented any individual large-scale supplier from dominating the decision-making process.

An important technical prerequisite for this type of collective dairy was a constantly operating centrifuge which could separate cream from milk in one run. Previously, this process had required patient skimming in a large vat. However, in 1878, L. C. Nielsen, a Danish engineer, developed a suitable centrifuge which soon came into production. This invention made it possible to produce butter of consistent quality, just as good as that produced by the manor-farm dairies. This device was the heart of the new collective dairies and also dictated their size, as the centrifuge was large enough to process all the milk from all the farmers in the area. Without this technology, the collective dairies could hardly have existed at all, as there would have been no incentive to work together. It is an intriguing thought that without the centrifuge, one of the largest revolutions in the history of Danish agriculture, the development of the co-operatives could not really have taken place. In this respect, the centrifuge had the same importance for Danish society as the invention of the spinning wheel had for Britain.[5]

The breakthrough of the co-operative idea is normally dated very precisely as having occurred on 10 June 1882, the day on which the first collective dairy in Denmark started production in the village of Hjedding, near Varde in west Jutland. This is perfectly correct, but overlooks the fact that the same idea, based on the model established in Britain by Robert Owen and William King and put into practice by a group of local weavers, who set up a co-operative purchasing association in Rochdale in the north of England in 1844 as a practical expression of the utopian socialism of the time, had already taken root in Denmark on the consumer side as a co-operative society. The first such society in Denmark was the Workers' Co-operative in Thisted, which was established in 1866. Many others soon followed, and in 1880 there were 119 co-operative societies across the whole country, mainly in rural areas.

The founding of the co-operative dairy in Hjedding was the first time the idea had been put into practice on the production side, was a success beyond compare in the history of Danish agriculture and had few counterparts in any other country. The co-operative idea in Denmark can well be described as a wave which swelled on the west coast of Jutland and swept across the country. Its progress eastwards transformed Danish agriculture and allowed it to emerge strengthened from the crisis which was provoked by the collapse of the grain market. The movement could justly be described as the first grass-roots movement in the long history of Danish agriculture, and even though it originated in British utopian socialism, it had a decisive influence on the formation of modern Danish self-perception. Around 1900 almost 950 co-operative dairies had been established, and on the eve of the First World War the total was 1150. Thus it would be fair to describe the spread of the idea as virtually explosive. However, the movement never fully achieved its goal of establishing a co-operative dairy in every parish. The trend towards concentration in the twentieth century meant that most of these dairies were eventually replaced by large regional factories, but these were still formed as co-operatives.

The co-operative movement triumphed in other areas as well. The co-operative purchasing societies, formed to allow the members to negotiate favourable prices, spread nearly as explosively as the dairies. Around 1900 there were over 800 such societies, and on the outbreak of the First World War, this number had risen to almost 1500. A large number of co-operative slaughterhouses were also established. Purchasing associations for feedstuffs and artificial fertilisers also mushroomed, as did co-operative banks, which financed local projects; health insurance societies, and, in keeping with the times, co-operative electricity-generating companies.

The fact that such critical sectors as electricity generation could be organised on a private collective basis without any legislative regulation was possible because Denmark chose from the start to use direct current on Edison's original model. It was only after the Second World War that there was a general conversion of the grid to alternating current, based on the Westinghouse system, which allowed electricity to be conveyed via high-voltage cables over large distances without any significant loss of output. Direct current, on the other hand, cannot be conveyed far without significant power losses, and this meant that the electricity had to be generated as close to the end user as practically possible, by local power stations which supplied the immediate area.

So right from the introduction of electricity, Denmark had a decentralised system with thousands of direct-current generating stations.

These were usually built through private initiatives and based on the model that the people trusted – the co-operative system. As these co-operatives were established without any central government regulation, once again, we can see a grass-roots movement. For nearly a hundred years, there was no legislation concerning electricity supply. It was not until 1976, after the immediately preceding oil crisis had painfully demonstrated just how reliant society was on electricity, that the Danish Parliament finally passed a general law concerning electricity to guarantee the highest possible reliability of supply even in times of crisis.

Electricity generation is one of many examples of how deeply the co-operative movement permeated rural Danish society at the end of the nineteenth century and had a significant effect on the towns. Co-operatives became the favoured form of organisation for small- to medium-scale farmers in virtually every aspect of economic life. Joining a co-operative brought a closely knit network of relationships with the rural middle class and put the farmers in a position to work together to solve problems without recourse to the government or the large local landowners. The movement allowed these farmers to surmount the crisis provoked by falling grain sales by effectively pulling themselves up by their own bootstraps. It could be said that the triumphant co-operative movement was to some extent the means by which the liberalised agricultural sector re-established the solidarity and community they had lost through agrarian reform, with the critical difference that the new collaboration was only amongst the rural middle classes, and so the aristocrats and the smallholders were excluded.

That this co-operative movement was essentially a preserve of the self-sufficient middle-ranking rural classes is confirmed by an examination of who exactly took the local initiatives. Typically it was affluent farmers who over a number of years had achieved prominence in local councils and boards and also participated in various aspects of the work of the society, and who had often attended the Folk High Schools in their youth. The farmer who founded the first co-operative dairy in Denmark in 1882, Niels Hansen Uhd, is a shining example. Poul la Cour, a physicist who taught at the most famous Folk High School in the country, at Askov, was able to state in 1897 that almost half of the chairmen or directors of the co-operative dairies had been to Folk High Schools, where they had learnt to be open to new ideas, to take the initiative and understand the importance of working together.

It would thus not be entirely unreasonable to describe the co-operative movement as a prodigy of the Grundtvigian Folk High School. These schools inculcated an enthusiasm for innovation and the drive to put it into effect and so offer a partial explanation for the explosive growth of the co-operative movement at the end of the nineteenth century. It should also be kept in mind that the movement originated in the period of provisional government, when the political struggle between the Conservative Party, *Højre*, and the Liberal *Venstre* was at its height. As previously mentioned, the co-operative movement was one of the first truly grass-roots movements in modern Danish history. The members were almost exclusively supporters of *Venstre*, which was deeply opposed to the dominant regime and distrusted the large land-owners and financiers of the towns.

It was therefore completely natural that they should attempt to organise themselves in such a way as to be independent from these interests to the greatest possible degree. A co-operative was the perfect vehicle for this, as it allowed economies of scale to be achieved in the vital area of dairy farming, without introducing dominating capital interests, which the independent farmers regarded as hostile. The co-operative movement, which arose as an alternative to the dominant types of structure, thus became the platform from which the independent farmers as a class took over economic leadership in the agricultural sector, and from the start of the twentieth century also became politically dominant in Parliament.

THE BEGINNINGS OF INDUSTRIALISATION

In the middle of the nineteenth century, the population of Denmark was around 1.3 million, not including the duchies which were lost in 1864. Around 1870, this number had grown to approximately 1.8 million, and by 1890 had reached 2.2 million. At the end of the First World War the figure exceeded 3 million. Thus, the population grew at a rate and to an extent unprecedented in the history of the country, although most European countries experienced a similar phenomenon during the same period. This rapid growth was related to the general European phenomenon often described as 'the demographic transition', meaning the change from high rates of births and deaths, such as can currently be seen in the developing countries of the world, to much lower levels of both. This transition started around 1750 and was largely complete by 1900, although in the case of Denmark it ended a little later.

In the first half of the nineteenth century, just as in other countries, the life expectancy of the population steadily rose, as a result of better nutrition, better hygiene and better medical care. However, the birth rate remained at its previous high level for several decades, only falling quite late in the twentieth century to a level corresponding to the lower mortality rate. This temporary imbalance is the main explanation for the growth in the population shown by the figures cited above. In turn, the pressure of increasing population was a key factor in the gradual transformation of an agrarian society into an industrial nation.

Despite the comprehensive modernisation and intensification of the agricultural sector, it was still not in a position to cope with such a level of growth. Many young people – especially those from the poorer parts of the country – decided to emigrate to North or South America, thus joining the large wave of migration which swept from Europe across the Atlantic at the end of the nineteenth century. In the 1880s alone, no fewer than 77,000 Danes left the country, most headed for the midwestern agricultural regions of the United States, where they made their livelihoods by cultivating the vast prairies. The majority of the rural youth, who at the time had no prospects of finding work in farming, moved to the larger towns, which consequently experienced rapid expansion after centuries of virtual stagnation. Thus, the population of the countryside remained fairly constant.

The number of inhabitants of Copenhagen almost quadrupled over these 50 years, growing from around 125,000 to nearly half a million. The same thing happened in Aarhus, where the population grew from 7000 or so to over 33,000, and in Aalborg, from roughly 7000 to 20,000 inhabitants. A number of other towns experienced similar growth, especially those which were well located for maritime commerce or industrial enterprise. In these years many of the towns shook off their medieval layouts, and new towering factory chimneys and multi-storey blocks of flats came to replace the Gothic church spires on the urban skylines. Denmark was finally on the way into the era of urbanisation and industrialisation, albeit considerably later than many other European countries.

In 1887, just as this process was starting, the political economist V. Falbe Hansen wrote an authoritative account of the statistics of Denmark, in which he described the Danish economy as follows:

Agriculture is by far our most productive sector. It provides employment for the vast majority of the population, its produce constitutes by far the biggest part of the goods we export, by means of which we pay for our imports. Agriculture is central to our production, and most other companies are based around it, either to produce commodities used in agriculture, or to process and trade the output.[6]

He thus identified an important characteristic of the budding Danish industry, that it mainly grew out of agriculture and was initially based on refining raw produce such as grain, milk and meat. In the early phases, the co-operative dairies and slaughterhouses made up a significant part of Danish industry. In 1897, the first year for which reliable figures exist, the food and beverage industry as a whole accounted for around 1000 of the total of 5000 companies with more than five employees in the country. This sector, which included food-processing companies, was responsible for about a third of the total of industrial added value, and employed 20,000 of the total industrial workforce of almost 100,000. These few figures illustrate the importance of agriculture as the dynamo for industrial development in Denmark, as well as underlining another important aspect – the decentral nature of the nascent industry and the dominance of small companies. Correspondingly, in 1897, the average size of a company, taking industry as a whole, was only 19 employees.[7]

Another important factor in the development of Danish industry was the location of the country near major sea routes. This made it easy both to import the raw materials which the country largely lacked and to export the finished products. In itself, this allowed the growth of an extensive metal industry, including such activities as shipbuilding, out of all proportion to the mineral resources the country possessed. Statistics from 1897 show that this sector was actually comparable to the agriculturally based industry both in size and production capacity. At that point there were just over 750 companies in the sector, employing over 21,000 people and contributing approximately a fifth of the total industrial added value. These were generally relatively small companies, in fact little more than large workshops with a dozen employees, making smaller tools and machines for the domestic market. There were, however, isolated examples of very large companies such as motor manufacturers, cable and wire producers, and, in particular, shipbuilders – the most famous of these was Burmeister & Wain in Copenhagen – employing thousands of workers. These were the exception rather than the rule, and even then, the enormous industries of the Ruhr district in Germany or the English Midlands dwarfed Danish heavy industry. As noted, the typical Danish industrial company in 1897 had only 19 employees.[8]

This pattern, which was established in the first wave of industrialisation at the end of the nineteenth century, remained remarkably unchanged through the twentieth century. The 1972 census of industrial production, on the threshold of Denmark's entry into the EEC, showed that there were over 7000 industrial companies, representing an increase of roughly 50 per cent compared to 75 years earlier. The total number of those employed in industry had more than quadrupled over the same period, to 400,000, giving an average of around 50 employees per company. The total added value from industry had increased over 30 times compared to 1897.

These gross figures, however, hide some important internal changes in the pattern of industrialisation during the twentieth century. The most striking is that the number of companies involved in the food and beverage sector remained largely unchanged at around 1000 – now representing just a seventh of the overall number of companies – and that the contribution of this sector to overall added value had fallen to around a fifth. The metal industry had developed in the opposite direction, the number of companies having almost tripled to around 2000, together contributing more than a third of the overall industrial added value in 1972. This pronounced shift away from purely agriculturally based industries to the high-technology metal industry is the main explanation for the high increase in added value in relation to the number of companies and numbers employed over a period of nearly a hundred years. The sector based on agriculture traditionally involves a relatively low amount of processing, and thus added value, whereas a specialised metal industry such as that which grew up in Denmark, producing niche products such as sophisticated measuring equipment, advanced pumps and radiator valves, typically has a very high level of value added per unit manufactured. So this move towards the industrial sectors with higher levels of added value, plus improved job training and an increase in real capital, explains the increase in the productivity of a Danish industrial worker measured as contribution to added value from a mere DKK 1000 in 1897 to DKK 97,000 in 1972 – an achievement which fully measures up to that of other European countries.

Although on the whole the development of Danish industry through the twentieth century has been in line with that of the large industrial countries, there have been some significant differences, such as the fact that it still includes a relatively large export-oriented food sector, and that it is still dominated by a large number of small companies, with fewer than 50 employees. Despite the shift towards the electronic and chemical industries, the continued importance of the food sector is such that it accounts for nearly a third of the total industrial production measured in production value. This is very similar to the pattern in the Netherlands, another primarily agricultural country, but far higher than that of the old industrialised countries such as Germany and Britain. Doubtless, this can be directly attributed to the basis of modern industry in the agricultural co-operatives at the end of the nineteenth century.

Even the turnovers of the largest Danish industrial companies – such as Danfoss, which manufactures thermostatic valves, Lego, the toy company, the A. P. Møller Group and the pharmaceutical company Novo Nordisk – are only enough, even at the end of the twentieth century, to come in at around 500th in European rankings of size, and more locally, the leading Swedish companies are much bigger. Companies employing between 10 and 19 people account for nearly twice as large a proportion of the total workforce as the EU average as a whole.

This trait must be seen in the light of the particular history of industrialisation in Denmark, with its lack of domestic supplies of natural raw materials, whereas in countries such as Britain and Germany, concentrations of heavy industry grew up around reserves of primary materials. Thus, Denmark does not exhibit the same pattern of industrial concentration. Instead, the centres of growth in Denmark grew up where individual companies that were able to succeed in competing with similar heavy industries abroad were founded. Danish industries were obliged either to produce for the limited home market or to find lucrative niche products which could be sold abroad. Both of these options favoured an industrial structure of many small companies, and it is in fact only now, with the open markets of the EU, that Denmark has started to see any change in this pattern, along with the emergence of larger concentrations of companies and large-scale industrial production.

Compared to the neighbouring countries to the west, south and east, industrialisation came rather late to Denmark and the move from being an agricultural country to an industrial nation was slow and gradual. It was not until as late as the beginning of the 1960s that the value of industrial exports overtook that of agriculture. The lateness of industrialisation affected not only the economic structure of the country in general and the nature of industrial companies in particular, as described, but also had a number of secondary social and political consequences.

One was definitely that a genuine working class arose much later in Denmark than in, for example, Britain or Germany. In 1872 there were only 35,000 industrial workers in Denmark – a negligible number compared to the huge groups of workers in the old industrialised countries. In 1914 this had increased to 138,000, or around 5 per cent of the total population, and the number of industrial employees in 2000 was approximately 475,000 – 18 per cent of the workforce, or under 10 per cent of the population.

Denmark thus never experienced any inherited class conflicts which could compare either in scope or intensity with those that resulted from the mass exploitation of the workers in the mines or large heavy industries in the countries which industrialised earlier. The first real organised labour movement did not start in Denmark until 1871. After a brief revolutionary period in the wake of the 1871 Paris Commune, this movement very soon took on a reformist approach, focusing instead on the gradual improvement of the conditions of the workers.

This peaceful, reformist approach was encouraged by the particular fact that, as we have seen, Danish industry grew almost organically from the agricultural co-operatives and small workshops which normally had very few employees, and so the social differences and mental distances between the factory floor and the management were very small. In fact, the working environments of the numerous small companies in the early phases of industrialisation were strongly reminiscent of those on the farms from which most of the first generation of industrial workers came. In both environments, there was a constant and close proximity between the employers and the employees, and in both it was perfectly natural for the owner to join in the daily work and move amongst his employees as the first amongst equals. The same situation can be found in many of the numerous small companies that still make up a large element of Danish industry, where the owner of the business wears overalls and is in direct contact with the workers. To a certain degree, it can be maintained that modern industrialised Denmark has continued to use the reformed patriarchal production methods of agricultural society and the same style of direct communication, and that this is one possible explanation for the relatively amicable industrial relations which typify the Danish labour market even in heightened situations such as crises and wars.

Of course, this is not to deny that there have been points of hard confrontation and conflicts of interest in Danish industrial relations during the turbulent twentieth century. There were general strikes and lock-outs in the 1890s, the 1920s, the 1930s and the 1950s. Yet there can hardly be any doubt that the late industrialisation and the resulting flat hierarchy in the structure of both companies and the labour market go a long way towards explaining how Denmark has escaped industrial relations conflicts as widespread and disruptive as those in, for example, the countries which industrialised considerably earlier. The first real test of this infant industrialised society came in the virtually permanent crisis which followed in the wake of the First World War.

THE POLICY OF REGULATION DURING THE FIRST WORLD WAR

Compared to the nations at war, Denmark, thanks to its neutrality, escaped rather lightly from the First World War. There was certainly a general feeling of panic on the outbreak of hostilities in August 1914, with widespread hoarding and huge price increases, and people overwhelmed the National Bank in their attempts to convert their paper currency into gold. This forced the government to rapidly introduce comprehensive emergency legislation – called 'the August Laws' – to suspend convertibility into gold with immediate effect and to authorise the government to intervene directly over levels of prices and take the measures necessary to ensure supplies to the Danish market.[9]

Ove Rode (1867–1933), the Minister of the Interior, was charged with administering these emergency powers. He set up an 'Extraordinary Commission' to assist him in his task. This very powerful commission, which included not just politicians but also representatives of key organisations and businesses, in effect suspended the liberal market economy. For the duration of the war, the market was in practice controlled by the state in close collaboration with commercial organisations. Although the policy of stringent regulation was relaxed again once the war had finished, it nonetheless created the pattern of the future for some time to come. A great deal of the emergency legislation of the 1930s and the implementation of the welfare state which started to take shape around 1960 was also conducted through a tightly knit co-operation between politicians, the state, and business and labour market organisations. Together, they took responsibility for the comprehensive regulation and limitations of the economic freedoms of the citizens necessary to ensure that everything continued to function.

This amalgamation of government power and the interests of business and other organisations, or, to put it another way, the merging of the state and civil society, has continued to be a characteristic of what has subsequently been called the 'Danish model'. As noted, the roots of this can be traced right back to early absolutism and were expressed in the agrarian reforms at the end of the eighteenth century, but the traces can also clearly be seen in modern times in the years of crisis during the First World War, which led to a general acceptance that the economic freedom of the individual had to be subsumed to the collective good, and that the interests of the whole could best be served through a close collaboration of public and private interests. With the policy of regulation during the First World War, the politicians definitely set off down the road which led directly to the comprehensively regulated Danish welfare state of the present day.

Even such tough regulatory measures could not, however, prevent the First World War from leaving a deep mark on the Danish economy. At the start of the war, farmers and the larger transportation and industrial companies earned handsome amounts by selling goods, often substandard, to the warring nations. Yet the rising prices of food mercilessly undermined the living standards of the workers and the middle classes, which in turn exacerbated class divisions and social tensions. An entirely new group of nouveaux riches suddenly appeared, profiteers who usually made money by speculating in very poor-quality foodstuffs before shamelessly displaying their new-found wealth to all and sundry. This group in themselves were a symbol that the old social order was rapidly collapsing. The bond of solidarity which had held society together was felt to be in danger of snapping, revolutionary movements started to arise, and only the policy of regulation, which had broad political support, prevented the descent into political and social anarchy.

The situation went from bad to worse on 1 February 1917, when Germany declared unrestricted submarine warfare, thus bringing the United States into the war on the side of the Allies. Britain could now rely on supplies from the United States, and so closed its markets to Danish goods while simultaneously blocking deliveries of raw materials to Denmark to ensure that they were not passed on to Germany. This was a virtual catastrophe. The submarine war caused the loss of 178 Danish ships, and even more were laid up. Agricultural production fell dramatically because fertilisers and feedstuffs were not available, coal imports decreased by a third, and industrial production was at a virtual standstill. Thus followed massive unemployment, explosive price increases, and heavy-handed rationing of most consumer goods. The profits the country had made from the first years of the war were more than lost in the last brutal phase. Although the losses Denmark suffered in no way compared with those of the nations at war, still the country was poorer in every respect at the end of the war in 1918 than it had been at the start in 1914.

Even so, most of the population of Denmark survived the First World War fairly unscathed. Of course, there was social hardship, and many of the worst-off were totally reliant on handouts of food from public charity kitchens, but at least there was nothing like the widespread famine that afflicted countries such as Germany and Russia. There were, naturally, shortages, but government rationing and regulation attempted to ensure a reasonably equitable division of the dwindling stock of goods there were. Above all else, there had been none of the wholesale destruction and colossal loss of human life which the countries involved in the war had suffered. They, indeed, effectively lost an entire generation of young men, and this was certainly not the case in Denmark. However, the war had shattered the old secure existence and crushed the embers of the bright faith in progress which had marked the years leading up to the war. Everywhere, there was nothing but disillusion and despondency, or, as in Germany and Russia, anarchy, revolution and economic chaos. The solid citizenship of the past, with its genteelness, strict morality and respect for authority was gone forever, and had been replaced by a new disquiet and uncertainty which could be attributed to the collapse of the trusty old standards while nothing new had come to replace them.

The harsh conditions that wage earners were suffering greatly strengthened the trade union movement. Union membership shot up from around 160,000 in 1914 to over 360,000 in 1920. At the same time the workers' movement became more radical, and one militant faction broke away to oppose the Social Democrats, who supported the regulation policy of the government. These syndicalists, as they styled themselves, drew inspiration from events in Germany and Russia and worked towards an overthrow of society to introduce socialism. In the next few years they organised a large number of strikes and demonstrations, although they never achieved their aims, not least because the Social Democrats unambiguously backed the existing government and united with it to oppose syndicalism.

This constant agitation nonetheless made it clear that Danish society was in need of comprehensive reform. The dramatic changes in the distribution of wealth through the war years had intensified this need, and the militant activities of the left wing had contributed to persuading most of those in power that such reforms should be democratic in nature, and in accordance with the rules which had been established through the constitutional struggle leading to the 1915 constitution. This wide consensus to abide by the principles of democracy carried Danish society safely through the interwar crises and difficulties which pushed many other European countries into dictatorships and totalitarianism.

LAND REFORM AND BANK FAILURE

The first essential was to provide reasonable improvements in the real wages of those who had suffered most in the whirligig economy of the war years. Under the pressure of growing social unrest, this led from 1920 to the implementation of the first collective bargaining agreements in the labour market, which incorporated an automatic regulation of wages through a price index so that increases in prices of staple goods were automatically compensated by adjustments in wages. This scheme, which provided a form of inflation protection for wage-earners, effectively remained in force until the 1980s, when a Conservative government abolished it as part of a thorough reorganisation of the national economy.

This innovation ensured that the financial circumstances of the ordinary unionised industrial worker would not be ruined by factors outside his control. There was still, however, a problem regarding the numerous agricultural workers who were not unionised, who often eked out a wretched existence and had no recourse to any collective system of agreements. The land-reform legislation of 1919, one of the most extensive land reforms in recent Danish history, was an attempt to alleviate the plight of this group. It was no accident that the date of these reforms was 1919, as the politicians feared that the revolutionary movements which were sweeping through Europe would find a foot-hold amongst the marginalised rural sectors of society. However, the laws also represented a somewhat late fulfilment of a promise made in the constitution of 1849 that the privileged right of ownership of land through entailed estates would be legally abolished, in accordance with the constitutional provision that all prerogatives of title, rank or class would be discontinued. The land reform of 1919 thus finally honoured this promise, albeit 70 years after it was made.

The Reform Act, introduced by the Social-Liberal government with the tacit support of the Liberal farmers' party *Venstre*, stated that all glebe land (i.e. land owned by a parish church or ecclesiastical benefice) was to be confiscated. The most important and controversial section of the law, however, was that stating that all existing '*majorat*' estates (a form of endowment) belonging to the previous counties, baronies and other entailed estates would come into free ownership. The previous owners of the *majorat*s were, however, allowed to keep their estates on the condition that they paid 10 per cent of the value of the estate to the government and handed over 25 per cent of their land, in return for compensation, with the aim of it being parcelled out to smallholders. As these *majorat*s constituted nearly 10 per cent of the entire agricultural land of the country, this provision was in effect a redistribution of ownership of an extent comparable to that under the large agrarian reforms. This time, however, it was not the independent farmers but the smallholders who benefited. Following the agrarian reforms, government legislation regarding land had been aimed at protecting the medium-sized farms. This did not change, but this time land was taken from the very big farms and given to the smallest.

The result was the emergence of getting on for 20,000 new small-holdings, each with enough land to support a family if run with suffi-cient thrift and diligence. So this created a completely new class of small, independent farmers who would otherwise have been forced to move to the towns and join the urban proletariat. Instead, the Social-Liberal Party, *Det radikale Venstre*, who initiated these reforms, gained a solid basis of support from this new class. The party, with its social-liberal leanings, was positioned in the very centre of the political spectrum.

In a wider context, the land reform of 1919 had at least two other long-term consequences. It meant that the social democratic move-ment never truly gained a foothold in the countryside and so could never win an absolute majority of votes. The large group of small-holders, as mentioned, threw their support behind the centre party, *Det radikale Venstre*, and henceforth collaboration over the centre ground became the very basis of Danish politics. This moderating political effect was in fact one of the important motives behind the introduction of the reforms. In a book written in 1928 about the smallholders, the political economist Jørgen Petersen expressed this basic philosophy very accurately:

> The higher the proportion of the population who support themselves through agriculture, the more solid the economic and social foundations will be and so the lower will be the risk of the storms of bad years sweeping society away. It thus follows that parcelling out land into small independent farms will stabilise the economic and social basis of the country.[10]

The key concept here is that of stability – economic, social and political. This was indeed exactly what the reform of 1919 achieved, as it transformed the potentially fanatical rural underclass into a group of politically moderate, small-scale, independent tradesmen.

To turn this around, the appearance of the numerous new communities of smallholders all over the country was the clearest sign imaginable that the days of the classic estate-ownership structure dating from the time of absolutism had finally gone. This reform marked a full stop for the aristocratic era in Denmark, and its ostentatious manor houses and oversized farm buildings now stood merely as a reminder of a time that had vanished, of a dead economic and social order. Only a small number of the previous large estates survived the transformation as independent units. The majority slowly disintegrated and sold off the remaining land, while the huge buildings gradually found other uses, such as training centres and conference facilities. The reform also took away the last real privilege of the Danish landed aristocracy – privileged ownership of land. Although the concept of nobility was allowed to remain in existence, it did so in name only. Since 1919 titled Danes have in every respect shared the same rights and duties as every other social class. Under the pressure of the revolutionary movements following in the wake of the First World War, Denmark eradicated the very last feudal elements from society. This opened the way for a modern egalitarian society where the frontiers were not between the privileged landowners and the downtrodden peasants, but rather between liberals and socialists, both of whom were of the moderate democratic type, the reforms of 1919–20 having actually removed the danger of a totalitarian solution to the crisis such as in Russia, Italy, and later Germany.

Notwithstanding this, in many ways the interwar years were a turbulent period for Denmark, as for the rest of the world. It started sombrely when the Social-Liberal government, which had borne the brunt of the stringent restrictions of the war years, was dissolved by the king in 1920, a move which brought Denmark closer to the brink of a republican revolution than it had ever been. The situation became even more precarious in 1922 when the largest bank in the country, Landmandsbanken, collapsed as a result of some disastrous commercial speculations in Russia and the Baltic States in combination with dramatic price falls on the world markets.

This unexpected collapse of one of the most respected financial institutions in the country sent a violent shock wave through Danish society. Many people saw it as conclusive evidence of what disasters could occur when capitalism was allowed to run rampant and unbridled, as it apparently had been under the ruling *Venstre* government. Large numbers of people rallied to the Social Democratic Party, which had put its revolutionary Marxist origins behind it and now simply wanted to counteract the excesses of free capitalism through government intervention. In other words, it was no longer part of the programme that capitalism should be abolished, but that it should be brought under state control. This programme appealed to a wide section of the Danish population in the light of recent events.

As a result of this moderate reformist track, the Social Democrats won the 1924 elections with a large majority, making them, for the first time, the largest party in the country – a position they maintained right up to the election in 2001 – and put them in government with their paternal chairman, Thorvald Stauning, at the head. With the exception of some short interludes of Conservative government, they remained in power for the rest of the twentieth century. This gave the Social Democrats, most often in collaboration with *Det radikale Venstre*, a fairly free hand in the long slow haul of implementing their programme of reforms. The result was the current Danish welfare state, which rests on the acceptance of capitalist methods of production with extensive government regulation.

THE CRISIS OF THE 1930S – COLLABORATIVE DEMOCRACY

The first true test of the sustainability of this policy came with the world crisis in 1929, which hit Denmark shortly after the newly formed Social Democratic radical government took office under the leadership of Thorvald Stauning and with the radical P. Munch (1870–1948) as Minister of Foreign Affairs. The crisis started with a dramatic fall in share prices on the Wall Street stock exchange, which forced American bankers to recall their investments from Europe and was especially damaging to the largest economies of the region, notably Britain and Germany. The immediate reaction was the introduction of protectionist measures which almost paralysed international trade. This was a catastrophe for a small country such as Denmark, with an economy which was totally dependent on export.[11]

The crisis really bit in Denmark in 1931 as agricultural prices fell drastically in the chief markets of Britain and Germany, and the attempts by farmers to compensate by increasing production made matters even worse. The fixed costs of farming did not decrease, and so many were driven from house and home. In 1930 farmers were forced to sell 1700 farms, whereas in 1932 this figure reached 4300. The problems faced by farming spread to the commerce of the towns. Unemployment in urban areas shot up from 14 per cent in 1930 to over 40 per cent in 1932. In this desperate situation, everyone looked to the state for help.

The first step the government took, with wide support in Parliament, was to suspend the convertibility of the Danish *krone* into gold and so preserve the national gold reserves. The same measure had been taken during the First World War, but had been reversed by a liberal government which made 'the honest *krone*' a major issue, to the considerable detriment of Danish trade with the rest of the world. Now the gold standard was again suspended to prevent any collapse of the country's financial system comparable to the national bankruptcy of 1813. As it turned out, it was never again reintroduced.

There was broad political agreement on all this. However, once it came to concrete initiatives to support the beleaguered agricultural sector, this unity crumbled. The Social Democrat-led government proposed that the farmers should receive direct emergency help from the government. This was strongly opposed by the liberal party, *Venstre*, which preferred cuts in public expenditure and tax reductions. These different approaches reflected two fundamentally opposed attitudes to resolving economic problems, which would become recurrent issues later in the century, namely state intervention versus faith in the mechanisms of the free market. Even today, this debate of principle still rages in various guises, even though the liberals have in the meantime moved considerably nearer to accepting government intervention and very high levels of taxation.

As the crisis became worse, *Venstre* had to shelve its liberal views in this particular situation and accept that the government had to manage the crisis in a way which, in force and scope, resembled the policy of regulation introduced during the First World War. In 1932 the government decided to institute an Exchange Control Office under the aegis of the National Bank, which actually turned back the clock to the days of the mercantilist policies against which liberals the world over had been fulminating since the days of Adam Smith. After this, any use of foreign currency had to be approved by the office, and so by the state, and was only granted to companies if they could demonstrate that the imports they required could be considered essential and to the benefit of society. This meant that anything which constituted a competitive threat to Danish products could be kept out of the country. The system also allowed the government to set up extensive bartering agreements with other countries. The regulation extended to production itself, with orders to limit production in an attempt to maintain prices. In farming, a system of what became known as 'pig tickets' was introduced, where farmers were only allowed to deliver their pigs for slaughter if they had enough tickets, or vouchers, for each one. As these pig tickets were in great demand, a black market for them rapidly developed.

The high point of the economic crisis was the winter of 1932–3, just as a major conflict in the labour market was coming to a head. It was not surprising, given the seriousness of the situation, that in a speech to Parliament on 26 January 1933, Prime Minister Stauning chose to take a sombre tone:

> Danish society is without doubt currently facing the most serious situation it has ever encountered. We are facing a situation where there are nearly 200,000 unemployed, in other words nearly one million people are affected by unemployment and do not have enough money to keep the wolf from the door. We are facing a situation where 250,000 farmers, with farms of various sizes, are hit hard by the crisis, which means there are yet another one million people without enough purchasing power to enable them to contribute to sustaining production.[12]

The Prime Minister estimated that over half the population of Denmark had no purchasing power and that the Danish economy was nosediving in an economic spiral without comparison.

This desperate situation gave rise to one of the most epoch-making compromises of modern Danish history, called the Kanslergade Agreement, after the street in Copenhagen where the Prime Minister lived, where his home was the scene of critical cross-party negotiations in the shadow of the impending conflict. The agreement was between the government and the largest opposition party, *Venstre*, and was finally concluded on 30 January 1933 – the same day that Hitler became Chancellor of the Reich in Germany.

It covered a number of profound political interventions, including a law extending collective agreements – the first of many to follow – a large devaluation of the *krone*, and emergency assistance for agriculture. The agreement also meant that *Venstre* had to abandon its previously vehement opposition to the proposals for social reform made by K. K. Steincke (1880–1963), Minister of Social Affairs. This huge package of social reforms simplified many points of the previously complex social legislation built on the principle of public assistance and private philanthropy, and proposed to replace it with a legal principle and fixed charges for social assistance. The principles of this legislation became normative for the design of the subsequent Danish welfare state.

The Kanslergade Agreement also laid the foundations for a more expansive state economic policy on Keynesian principles. Afterwards, the crisis was tackled systematically by under-budgeting to buoy up purchasing power and increase employment. This was only possible because the Exchange Control Office could ensure a reasonable balance between imports and exports. Fortunately, the result of all this was that unemployment began to fall steadily. For the rest of the 1930s, unemployment stayed at around 20 per cent, which was admittedly high, but no higher than it had been in the 1920s. Agricultural earnings also rose, shown not least by the fact that the number of forced sales fell to around 2000 a year at the end of the 1930s.

There were also longer-term results from this major agreement. The hard negotiations knocked some of the ideological edges off the parties. Most obvious was the retreat of purely liberal ideas, corresponding to the Social Democrats definitively abandoning their original Marxist philosophy and changing into a broader party of the workers and the people with considerable popular appeal. This ideological shift was very clearly shown in Stauning's manifesto of 1934, often referred to as 'Denmark for the People'.[13] Through this process the four old parties gradually became closer to each other. Indeed, together they had shouldered the responsibility for the emergency legislation and steered Denmark through the crisis with a steady hand. With their large parliamentary majority, they represented the 'collaborative democracy' which came to be a guarantee that extreme parties on the Left or Right could not win the power they sought. The extensive collaboration of the old parties thus ensured that Denmark weathered the storms of the 1930s and kept democracy and parliamentarianism intact. The emergency policies also meant that a closer co-operation developed between the government, commercial organisations and the parties in the labour market, another clear indicator of the collaborative style which would help to create the welfare state after the Second World War.

In the interwar years, Denmark was a society undergoing major changes. This was not just because of the recurrent crises of the international economy, but also because of profound structural reorganisations as part of the process of moving from an agrarian to an industrial society. The chronology of this process can be seen from the changing patterns of employment. Until 1930, nearly half of the entire workforce of the country was employed in agriculture, and around a third in industry. On the eve of the Second World War, these proportions had been reversed: in 1940 less than a third of the workforce was employed in agriculture, while industry accounted for towards 40 per cent. In real terms, this corresponded to a virtual doubling of the industrial workforce, which can partly be explained by the fact that most of the Danish industrial production was intended for the home market, which was robustly protected by the Exchange Control Office.

Although those who stood in the long lines of the unemployed in the 1930s hardly noticed, Danish society as a whole became markedly richer between the wars. Measured as production per head, every single Dane had nearly half as much again at his or her disposal in 1940 than in 1920. This economic progress was admittedly distributed very unequally, and the large number of the unemployed saw very little of it. This, in turn, heightened political tensions. The extensive social reforms which started in 1933 can be interpreted as an attempt on the part of the government, led by the Social Democrats, to reduce these tensions by turning the task of helping the needy into a common social responsibility. This attempt can be described as a success in that it actually succeeded in mitigating the worst effects of unemployment and in the process denied any significant influence to the political extremists. Neither the tiny Communist Party nor the even tinier Nazi Party managed to challenge the dominance of the four old parties, with their 'collaborative democracy', or the broad consensus behind the firm policy of regulation which carried the country safely through the storms of the 1930s.

IN THE SHADOW OF THE SECOND WORLD WAR

As already mentioned, Denmark was occupied by German troops within just a few hours on the morning of 9 April 1940, almost as a side effect of Hitler's campaign against Norway and its strategically important Atlantic ports. The invasion was followed by a German ultimatum not to offer resistance in return for a promise that Germany would respect the political independence of the country. The government and Parliament decided to bow to this pressure, and thus pave the way for what was called the 'peaceful occupation', built on the fiction of the continued independence of Denmark. This somewhat unusual situation continued until the end of the Second World War in 1945, and with few exceptions, the contacts between Denmark and Germany were conducted through the respective Foreign Ministries during the whole period – in the sacred name of fiction.

No one, either in Denmark or elsewhere, really believed it. It was clear to most people that with the occupation, Denmark had become a protectorate of Hitler's *Neuropa*, and, taking their lead from the government, businesses organised their activities accordingly, with the exception of the merchant navy. Two-thirds of the ships happened to be in neutral ports or ports belonging to the Western Allies on 9 April 1940, and so they continued to sail in the service of the Allies for the rest of the war.[14] Danish exports now went to Germany, which direly needed the agricultural produce and paid good prices. In return, the Germans supplied coal and other raw materials, allowing Danish companies to function for most of the war as if nothing had happened. These were good times, especially for the farmers. They could sell everything they could produce at favourable prices, and so they did. It has in fact been calculated that the volume of food Danish agriculture supplied to the German Reich was the equivalent of one month's consumption for each year of the war. It is therefore no wonder that in the first years of the war the British organisation for subversive warfare, the Special Operations Executive (SOE), identified sabotaging the Danish supplies to Germany as its key goal for operations in Denmark.[15]

From the start of the occupation, wages were frozen and rationing was introduced, which lowered the real wages of the industrial workers and caused unemployment to rise. On the other hand, the large-scale construction work on the west coast of Jutland to form part of Hitler's Atlantic Wall provided a great deal of employment. It has also been calculated that this cost approximately DKK 5 billion, and was financed by German withdrawals from the Danish National Bank. Alongside the profits from exports of around DKK 3 billion, this constituted a considerable injection of purchasing power into the Danish economy. The result was a rapid rise in prices leading to yet a further fall in the real wages of industrial workers. Yet, all in all, compared to their European neighbours the Danes escaped very lightly indeed from the war and the occupation. There was rationing, it is true, but no one went hungry, and after the occupation the Danes were much better nourished than most other people in Europe. Also material damage was very limited, and the apparatus of production was left largely intact. Whether this was really worth the price in terms of the damage to Danish self-respect resulting from Allied accusations of craven opportunism is, of course, a matter for debate. That is another story, which does not belong here.

In any case, it was not for a dozen or so years after the end of the war that Danish society fully recovered from the long-term effects of the German occupation and the crisis of the 1930s and so could once again join the club of the affluent countries of the West. Between 1945 and the middle of the 1950s, Denmark showed the lowest economic growth of any of the Western countries, and unemployment constantly hovered at around 10 per cent of the working population. During these years, Denmark was, like many other European countries, a grey, semi-impoverished society with shortages, exchange controls and rationing. There were several reasons for this lack of growth. One was that there was virtually no new investment during the occupation, which left the production apparatus worn down and antiquated. Next is the fact that exports to the critical German market stopped for a period, while Britain, a traditionally important market, was struggling with a deep postwar economic crisis. Once trade with Britain resumed in 1945, the Danish government, partly as a penance for the country's equivocal position in the war, had to accept somewhat lower prices for the important exports of bacon and butter, but had to pay a premium price for British coal. Under these conditions it was more than merely difficult to earn enough foreign currency to cover the import of ordinary foodstuffs while also finding the resources for industrial investment.

In the years immediately after the war, Denmark was hopelessly caught in this foreign currency squeeze which hindered development and disappointed the population. In an opinion survey in 1949, as many as a quarter of the inhabitants expressed a desire to emigrate to the United States. This vividly reflected people's frustration over the difference between their expectations of postwar life and the shabby and depressing economic and social realities. Light only began to appear at the end of the tunnel when Marshall Aid started to flow in.[16]

The extensive help that America gave in the reconstruction of Western Europe from 1948 was an attempt to stem the advance of the Soviet Union and Communism. It took the form of dollar aid, earmarked for buying US goods. This aid was bestowed on condition that the recipient countries signed up to the OECD, a new co-operative economic organisation which obliged member states to remove the import regulations imposed during the crisis of the 1930s. Denmark received its share of the cash aid. This immediately alleviated the economic hardship, but it was not until the end of the Korean War that conditions were such as to allow the gradual lifting of government import regulations and the complete end of rationing. Finally, the way was paved for the welfare revolution which, in a surprisingly few years, transformed Denmark from a grey land of shortages to an affluent society on a par with the leading Western countries. The welfare revolution, which coincided with the sustained boom in the West from 1953 to 1973, can be roughly divided up under three main headings: the dramatically dwindling importance of agriculture to the overall economy; the second industrial revolution, and the emergence of the service society.

AGRICULTURE IN RETREAT

In 1950, a quarter of the total Danish workforce was still employed in agriculture. This figure fell to 18 per cent in 1960, and to around 10 per cent in 1970, and then continued to fall steadily to the point where at the end of the century, jobs in agriculture and related businesses accounted for just 8 per cent of the total.[17]

This trend was fuelled by stagnating prices for agricultural produce coupled with rising wages, which forced the sector to mechanise and rationalise extensively. Helped by Marshall Aid, tractors and combine harvesters started to take over the work on the farms from the 1950s. In 1948 there were only 6000 tractors in Denmark. By 1965 this had increased to 133,000 and the number was still rising. Mechanisation allowed a huge reduction in the number of workers – in 1950 there were 122,000 employees, but by around 1975 this number had fallen to just 14,000.

There was also an enormous restructuring which marked a clear break in the trends of the preceding hundred years. Whereas in the past, the trend was to parcel out land to smallholders, the new mechanisation reversed the process. In the decade after the war 9000 independent farms disappeared, followed by another 75,000 between 1956 and 1976, when the total number of farms was 124,000 as against 208,000 just 30 years previously. The move to large-scale operation continued unabated over the subsequent decades, to the point where in 2000 only 20,000 farms remained, with an average size of 100 hectares, which is more or less the area a single man can cultivate with the use of modern machinery.

This huge exodus from the land did not, however, lead to any reduction in production; on the contrary, this grew considerably. Today the remaining Danish farmers produce enough food to support 15 million people, three times the total population. In other words, the rationalisations generated an increase in productivity without any parallel in the long history of the sector. Yet the stagnation of prices did not allow the remaining farmers to maintain a standard of living which more or less corresponded to their efforts. From around 1960 the average income of farmers was a little lower than that of industrial workers, and from 1961 the state had to provide direct subsidies, which grew year on year until Denmark joined the EEC in 1973 and the schemes were included in the comprehensive EEC subsidy system.

This metamorphosis of a self-sufficient business with strong liberal traditions into a state-assisted activity deeply dented the self-image of the farmers. For centuries they had been responsible for running the country's most important sector and their voices carried weight in local communities and the national legislative assembly. After 1960 they had to watch helplessly as they lost their standing to the ever-advancing industrial sector, and at a national level they were too few and too dependent on state subsidies to play any important role. In many ways, the situation in which they found themselves was reminiscent of that the great landowners had faced after the agrarian reforms in the late eighteenth century, when the independent farmers took over their position of power and their role in society. Both of these developments were part of the protracted process of modernisation in Danish society which started in 1800.

The industrialisation of agriculture sounded the death knell for a style of life which had existed for centuries, with its quadrangular farm buildings – themselves the very image of the old Danish rural culture. The old society could close itself off from the outside world, but even so had built close links to the world economy since the emergence of the co-operative movement, and had created the framework for a small, self-contained society. Now all of this became no more than a nostalgic dream of the good old days before the world went out of joint. It was hardly coincidental that Danes in town and country alike flocked to the cinemas in the 1950s to watch films based on the novelist Morten Korch's naive dramatisations of a rural life which had already become a thing of the past. It was a romanticised revisiting of a rural culture which no longer existed, a trip back in time to the rosy world of yesteryear.

THE SECOND INDUSTRIAL REVOLUTION

The second large wave of industrialisation rolled over Denmark in the 1950s and 1960s, speeded on its way by the large reserve of labour which was released by the rationalisation of agriculture. The number of industrial workers grew in step with the exodus from the farms, from 200,000 just after the Second World War to 315,000 in 1972. There was also a rapidly growing body of white-collar workers involved in product development, sales and administration. The numerous small industries, some of which have since become very big, mainly focused on niche production, such as radiator valves, plastic toys and specialised pumps, or pharmaceuticals based on agricultural production, such as insulin preparations for diabetics. These product areas all required a high level of know-how. Denmark, with its lack of raw materials, could hardly offer fertile ground for the development of any true heavy industry.[18]

The fact that the industrial products were highly refined and specialised explains why their value grew much more rapidly than the number of industrial jobs. In real terms, the value of Danish industrial production in 1973 was three and a half times higher than in 1947. This productivity increase, like that in agriculture, was achieved through automation and investment in modern production equipment. Two especially successful examples of this automated niche production are the valve manufacturer Danfoss and the toy producer Lego.

In 1933, Mads Clausen, a talented engineer working in an outbuilding on his parents' farm on the island of Als, developed an expansion valve suitable for applications in heating and cooling systems. On the basis of this invention, he set up his own company in Nordborg on Als, where he lived. The postwar boom created a strong demand for oil-fired heating, refrigerators and washing machines, for which the Danfoss valve was an essential component. This in turn created an international demand, and Danfoss grew meteorically in the years following the war. Around 1960, Mads Clausen's company had become the largest in Denmark, with roughly 4000 employees. An entire town grew up around his family farm.

In the sleepy little village of Billund in the 1930s, Gotfred Kirk Christiansen ran a one-man company called Lego, making wooden toys. After the Second World War he started to use plastic, and in 1958 he finally developed the bricks which could be put together in innumerable ways which became famous all over the world as Lego bricks. This worldwide success meant that the Lego group grew through the 1960s into one of the biggest companies in Denmark. At the same time, Billund grew around the factory and now has the second busiest international airport in the country. The huge amusement park, Legoland, with its replicas of famous buildings constructed with Lego bricks, has become one of Denmark's major tourist attractions.

Danfoss and Lego are the two most conspicuous examples of companies which started with a single, powerful idea and then grew in the locality where the idea was hit upon to achieve a size where they dominated a whole area of the country and an entire sector on a global scale. Yet the typical pattern of the second wave of industrialisation was the dominance of small companies, usually developments of an existing workshop, which produced goods for a longer or shorter period and then vanished once more when the market conditions turned unfavourable. In 1973, around 20 per cent of Danish companies had fewer than 10 employees, and only 25 per cent had more than 50. This particular structure had advantages and disadvantages. The advantage was that it provided the flexibility to adapt to market conditions without any widespread social consequences. The disadvantage was that the small companies found it very difficult to manage product development and marketing on a scale suitable for the international market. There was a pronounced trend after the establishment of the internal European market in the 1990s for Danish companies either to merge or to enter strategic alliances with similar but larger foreign concerns. This process could with some justification be described as the third industrial revolution, and has developed in the high technology and biochemical sectors in particular.

The breakneck speed of the development of the industrial sector put companies in a position to absorb the labour force which the rationalisation of agriculture had released. Unemployment fell around 1960 from a level of approximately 10 per cent, which was pretty much the normal level after the war, to low single figures little higher than the structural unemployment which is inevitable in any society experiencing rapid change. In fact, the demand for labour was so high, and families' needs for new consumer goods such as cars, televisions and white goods so pronounced, that the majority of Danish women entered the labour market during the 1960s, with the effect that the overall working population grew by around 12 per cent over this decade. In turn, this meant that most households had two incomes, and so could afford more and more consumer goods, which fuelled the production even more. In this period, the country previously typified by shortages exploded into a truly affluent society.

THE WELFARE STATE AND THE SERVICE ECONOMY

It is quite clear that the social and economic changes described above placed a completely different and much bigger demand on social services than the preceding social structure, which to a large extent relied on itself. The citizens of a now affluent society made increasing demands for the public provision of services in such forms as childcare institutions, better education and extended home help and nursing for the elderly and ill. All of these needs had previously been catered for largely by families themselves or those close to them. The response to these numerous requirements and challenges was the welfare state, which truly came into being in Denmark around 1960.[19]

The concept of the welfare state, albeit – quite naturally – in various forms, originated in Western Europe in the aftermath of the Second World War. As already discussed, it was a central principle for the Danish Social Democrats, who formulated the main outlines in their manifesto entitled 'The Denmark of the Future' as early as 1945, and fleshed out the bones in their 1961 manifesto. According to this, the public sector did not just have the responsibility of alleviating immediate need, but also of ensuring that every citizen could enjoy a decent standard of living and have access to health care and education. This was to be financed through progressive taxation, where a larger burden fell on the higher earners and the welfare services were thus to be in a certain way 'free of charge'. Although originally the welfare state was the project of the Social Democrats, the concept was gradually accepted by the Liberal and Conservative parties. So the subsequent discussion was not about whether Denmark should become a welfare state or not, but a debate over the extent of welfare legislation.

The creation of the welfare state and the service society led to an explosion in the number of civil servants. In 1950 there were 168,000, of which 73,000 were employed in health and social services. By 1960, this had grown to 234,000, with 101,000 in the health and social services. By 1970, the figures were 444,000 and 200,000. In 2000, the public sector employed approximately 900,000 – just about a third of the entire working population. This naturally corresponded to a growth in public expenditure as a proportion of gross domestic product. In 1950 this amounted to just 23 per cent, but since 1970 it has been around 50 per cent, although there has been a slight decrease recently. Taxes rose in step with the expansion of the welfare state. Until 1960, Danes paid around a quarter of their income in tax. This then doubled, to 50 per cent, and in 2000 the figure had reached 51 per cent.

These figures could not more clearly demonstrate the colossal expansion of the welfare and service society in the second half of the twentieth century, carried forward by the sudden affluence of the 1960s. Neither the crises of the 1970s nor the 1980s could halt the further growth of the welfare state. Danes themselves had so identified with the system that it would have been electoral suicide for any politician to even suggest abolishing it, despite the fact that more or less everyone in any position of responsibility could see that the system could not continue to expand without serious repercussions for businesses of all kinds, which at the same time were having to compete ever-more keenly in international arenas. To be fair, the politicians who launched the system had every reason to believe that the need for social services would fall as general prosperity increased. In the real world, virtually the opposite was true. Needs and requirements have actually grown with the increase of social and medical provision, and there are no signs that they will diminish.

There is a way in which the Danish welfare state, with its comprehensive social safety net and high level of collective responsibility, can be perceived as a modern, national version of the old village collectives from before the time of agrarian reform. These created a secure framework for the everyday life of the Danes over centuries and shaped their behaviour and norms to the point of defining what it meant to be Danish. The welfare state, with its innate security and collective protection against threats from both within and without, touched on something very deep in the heart of the Danish sense of nationality. This could go some way to explaining the reluctance to change the system despite the recurrent complaints about the level of taxation. Politicians therefore need to be very sensitive indeed when trying to limit the growth of this welfare state. Even the Liberal-Conservative government which was solidly supported by the middle classes in the 2001 election has refrained from cutting services. They have limited themselves to a simple decision not to increase taxes further. Given the current levels of taxation, this can only be seen as a very limited and modest step.

THE DANISH WELFARE STATE AND THE WORLD ECONOMY

The real architect of the welfare society, Jens Otto Krag, who was, as mentioned before, a Social Democratic Prime Minister, considered right from the start that the welfare state was a project which would hold Danish society together in the difficult years after the war and deafen the Danes to the ideological siren songs from the East during the Cold War. In his eyes, it was a national project intended to protect the tiny Danish society from external threats. He was equally clear that economic growth was a precondition for the success and enhancement of the project. As Denmark was so reliant on exports, continued growth required unhampered access to export markets. West Germany and Britain were the two of most important. So, he saw the most pressing political objective as ensuring that Denmark was not excluded from these essential markets. This was not so straightforward in the light of the prevailing market situation in Europe. It is to his eternal credit and glory that he succeeded, albeit only after an enormous personal effort, and at the same time steered his overriding objective – the welfare state – through the treacherous waters of the 1960s.

The Common Market was established in 1957, and consisted of West Germany, France, Italy and the Benelux countries. This was the germ of an extensive economic and political collaboration, which first took the form of a customs union and some agricultural agreements to set a minimum price for produce. Denmark considered applying to join, but decided against as Britain and the other Nordic countries were unwilling to go along.[20] Two years later, Denmark joined EFTA instead, a free-trade agreement led by Great Britain. Portugal, Switzerland, Norway, Sweden and Finland joined too. From a Danish perspective, one clear drawback to this free-trade agreement was that it did not include agricultural produce, still the country's most important export, added to which it made exporting to the Common Market more difficult. The agricultural lobby wanted to join the EEC, preferably alongside Britain.

In the longer term, the division of Europe into two trading blocs posed problems, not least for the EFTA countries which had to stand on the sidelines and watch the German economic powerhouse build up steam in the EEC while the EFTA region remained rather less dynamic. Great Britain applied to join the EEC in 1961, and Denmark put in a parallel application. After a long series of fruitless negotiations through the 1960s, which ended when the French President, Charles de Gaulle, vetoed British entry at the last moment, an agreement which met the British conditions was finally reached in 1972. Thus, Denmark too felt able to sign the Treaty of Rome.

This also suited Krag's vision, even though the road had been long and all alternatives had been exhausted, including an exclusively Nordic free market, Nordek. The horrific scenario that Britain might join without Denmark was now a fear of the past. However, one hurdle remained: winning a referendum. In the internal campaigns leading up to the referendum, the supporters of the EEC focused on the economic arguments for membership, whereas the opponents insisted that joining would mean that Denmark would surrender its independence to the transnational European institutions and that the level of welfare in Denmark would be jeopardised.

This set the terms of the debate which would run again and again with every subsequent vote about the enlargement of co-operation with the EEC. Oddly enough, even though it was the starting point for Krag, the supporters of membership did not succeed in communicating to the people that joining involved much more than purely economic issues, but also the preservation of the most important icon of modern Denmark – the welfare state itself. This allowed opponents to get away with presenting the EEC as a threat to the welfare state and to the very concept of Danishness, which, to put it mildly, hardly reflected the political and economic realities of the issue. This odd mix-up of roles and unsubstantiated argumentation has actually been the bane of the Danish debate about Europe ever since 1972, meaning that it has been exceptionally difficult to conduct any sensible public discussion of what is probably the most critical issue for Danish society in the late twentieth and early twenty-first centuries: the position of Denmark in an ever-more encompassing European collaboration. Despite these fundamental obfuscations, the referendum of 2 October 1972 showed a clear majority for joining. Despite the fact that the Norwegians had rejected membership to the concern of Danish supporters of the EEC, 63 per cent of Danes voted for and 37 per cent against. So, on 1 January 1973, Denmark became a fully-fledged member of the expanded EEC, which now incorporated all the export markets of importance for continued economic growth in Denmark, and thus for the continuation of the welfare state.

For other reasons too, 1973 was a watershed in modern Danish history. As mentioned before, it was in this year that a number of protest and single-issue parties won enough seats in Parliament to destabilise the political consensus between the four old parties which had led to the creation of the welfare state and the entry into the European Common Market. This marked the beginning of a long period of political instability. It was also the year when the international oil crisis really hit the country hard and threw the vulnerable economy into a long recession which led to innumerable bankruptcies and rapidly rising unemployment. Not only did this halt economic growth for a long time, it also endangered the very existence of the welfare state. The whole system had to be slimmed down in order to be able to function in times of low growth or no growth at all. This issue, in combination with ensuring the survival of business life through the storms of the 1970s and the 1980s, determined the political agenda for the remainder of the century.

Things were not quite as black as they could have been, as the sky-high price of oil made it economically viable to exploit the reserves of oil and gas in the Danish sector of the North Sea. The shipping company Mærsk Mc-Kinney Møller was the biggest operator here. As a result, Denmark has been self-sufficient in energy since 1997 – a situation without parallel since the early modern society, with its low energy requirements. The price of coping with the turbulent world economy of the late twentieth century was a greater inequality within Danish society.

Even though the personal consumption of Danes rose as a whole by nearly a third from the crisis in 1973 to the end of the century, this growth was distributed more unequally than before. An entirely new and constantly growing group arose, consisting of the long-term unemployed, social security clients and – as in other Western countries – drug addicts, all of whom were permanently reliant on the social services and so did not experience much of the general increase in incomes. On the other hand, the economic instability of the 1980s was especially favourable to speculative businesses, and small groups of young high-fliers amassed tremendous fortunes, which were often lost just as quickly as they had been gained. In its volatility, the situation resembled to some extent that of the mercurial years after the First World War. Although throughout the period approximately 30 per cent of domestic product was redistributed through the mechanisms of the welfare state, this was not enough to prevent social divisions from widening. This trend was reinforced by the rapidly increasing numbers of immigrants and refugees from the so-called Third World. In 2000, there were around 300,000 of these in the country, rising to around 400,000 in 2010. Just like the 'residual groups' described above, the majority of the newcomers were also dependent on state transfer payments, to some extent because of a poor integration policy.[21]

THE RELUCTANT EUROPEANS

As already mentioned, the majority of Danes saw entry into the EEC as part of a national project to protect the Danish economy and rescue the welfare model. As an extension of this standpoint, the Danes, like the British, were functionalists in that they wanted European co-operation to be limited to practical matters of economics and not to move towards political union. This conveniently ignored the fact that the central concept of the original common market was federalist, with the long-term vision of uniting Europe politically. Economic co-operation was simply a beginning and a tool to achieve this end. This difference of perspective is clearly one of the main reasons for the reluctance and reserve which has since been the hallmark of Danish attitudes to the plans for expansion.

For the first dozen or so years after Danish entry, the plans for union moved very slowly – the countries involved were preoccupied with warding off the acute effects of the oil crisis. Indeed, in 1979, direct elections were introduced for the European Parliament, which at the same time was given budgetary control over the European Commission. Yet although this smacked a little of the formation of a union, it did not attract much attention, as it did not interfere with the sovereignty of the member states.

During the 1980s, however, the plans for union gathered speed. In 1983 the member countries issued a declaration in which they committed themselves to working towards a union. Three years later, the heads of governments adopted the Single European Act, which included provisions for the removal of all technical and fiscal trade barriers by 1993, with the aim of creating 'the internal market'. There was also agreement over implementing wide-ranging harmonisation, including areas which were not directly related to economics and trade. Most significantly, these harmonisation measures could be implemented by majority voting in which no individual country could exercise a veto.

Such extensive decisions undeniably smelled strongly of union, which was undoubtedly why Poul Schlüter (b. 1929), the Prime Minster at the time, was unable to win the required majority in Parliament. His Conservative government chose instead to call a consultative referendum, which, however, given the nature of the issue, would actually be binding. Just as in 1972, the discussions centred less around the concrete issues than the question of membership or not. In a moment of weakness in the heat of the battle, Prime Minister Schlüter described the idea of union as being as dead as a doornail, thereby flying in the face of the evidence. This, to put it bluntly, did little to encourage an objective climate for debate. Nonetheless, it became apparent that the government had judged the referendum correctly. The actual result was that a little more than 56 per cent voted for the Single European Act, and just under 44 per cent against. All subsequent polls about the expansion of the community have divided the Danish people roughly in half, sometimes with a slight majority saying yes, sometimes with a slight majority saying no.

This became especially apparent with the Maastricht Treaty of 1992, officially called 'The treaty on political union'. This consisted of a large number of agreements, all of which extended collaboration and made it more binding. The key point of the agreement was economic and monetary union, with a common central bank and a common currency, which would change the previous economic common market into a close supranational co-operation on a federal pattern. This move was a natural consequence of the collapse of Eastern Europe and the reunification of Germany after the fall of the Berlin Wall in 1989. This created an understandable desire amongst the member countries to lock the new united Germany into a union agreement which could counterbalance it and at the same time create a stable alternative to the instability in Eastern Europe.

This treaty made it absolutely clear that the union was by no means 'dead as a doornail', as Schlüter had rashly claimed. As the treaty involved the surrender of sovereignty, the constitution dictated that there had to be a referendum. For the first time, the debate leading up to the referendum focused seriously on the political aspects of the project rather than just the economy. Those who spoke for the parties which opposed the treaty were able to successfully play on the fears of the Danes that they would lose their cherished welfare state and be overrun by obscure foreign interests. Against this argument, the attempts of the supporters of the treaty to convince the population of the political and security aspects of the project had little chance of success. The result was a narrow defeat for the supporters, with 50.7 per cent voting no, and 49.3 per cent yes. And so, as far as Denmark was concerned, the proposal was defeated.

The result sent shock waves through the political establishment both in Denmark and abroad, as any alteration of the European treaty required the agreement of all the members. Naturally enough, the other countries found it unacceptable that the whole process of integration could be abruptly terminated just because of little Denmark. A solution was found in the form of the Edinburgh Agreement of December 1992, which gave Denmark the right to opt out of four specific areas. These were: the question of common citizenship of the union; the common currency; defence policy; and legal co-operation. The following year, this new agreement was put to a referendum in Denmark. This time nearly 57 per cent voted for it, and a little more than 43 per cent against.

It would later become apparent that Denmark had shot itself in the foot by opting out of precisely the areas in which the union developed most strongly in the next few years. In 1994 the EEC changed its name to the EU – the European Union –as a symbolic expression of the closer collaboration. Once Sweden, Finland and Austria joined as full members in 1995, it became even harder to imagine a future for Denmark outside the EU in which, following the Edinburgh Agreement, the country had only partial membership. The half-hearted nature of this membership was even more strongly underlined when in yet another referendum, in September 2000, 53.1 per cent of the population rejected joining the third phase of economic and monetary union, which included the introduction of the euro as a common currency. Once again, this highlighted the pronounced Danish popular scepticism towards the EU project, which many perceived as elitist, and far removed from the realities of daily life and work.

A good illustration of the contradictions of the Danish attitude to the EU project is that the very effective Danish presidency of the EU in the autumn of 2002 was a key factor in concluding the agreement to expand the membership still further, this time by preparing to admit ten more countries These were the three Baltic States, Poland, the Czech Republic, Slovakia, Hungary, Slovenia, Malta and Cyprus. This not only pushes the fulcrum of the union to the north and east – that is to say nearer to Denmark – but has also thrown Denmark's ambiguous attitude into stark relief. Thus, in 2002, it is even harder to imagine a future for Denmark outside the EU than it was after the previous enlargement in 1995. Yet still about half of the population remain steadfast sceptics.

THE HALF-HEARTED, PIONEERING COUNTRY

At a certain point in the 1990s, the then Social Democratic government launched the slogan 'Denmark as a pioneering country'. According to this rather pathetic slogan, Denmark was to project itself as an example to other countries in the area of welfare, not just in education and health care but also in a number of other important fields related to welfare in general. The slogan had scarcely seen the light of day when a range of comparative international studies pricked the balloon of smug complacency which it represented. These reports showed that Danish school students trailed behind those in the other countries with which Denmark normally compares itself in terms of knowledge and ability, and that with very few exceptions, the Danish educational system was too expensive and inefficient. They also showed that despite the very high costs, in many respects the Danish health service was no match for that of, for example, France, and was plagued by long waiting lists, decaying buildings and obsolete equipment. Report after report presented a depressing picture of the standards of the core welfare services in Denmark, which stood in glaring contradiction to the fine words of the government's slogan. These conclusions were a harsh blow for many Danes and triggered the first really serious and unbiased debate about the priorities of the welfare system and the limits to welfare.

Through this debate, it became crystal clear that it was no longer enough simply to continue to expand the Danish welfare model along the lines which had been staked out in the 1960s, as the pressure of the new globalisation following the fall of Communism was creating ever more rapid changes for Danish business and society. It was becoming essential to adapt to the circumstances of an expanding Europe with fewer borders. This growing tension between a desperate desire to cling to the old familiar patterns and the relentless need to adapt and change to meet the demands of globalisation, even in the very areas – such as the welfare state in its classic form – which many see as being of central importance in maintaining a particular Danish identity, is the biggest challenge Denmark faces in the twenty-first century. A great deal depends on how far it can meet this challenge.

Let us return for a moment to what Sir James Mellon said about the Danish economy in the broadest sense, that it had to serve two purposes: one, to create the basis for a reasonable standard of living, the other to protect the very concept of Danishness. It could be said that the dilemma facing Denmark in the years around the change of the millennium was in essence, that the globalised economy of which, for good or ill, Denmark was a part was developing in directions which diverged in many respects from those that the Danish welfare society – the single outstanding element in the identity of the modern society – was designed for or able to deal with. An essential precondition for the Danish economy to return to a position where it can fulfil both of the purposes Sir James identified – an efficient welfare system without a lowering of competitiveness or living standards – is the willingness to change. Denmark does not have the power to change the global patterns, and so the difficult task consists of adapting to them without losing identity and social values in the process.

The story which has been presented here, of the development of Denmark from an impoverished country with many shortages into one of the richest countries in the world, shows that previous generations of Danes had in fact mastered this difficult art at crucial moments in history. This gives cause for hope that the current generation will be able to work the same magic and find the balance which will make it possible to maintain and improve Denmark's economic position in an ever-changing world, without obliterating the Danish character.

After the fall of the Berlin Wall and the rise of the Asian tiger economies, the world and its economy shifted closer to Denmark. However, as the ambiguous attitude to the EU serves to demonstrate, it is unclear how far Denmark has really moved towards the rest of the world, and specifically, how far Danes actually wish to go out into the rest of the world. A clarification of this question and a calculation of the consequences is urgently required, and is indeed critical for the future economic standing of the country.

8
. . . .
The Danes – A Tribe
or a Nation?

DANISHNESS IN THE LOOKING-GLASS OF HISTORY

In many respects, at any given time, there is an intimate interplay between the fashions in historiography and the contemporary self-image of the inhabitants of a country.[1] The particular interpretation of the past that becomes dominant largely defines how the people of a nation see themselves, their region and their country in relation to their surroundings. This is also determined by the current utopias of society, meaning the conception of the direction the society should be taking and how the members of society can best accommodate each other. Thus, the writing of history will, at any time, be a reflection of the prevailing collective identity and the common utopias.

This effect works in the other direction as well. The coherent interpretations of the past of a nation are also a record of collective consciousness, stretching far beyond the limits of the recollections of any individual, and so contribute to a crystallisation of individual memories and perceptions of the surrounding world into certain patterns, created and limited by the interpretations which form the foundations of the structure of the larger narratives about the collective past of the nation. The nature of these interpretations therefore has a powerful influence on the continued development of collective identity and self-image. So the very writing of history is both a mirror of the present and an important tool of consciousness, as it plays a key role in preserving tradition and developing identity. A study of the lines of interpretation which dominate the writing of a nation's history must therefore be able to reveal something of significance about the way in which that nation currently perceives itself, and its hopes and expectations of the future. Of course, this is equally true when it comes to Denmark.

Key aspects of the way in which Danes perceive themselves could thus be said to have been formed by two main currents in recent Danish historiography, which together have made a decisive mark on the Danish collective consciousness. One is what is known as the radical tradition of history and the other has appositely been called the 'farmers' approach' to recording Danish history.

The radical tradition of history had its origin in the atmosphere of defeat which settled over Denmark in the decades following the catastrophic – and largely self-inflicted – defeat at the hands of Bismarck's Prussia in 1864, which once and for all made Denmark a midget state. It is named after the political convictions of a small group of talented historians who at that time were in the vanguard of what was known as the 'critical breakthrough', when the discipline of history as an academic subject became a truly modern science, with its own methods and fixed scientific norms. These pioneers were nearly all adherents of the intellectual, radical (this is where the name derives) wing of *Venstre*, then the party of opposition. Unlike the mainstream of the liberal party of opposition, the radical wing strongly advocated that Denmark should adopt a pacifist and neutral foreign policy in recognition of the fact that after the defeat, the country could no longer defend itself militarily. Instead of defending the country by use of arms at the borders, the survival of Danishness should be ensured by turning outward loss into inward gains, both in purely material terms by cultivating heaths and bogs, but also by reinforcing Danishness through enlightenment, education and character development, at the same time as accepting the powerlessness of the country in international terms, and adopting an appropriate foreign policy.[2]

These radically oriented historians built these fundamental ideas, in combination with the conviction that the long-term survival of the country depended on the industry and inventiveness of the ordinary Dane, into their trendsetting interpretation of the whole of Danish history. The hidden agenda of their work was to teach the Danes about the disastrous results throughout history of an aggressive foreign policy, and the blessings which would accrue if people simply looked after their own affairs peacefully while Denmark accepted its own insignificance and powerlessness and acted accordingly. Their interpretations of Danish history were correspondingly marked by a pacifist philosophy and a strong emphasis on the value of the efforts of ordinary, hard-working Dane, in contrast to the useless landowning classes and the foolish, parasitic rulers. This attitude was most clearly expressed by one of the leading figures of the next generation within this tradition, Professor Erik Arup, in his history of the Middle Ages, written in 1926. He described the gruelling toil of the Danish peasants to make the land fertile, and showed his historical credo when describing the farmer Bjørn: 'It was men like Bjørn and his sons who in their time made the country rich through their work, and their deeds deserve just as high a place in history as those who went on the crusades against the Wends or the Estonians.' In short, the unobtrusive daily toil of the farmers to make Denmark a fertile country was far more important than all these kings and wars.

In accordance with such basic views, the radical historians presented the history of Denmark in conformity with how it appeared through the lens of the late nineteenth-century midget state. In defiance of the historical facts, they represented it as if Denmark had always been a small state in a European context, and so interpreted political developments from this standpoint. Judged in this way, things went wrong for Denmark every time the ruling politicians had forgotten that Denmark was only a small, insignificant country and had tried to sup with the big boys.

In this interpretation, Denmark's problems started when Christian IV, in a fit of megalomania, cast the country into the Thirty Years War, which resulted in the catastrophic defeat by the Catholic forces at Lutter am Barenberg in Harzen in 1626. This conveniently ignores the fact that at the time Christian IV actually commanded one of the biggest and strongest polities in Northern Europe. From this point on, still according to the radical historians' reading, the long decline set in, due exclusively to a rash and aggressive foreign policy which failed to take into account the postulated insignificance of the country.

The key points in this long, and according to the radical historians' perspective virtually inevitable, tale of ruin, were years such as 1645, when the province of Halland was ceded to the Swedes; 1658, when as a result of a self-inflicted war Denmark lost the rest of the Scanian provinces to its Swedish rival; 1801 and 1807, when Britain, a world power, bombarded the very capital of Denmark into submission and deprived the country of its critical means of defence, the fleet; and 1814, when Norway fell out of the dual monarchy and entered a personal union with Sweden. Then finally came the ultimate catastrophe of 1864, when Denmark lost the duchies of Schleswig and Holstein to Prussia and so was reduced to its smallest ever, cut down to a size which approached the critical minimum for it to exist at all as an independent state.

It was at this absolute nadir that the radical historians perceived the situation and interpreted it as the result of several hundred years of misguided foreign policy built on the politicians' lack of understanding of the weak position and resulting limited freedom of action. The doctrine which, on this basis, they passed on to their contemporaries and successors was that the continued existence of Denmark as an independent nation required the country to act as unobtrusively as possible in the international arena and to refrain from intervening in international politics by, for example, siding with any of the conflicting parties.

The key words in this doctrine, drawn from the disasters of the past, were thus neutrality and pacifism – two concepts which seeped deeply into the Danish self-image through the twentieth century. They formed the basis for the policy of unarmed neutrality which dominated Danish security policy in the first half of the century, and did not really crack until the German occupation of the country under Hitler in 1940, which then led eventually to the country joining NATO in 1949, marking a clear break with this long political tradition. This is also a large part of the explanation of the widespread reluctance of Danes to commit actively to the European Common Market – later the EU – as such engagement with its political exposure and active international conduct would be in contradiction to the historical lesson not to mix with the great and powerful which the radical historians had inculcated.

It was a long way into the second half of the twentieth century before this interpretation of history began to loosen its grip on the mentality of the Danes, and people began to put the whole 'post-1864 syndrome' behind them in favour of a self-image which replaced the inward-looking fear of the outside world with a broader understanding. Yet even on the threshold of the new millennium, there are still clear traces of the older mindset, both in the current political debate and opinions in general.

The historical legacy of the theory which historians and other intellectuals constructed from the catastrophe of 1864 and the long string of misfortunes which preceded it made a deep and indelible impression on the nature of the Danish character in the twentieth century. Foreign observers have often interpreted this as self-containment, self-indulgence and defeatism. For example, Rodney Gallop, First Secretary of the British Legation in Copenhagen, made the following remarks about the general Danish character in a report he sent to the Foreign Office in London in October 1939, shortly after the outbreak of the Second World War:

> A few decades of material prosperity and the ministrations of an over-paternal government seem to have sapped the spirit of a Viking race which can point to 1500 years of vigorous and independent history ... . In Denmark today spiritual values are at a discount, and I doubt whether, if the country were overrun by Germany, the population would oppose even a reasonable degree of passive resistance let alone that desperate fight against overwhelming force which counts all well lost if a nation's soul be saved.[3]

With these words, Gallop drew a censorious picture of a cosseted, defeatist people whose self-respect had been destroyed by a paternalistic government and some years of material progress. Naturally, his views cannot be divorced from the serious situation that his own country was immediately facing. Nonetheless, ignoring the negative prejudices shown in his choice of words, this extract shows the essence of a very widespread attitude which took hold after 1864 and which determined the politics of the country up to the Second World War.

What he missed, or turned a blind eye to, in his enthusiasm to condemn the easygoing Danes was precisely the fact that the attitude he described so cuttingly resulted from hard-earned historical experience interpreted through the radical historical tradition and which, in point of fact, was a method of survival for a tiny nation whose country had become so small that one more mistake in international politics might spell its demise as a state. This position could only invite political caution, and this permanent sense of being poised on the verge of extinction as a state and an independent nation was the element which really held together the self-image and perceptions of the outside world of the radical tradition, and even its historical interpretations. The last remains of this fear only really disappeared with the end of Communism in 1989. Significantly, it was also from this point that the radical tradition started to make way for a different and more outward-looking mode of seeing the world and Denmark's place in it.

THE 'FARMERS' APPROACH'

The other great interpretation of history which has left a deep mark on Danish mentality is, as mentioned at the start of this chapter, what is called the 'farmers' line'.[4] In its power and interpretative impact, this particular interpretation bears comparison with the 'Whig interpretation of British history', so incisively described in the well-known work of 1931 by the philosopher Herbert Butterfield. Naturally enough, it originated in the agrarian reforms of the end of the eighteenth century and slowly developed through the nineteenth century to become a coherent interpretation of the main lines of development in more recent Danish history and the principal driving forces within it.

This interpretation started from the point when the peasants – the rural middle classes – were granted their independence through the reforms, and their gradual seizure of economic and political power in the following century. The nature of this interpretation is to place Danish rural society, represented by these independent farmers, at the centre of the understanding of Danish history as a whole, and push the history of all other groups into the wings. Thus, the history of Denmark in the nineteenth century became synonymous with the history of the victorious farming class, while the contributions of estate owners, agricultural labourers, urban traders and mariners were seen as insignificant.

In the later years of absolutism, a loose coalition of agrarian historians, urban nationalist liberal intellectuals and aggressively egalitarian thinkers developed this into a coherent image of Danish society, one-sidedly focused on the middle-class farmers and the liberal ideology which they espoused. Supported by the co-operative movement, a view of Denmark as an agricultural country and the Danes as a nation of farmers gradually took hold. This lasted well into the twentieth century, decades after Denmark had actually changed into an industrial nation. Just as the radical historical tradition had a critical influence on how Danes perceived the world, this 'farmers' line' created a self-image amongst the Danes as being a nation of equal farmers, who through their own hard labour on the ancestral soil had managed to get along quite nicely without anybody's help.

It would be a very interesting thought experiment to imagine what it would have meant for the self-image of the Danes, in terms of extroversion and openness, had the seafarers and fishermen been allowed to set the agenda for the interpretation of history, as might well be considered natural for a country with such extensive coastlines and extensive maritime activity. Had this been the case, the Danish character would certainly be closer to that of the British or Dutch. Instead, the ideological dominance of the independent farmers during the nineteenth century and the traumatic experience of the crushing defeat in 1864 determined the formation of the collective mentality, defining the society as agricultural and the country as a trivial midget state with no international role to play. Thus, the contours of the Danishness which prevailed through most of the twentieth century were drawn. However, no concept ever remains static, not even that of Danishness. The remainder of this concluding chapter will thus be dedicated to an attempt to define what is particularly Danish about the Danes from a longer historical perspective.

THE MULTINATIONAL STATE AND DANISHNESS

Recent research in Britain has employed the term 'Britishness' to describe the overarching feeling of identity which is assumed to unite the English, Scots, Welsh and Northern Irish in one entity – the British – despite the old internal boundaries of the United Kingdom. This overall common identification is generally considered to have arisen during the Reformation, as part of the mutual struggle against the Catholic Church, and then to have been reinforced when Britain was the hub of a worldwide empire, the management of which brought the diverse elements closer together and slowly dissolved their internal differences. Extending this argument, many people see the collapse of the Empire, with its common political and administrative burdens and obligations, as part of the reason for the re-emergence of the old identities – English, Scottish and Welsh – in the second half of the twentieth century, and the diminution of the concept of 'Britishness'.[5]

In many ways, similar crises of identity can be found in Danish history, even though there are many differences, including the obvious one that the Oldenborg state was never the centre of an empire on the scale of that of Britain. The region we call Denmark today, as explained, was actually part of a large multinational state up until 1864, called the Oldenborg Monarchy, the dual monarchy or the Union, in which each part had its own linguistic, cultural and national identity. The only element which actually united this complicated and diverse state was the common monarchy, which attempted to overcome the regional differences and become the overall object of identification for all subjects, whether they were fishermen in northern Norway, merchants in Altona or farmers on Zealand. It is pretty much self-evident that the state, faced with these circumstances, had to attempt to reinforce the 'supranational' bonds of loyalty and dampen regional feelings and movements which could lead to division or separatism. In this way, the actual political agenda was not dissimilar from that of promoting the concept of 'Britishness'.[6]

It is clear that the circumstances for creating this special collective Danish identity were not especially propitious – in any case not in the sixteenth and seventeenth centuries, when the state's grip on power and opinion formation was fixed and undiminished, and there was no middle class able to dictate the agenda. The only unifying element in shaping public opinion – the Church – was under the exclusive control of the state. Also, at least until 1660, the only common organ was the state council and the upper crust of the Danish nobility, which, by virtue not least of their traditional military function, developed a kind of patriotism, specifically attached to the Danish territories. The quotation from Lord Admiral Herluf Trolle in 1565 in Chapter 3 serves to demonstrate this. The council also came to regard itself as representing special Danish interests, which was particularly clear with their stubborn resistance to the wishes of Christian IV, first to wage war against Sweden and then to enter the Thirty Years War. In both instances, the council emphasised that war was against the interests of Denmark, which had no quarrel with the German emperor. In both cases, the king replied that war would serve the interests of the larger state, which he was charged with protecting, whereafter he imposed his plans, in the first instance by threatening to declare war in his capacity as Duke of Holstein and in the second to follow up on this threat, which produced exactly the consequences feared, especially for the Danish part of the entire kingdom.

If there was any sense at all in talking of a particularly Danish patriotism fostered by one form or another of solidarity linked to the territory and its inhabitants, then it was the native nobles, and especially the higher stratum of this nobility, who carried it. The very small number of nobles lived a life secluded from that of the vast majority of the population. Also, under the influence of the Renaissance, their cultural ideals became ever more cosmopolitan. Taking these two factors into account, the most that could be said of the Danishness of this group is that it took a somewhat elitist form, and was not rooted in the population at large, who mainly felt linked to their immediate local communities, and hardly took the time to think about whether, beyond being the humble subjects of the king and members of the collectives in the town and country, they were Danish in some higher abstract way.

The first time there was any sign of real efforts to form a special mutual Danish identity came in the decades after the change of the regime in 1660, when the most important frame of reference became the language and the old noble elite was replaced by civil servants of largely middle-class origins. It was probably also significant that at this time the Swedish government was in full swing with a very determined campaign to make the conquered Scanian provinces truly Swedish. The trend in Denmark could be seen as a reaction to this and an attempt to find a new common frame of reference after the territorial amputation following the Karl Gustav Wars.

Arne Magnussen received support from the government to visit Iceland, the country where he was born, to extensively and systematically collect old Nordic manuscripts. He unearthed a rich and previously disregarded source material for the Icelandic sagas, which cast light on the first origins of Danishness. A large part of this collection of manuscripts was returned to Iceland at the end of the 1960s and is now housed in Reykjavik. In addition, work on a comprehensive historical topography of Denmark was set in motion, using material collected from all corners of the country; and philologists and other men of letters energetically threw themselves into the task of normalising the mother tongue, using the dialect of Zealand as the basis. In this period, a large number of grammar primers and spelling dictionaries were published. The senior civil servant Matthias Moth devoted all his spare time to collecting material for a major dictionary of the Danish language. Although he never completed his life's work, he did produce no fewer than 60 large folios. The poetic masterpieces of the time were written by Bishop Thomas Kingo (1634–1703) – incidentally, a descendant of a Scottish immigrant – who wrote a large number of poems and hymns in the sonorous baroque Danish style then in vogue. Kingo's work brought Danish vernacular psalmody to a peak which would not be surpassed until the arrival of N. F. S. Grundtvig a good hundred years later.

All these initiatives, along with similar, slightly later developments in the area of national historiography, where the leading name was the Enlightenment philosopher, playwright and historian Ludvig Holberg (1684–1754), clearly point to a concerted attempt to give Danishness, and especially the language, a sufficient solidity, shape and content for it to serve as the basis for a feeling of solidarity throughout Danish territory. This seems at least to have been the intention, although in practice the effect was limited to the literate section of the Danish population, which at the time was of a rather modest size. These many signs of a dawning of a common feeling of Danishness which appeared in the decades around 1700 can certainly be attributed to the heightened general sense of crisis following on both the defeat in the Swedish Wars, and the reorganisation of the state in 1660 which created a comprehensive transformation within the Danish elite.

DANISHNESS AND ABSOLUTISM

However, it is worth emphasising that the whole undertaking could not move forward unless it was approved and supported by the absolutist regime itself. Its objective in supporting this was hardly motivated by national politics, but should rather be interpreted as an attempt to impose the order, uniformity and collectivism which was part of the very nature of the absolutist system itself on the cultural area too. As, according to absolutist ideology, the king was effectively considered as the sole owner of the entire territory over which he ruled, after 1660 there was in principle no difference between the position of Norway, Denmark or Schleswig in the monarchy. It was therefore no longer necessary to balance the special interests of the different parts of the kingdom, and the regime could, without any serious risk, set in motion and support a harmonisation of culture throughout the territory on the basis of the dominant Danish element. So perhaps, in point of fact, these numerous initiatives were not so much an expression of a blossoming sense of Danishness growing from below as a large-scale imperialist cultural offensive by the government to create a more uniform absolutist state.

If this statement holds water – and in the light of the numerous efforts already mentioned to achieve uniformity in the administrative, religious and legal spheres, there is much to suggest it does – then it must also be added that the initiative was living on borrowed time. Any such enforced orthodoxy could only have any prospects of success in a pre-national social structure, and in a society without an articulate middle-class public in the form of media which could give room for perceptions other than those of the government. Denmark, along with other Western European countries, saw the emergence of just such a middle-class public from the middle of the eighteenth century. With it, the role of the absolutist regime in the politics of nationality and culture shifted from being proactive and setting the agenda to being defensive and reactive.

It was apparent that the public debate during the course of the second half of the eighteenth century came under the influence of the dawning nationalism of Europe and turned more and more towards a discussion of the relationship between the Danish, German and Norwegian sections of the population of the Oldenborg state. At critical junctures, this discussion threatened to run out of control and pit the different groups of the population against each other, with the implosion of the state itself as a possible consequence. The short-lived rule of Struensee's regime, 1770–2, gave especial rise to animosity, as many people saw it as almost akin to the German-speaking section of the population annexing the power of the state. Struensee, in keeping with the Enlightenment doctrine of the freedom of opinion, totally abolished censorship, which resulted in a deluge of public criticism and lampoons directed at the 'Germans'. The government had to tread carefully in this critical situation to avoid the state disintegrating into its linguistic and cultural components.

In 1776 it passed a law on nationality, the key provision of which was that only those born within the borders of the state could hold public office. This, of course, excluded the severely rebuked Germans, who had been born south of the border. On the other hand, the law also stated that all citizens could hold government posts, irrespective of whether they spoke German, Danish or Norwegian. This firmly established the equality in principle of all parts of the realm. However, to pre-empt any dissatisfaction on the part of the Danish population, the government simultaneously launched a grand propaganda offensive consisting of huge celebrations in the larger Danish towns, where it was made very plain time and again that the law was actually a huge triumph for Danishness. The Royal Copenhagen Porcelain Manufactory also produced a figure which allegorically symbolised the unity of the realm, and one of the biggest men-of-war was christened *Indfødsretten* – 'the nationality law'.

The government won various advantages through this trick. First, it averted the threatened internal split and turned it into patriotic enthusiasm. Second, through its adroit handling of the issue it managed to present its legitimising of the patriotic identity as a gift to the inhabitants at a time when the shift of emphasis from subjects to citizens and from a monarchy to a state was creating problems in many other places. Perhaps most importantly in this situation, the government rammed home the message in a way that no one could fail to understand that the fatherland was synonymous with the whole realm and that the king and his government personified both.

With this move, the monarchy won over the political loyalty of the citizenry towards absolutism for a long time to come and kept a tight rein on the development of the national identity. In addition it succeeded in neutralising the tensions between the groups of the population in this multilingual and multinational united monarchy. These were significant victories which bore clear witness to the remarkable ability of the late absolutists to negotiate skilfully through a minefield – a feat which the government repeated some years later in regard to land reform, as described previously. To drive the point fully home, the next year the government commissioned the author and civil servant Ove Malling to publish a work entitled *Great and Good Deeds of the Danes, Norwegians and Holsteiners*, which was considered an exemplary textbook for use in the grammar schools, to show how outstanding and deserving citizens of the entire realm had contributed to the well-being of the absolutist state through their diligence, resourcefulness and patriotism. The examples were very carefully chosen to cover all the groups within the population, and the message could not be misunderstood: linguistic affiliations were of minor importance; what mattered was to be a useful citizen of the entire realm. Doing this fulfilled the patriotic duty owed to king and country.

This delicate balance between patriotism to the whole kingdom, which can in many respects bear comparison with the 'Britishness' discussed above, and the nascent nationalist movements inspired by the French Revolution and the waves of German Romanticism was successfully maintained until it was finally swept away in the storms of the Napoleonic Wars. The British assaults on Copenhagen in 1801 and 1807 and the subsequent naval war triggered a strong feeling of Danish nationalism, which was reinforced by the loss of Norway in 1814. It was no accident that during this time Danish poets and authors produced a stream of important works in which they consciously turned their backs on the current hardships and focused on a distant, golden age. The national bard of the era, Adam Oehlenschläger (1779–1850), celebrated heroic Nordic antiquity in a number of grandiose plays; N. F. S. Grundtvig wrote his trailblazing works on

Nordic mythology, while the hymnodist B. S. Ingemann (1789–1862) became the most widely read author of the time with his numerous novels, taking inspiration from Walter Scott and based on motifs from the Danish Middle Ages. The underlying purpose of the hectic literary activity during these years of turmoil was to convince the Danes that despite the crises and setbacks of the moment they still had a role to play as a nation with a valuable cultural heritage. This was also the main theme in the deluge of patriotic songs that flowed from the pens of such authors as Grundtvig and Hans Christian Andersen. These many manifestations of budding literary nationalism together served to paint a new popular picture of Denmark, and left deep traces on the subsequent Danish self-image.

The national anger was not just levelled at the British, whose actions had forced the country into an impossible situation, but also at the absolutist regime that had proved itself incapable of averting the catastrophe and was equally unable to prevent the long-term effects, which sank the country into hardship and poverty.

In the lean years after the war, the critics of the system assembled into two camps, inspired by the two large and powerful currents stemming from the French Revolution: nationalism and political liberalism. The nationalists' aim was to create such a strong identity between the nation and the state that they were indivisible, at the expense of the multi-national absolutist united monarchy. The liberals, on the other hand, saw their objective as democracy, which equally would lead to the end of absolutist government. The reason that these two movements made only limited progress in the 20 years following the end of the war was that they found it very difficult to work together, even though their objective, a change of the system, was identical. The problem was, in brief, that the nationalists were not liberals, but mainly conservatives in the German Romantic style, and that the liberals were not nationalists in the Romantic sense of the word, but more internationalists who were simply using nationalist arguments as a vehicle to achieve emancipation and democracy.

It was not until the 1830s that the two camps combined in a powerful national liberal movement headed by the middle-class intellectuals of Copenhagen. From this moment the days of absolutism were numbered, as were those of the Danish–German state. The political agenda was now being set by the Danish National Liberals, who defined what being a citizen of Denmark actually meant. This resulted in the changes of 1848 and the new democracy, dominated by the National Liberals.

The new bearers of Danish identity were the intellectual middle classes, mainly in the capital, and their perception of Danishness was largely dictated by the difficulties between the Germans and Danes in the duchies. Thus from their perspective Danishness was more or less the opposite of Germanness, and represented all the positive values, while Germanness was not only negative, but also menacing. This national liberal mode of defining Danishness in contrast to Germanness survived for a long time, and continues in a diluted form even today, fuelled by the bitter experiences of the Nazi era as well as the traumatic defeat in 1864 at the hands of Bismarck's Germany. It was only in the twentieth century that the torch of Danishness passed from the middle classes to the farmers and then in turn to the social democratic working class.

THE 1864 SYNDROME AND DANISHNESS

As already emphasised at the start of this chapter, a great deal of modern Danish identity – of what it means to be Danish – was formed in the years after the defeat of 1864. The atmosphere of easygoing arrogance which followed the partial Danish victory in the Schleswig-Holstein uprisings in 1848–50 was abruptly shattered and replaced by a crushing defeatism and fear of disaster. Just how deep the despair was is graphically illustrated by the decision of D. G. Monrad, the Prime Minister who had led the government during the war, to go into immediate voluntary exile. He emigrated with his family to New Zealand, where he tried out life as a settler, before returning home in 1869 to become a clergyman.

The immediate reaction to the defeat was a profound doubt as to how far Denmark would be able to survive this dismemberment of the state. This was followed by a demonisation of the Germans and everything German, as they were the cause of the downfall of the country, with a corresponding increase in enthusiasm for anything pan-Scandinavian or English. The third phase was a certain defiant common will to carry the remains of the realm safely through the trials it faced. This will to survive was pithily formulated in 1872 by the poet H. P. Holst, who penned the following words for a medal struck for an industrial exhibition:

> Every loss can find a recompense again!
> Each outward loss must turn to inner gain!

This has become something of a motto representing the mood of the time.

After the humiliating defeat of 1864 and Bismarck's equally convincing victory over the France of Napoleon III in 1871, it was clear that there could be no hope of revenge. For many years following this, Denmark's security policy was almost exclusively dictated by the country's position as a tiny neighbour to the new united Germany. So attention turned inwards, and the struggle to define a new national identity under the new reduced circumstances started.

War and adversity had effectively prepared the ground for an outburst of nationalist feeling. Before the war this had been the preserve of a relatively small, tightly knit elite, but through the war and its sacrifices, it spread to the public at large, many of whom had lost their conscripted husbands and sons to the war. Under these circumstances, very few people could see any positive side to the defeat. One who could, however, was the old leader of the National Liberals, Orla Lehmann. Very shortly after the war he made a number of speeches drawing attention to the fact that as things had turned out, Denmark had become an example of something unique. In its reduced condition it now had a virtually total correspondence of the people, the nation and the state. Thus, through hardship and territorial losses – albeit unforeseen and unwilling – almost ideal conditions had been created for the development of a common national identity, an opportunity which simply could not have existed in the old two-nation state. The only remaining question was just what form this identity was to take.

In the process of answering this question, over the next decades Denmark became the stage for a discourse which at times turned bitter, and which was closely interwoven with the constitutional struggle and the rapid modernisation of production previously described. For the most part, there were four factions in this discourse.[7] The first was Conservative Denmark, represented by the old landowners and the remains of the right wing of the National Liberal Party. Then there were the Grundtvigians, the right wing of the liberal party *Venstre*. The third group was the left wing of the same party, which subsequently formed the party *Det radikale Venstre* in alliance with the remains of the left wing of the National Liberal Party, who were mainly Copenhagen intellectuals. The fourth faction consisted of socialists with their origins in the rapidly growing working class. Each of these four factions asserted their own perception of what it meant to be Danish. A key issue in this dispute was the relationship to Germany and the question of defence: to what extent Denmark could defend itself militarily in the new circumstances.

The Conservatives quickly associated Danishness with the will to defend the country. They had no delusions about any peaceful intentions on the part of the new Germany. Under the firm leadership of Prime Minister J. B. S. Estrup, they made defence, and especially the fortification of Copenhagen, their leading and most passionate cause. In their campaign, agreement on the issue of defence became the very touchstone of Danishness. Anyone who opposed a strong line on defence and especially the fortification of Copenhagen had, in their view, no claim to be a true Dane. This conservative nationalism attached itself to the flag, the king and the state, as the question at issue was defence through military power. For them the constitutional struggles in the 1880s and 1890s were a matter of nationality, where Danishness, defence and government power were combined in a single higher entity. As already recounted, they lost this struggle as part of the great political agreement with *Venstre* in 1894, after which the role of the state-oriented National Conservatives in setting the agenda was largely played out.

That part of the liberal party *Venstre* which originated in the flourishing Grundtvigian Folk High School movement and the emergent co-operative movement considered the concept 'the self-determination of the people' as being synonymous with true Danishness, in clear opposition to the nationalism of the conservatives, where the focus was on the king and the state, all too reminiscent for the Grundtvigians of Bismarck's model of nationalism in Germany. The key issue for them was the requirement for popular parliamentarianism, as a popularly elected assembly was for them the most genuine expression of the right to self-determination of the Danish people.

By far the majority of this group had affiliations with the Folk High School movement or else had studied at a Folk High School in their youth. While there, they had sung innumerable patriotic songs, many of them written by Grundtvig himself. This treasury of song was collected in the *Folk High School Songbook*, first published in 1894, which quickly became an icon in itself for the perceptions of the 'high school liberal' concept of Danishness. They had also learned that the common people – the wholesome and uncorrupted farmers – were the true backbone of the country and the group on which the future of the country would be built. From the Folk High Schools they also brought the particularly Grundtvigian view that social responsibility, Christianity and national identity were inextricably linked in a higher entity – that of Danishness. Carrying this ballast, they entertained no doubt that they were the true torch-bearers of Danishness and as such had a self-evident claim to power. It was this conviction that they spoke for real Danishness and were fighting the good fight that gave them the zeal and energy to take up the constitutional battle against the ruling right-wing regime – a battle they won with the change of the regime in 1901, which actually accepted their view of Danishness as the correct one, at least for a time.

However, there were two circumstances which meant that their ideological victory was not complete and that they subsequently had to give some ground. One was the issue of defence, on which they found it hard to make a decision. In their heart of hearts they agreed with the Conservatives that military defence was essential to protect the nation, but they also feared that the establishment of too powerful a military would strengthen the government so much that the freedom of the people would be endangered. So, instead, they put their faith in the spiritual strength of the people and supported a popular defence based on general conscription – a solution which could hardly be considered appropriate in scale to the threat posed by Germany. The second factor was their partisan definition of the rural middle class – the prosperous farmers – as the only legitimate carriers of Danishness. In this, they excluded two other large groups of the population from the company of true Danes, namely the smallholders and the agricultural labourers – not to mention the quickly growing class of industrial workers. Seen this way, the concept of Danishness espoused by the Grundtvigian liberals was to some extent as exclusive as that of the Conservatives.

THE PREVAILING IDENTITY

These uncertainties and difficulties eventually led to the left wing of the party splitting off and significantly choosing the name 'European *Venstre*', with Viggo Hørup (1841–1902), a journalist and outstanding political debater, as the leading figure. This faction was the fore-runner of *Det radikale Venstre*, which was founded as an independent political party in 1905. For Hørup and his supporters the Schleswigian Wars and their tragic outcome were not in any way an expression of inner or outward betrayal, as *Højre* and the Grundtvigians were inclined to assert. On the contrary, they were an expression of a lack of realism in Danish National Romantic circles. Instead, it was a question of 'the European imperative', where the weak had to give way to the strong. The way to ensure the continued survival of Denmark was therefore to forget all the nationalist attitudes and cravings for revenge which had dominated the debate thus far, and instead to make a realistic assessment of Denmark's true position and future potential in the existing international political situation.

On the literary front the same idea was powerfully expressed by the literary critic and academic Georg Brandes (1842–1927). His magnum opus, *Hovedstrømninger i det 19de Aarhundredes Litteratur* ('Main Currents in Nineteenth-Century Literature', published 1872–90), was not just a merciless revolt against self-sufficient Romantic Danish nationalism, but also a profound critique of civilisation which attracted a great deal of attention throughout Europe, especially amongst intellectuals. This and some of his other works were translated into ten languages and made Brandes the most internationally famous Dane around the turn of the century. He remained one of the most influential critics in the intellectual Parnassus. Viggo Hørup and his followers were closely linked to Brandes's circle.[8]

Hørup and his circle were, in other words, trying to persuade the people to abandon all the illusions which had set the tone for the debate, and look reality in the face. The reality was that Denmark could not defend itself by military means. As a result, this wing of *Venstre* adopted a clear anti-militarist approach and called for complete disarmament. Such a programme could easily be interpreted as unpatriotic, and indeed many people perceived it as such. Yet even though Hørup and his sympathisers were indeed keenly anti-militarist, they cannot truly be described as unpatriotic or even as a-national, as became very clear when in one of his numerous speeches he explained what was essential from a Danish viewpoint with regard to Germany:

> namely peace, international neighbourliness. There must be no shadow of a doubt that we are a trustworthy neighbour to Greater Germany, with no reservations or back-stabbing in any circumstance. ... Yet this policy is not the fruit of any special love of Germany or infatuation with the state and nature of Germany; it is dictated by a love of Denmark. Self preservation obliges us to take this position, not for the sake of Germany, but for our own.[9]

The lack of illusions expressed here was very closely echoed in observations made much later by Erik Scavenius, Prime Minister and Foreign Minister during the Second World War, who has been mentioned before and was a disciple of Hørup. The last part of the quotation, in particular, clearly underlines the fact that Danishness and the survival of Denmark were of central concern in this approach. The Danishness which Hørup, and later *Det radikale Venstre*, championed was based on an inner mental preparedness and a genuine democratic feeling of nationality, carried by free and enlightened citizens from all walks of society without excluding any particular group from the community of the nation. Because of this all-embracing concept of Danishness, including everyone irrespective of condition or calling, Hørup and his supporters appealed especially to the previously marginalised smallholders and workers in an attempt to involve them in the solidarity of the nation and involve them in the mental preparedness which they considered to be the only way to ensure the survival of Denmark in the longer term. In other words, this was a perception of Danishness with clear socio-political overtones, directly pointing the way to the subsequent close identification of the welfare society and the nation state of Denmark in the twentieth century.

The Social Democrats' perception of the special Danish nation actually ended up in the same place, although it had a very different starting point. The socialist workers' movement which was established in Denmark in 1871 was in its very origins anti-nationalist and international, in keeping with Marx's doctrine that workers had no fatherland. From the very start, this meant that it was accused of being 'un-Danish'. This appeared to be confirmed when the Danish social-ists encouraged the pro-Danish workers in Schleswig to vote for the German Social Democratic candidate in the German Parliamentary elections of 1872, in preference to a Danish national. The request created an enormous public outcry and was interpreted as conclusive evidence of the absence of any patriotism amongst the socialists. The critics, though, overlooked the fact that the Social Democratic candi-date had included a promise in his manifesto that he would support the right of the northern Schleswigians to self-determination, in other words, the opportunity for a peaceful reversion to Denmark. So this, indeed, was very far from being unpatriotic.

The socialist workers' movement slowly and steadily replaced their international approach with a more national angle, and so moved very close to the position of Hørup and *Det radikale Venstre*. Immediately after 1900, the leading Social Democrats decided that there was in fact no contradiction between internationalism and nationalism, but that these were complementary dimensions of the same struggle against capitalism, and in no way meant that workers had to love their country any less than anyone else. The leading ideologist of the party, Gustav Bang (1871–1915) – and, incidentally, married to Nina Bang (1866–1928), a leading social democratic politician who in 1924 became the first female minister in the world – expressed this sentiment as the fact that the Social Democrats wished to win back patriotism from the middle classes and purge it of militarism, royalism and stereotypical hostile images and enrich it with democratic and social values. He nonetheless maintained that a worker is not first and foremost born Danish. He is born a worker. Being Danish is something that has to be acquired. For him, social identity was primary, nationality secondary, and this would remain the case until the two identities could be united in the final goal of a socialist Denmark. As the Social Democrats worked towards this socialist goal, in reality they adopted a real feeling of nationality where the social and the national combined in a greater entity.

This absolute connection of the social and national projects was fundamentally very similar to the perception of *Det radikale Venstre* and was given a push forward when the events of the First World War dealt a deathblow to internationalism. The debate between the four approaches to the real nature of Danishness outlined here raged from the defeat of 1864 to the outbreak of the First World War. Finally, it was the latter two views, those of *Det radikale Venstre* and the Social Democrats, which won the day, although, notably, with the addition of some Grundtvigian elements. Today, the *Folk High School Songbook* is much more common than the *Workers' Songbook*.

The old conservative perception of Danishness slid into a torpor approaching oblivion, and significantly enough, the old party of the right, *Højre*, changed its name in 1915 to the Danish Conservative People's Party when the privileged voting rights of the landowners were abolished by the constitutional reform of the same year. The party introduced a socio-political programme as part of its working basis that in most respects followed the line of the victorious concept of the equivalence of social responsibility and Danishness. Thus, after decades of bitter struggle and heated debate, a national consensus was finally formed which paved the way for the project which was to become the most important rallying-point of Danishness and its most striking manifestation in the twentieth century – the all-inclusive and all-embracing welfare state.

Paradoxically enough, the very icon of consensus-based Danishness, the welfare society, was the result of the traumatic defeat in 1864 and the deep popular and national divisions which followed in the succeeding decades. Quite what form Danishness in that sense would have taken without this trauma is impossible to say. It is fairly certain, though, that it would have taken a very different shape. Modern Danish identity in all its facets would be inconceivable without the 1864 defeat. Yet while this is without any doubt an essential part of the explanation of the nature of modern Denmark and its inhabitants, it is not exhaustive or complete. Perhaps, therefore, to provide a more complete explanation, it would be useful in moving to the conclusion of this account, to take a longer time perspective in examining the questions which have been posed in the previous chapters.

PERCEPTIONS OF NATIONALISM

The dominant trends in modern research into nationality suggest that an essential precondition for the development of a collective national identity is the existence of a middle class able to formulate and present such a common identity. Such a class first truly emerged in Europe, and Denmark, around the middle of the eighteenth century. The next element, according to that part of the study of nationalism which can be described as modernist, was a widespread agreement to link the development of nationalism with what has been called the 'dual revolution' around 1800, meaning the rise of large-scale popular move-ments and the Industrial Revolution, and the subsequent growth of civil democracy and the corresponding growth of the middle-class public. Most scholars thus place the first inklings of a feeling of nationalism in modern terms as occurring in the first half of the nineteenth century. This is to say that the development of a collective national identity is normally considered to be a modern phenomenon, and perhaps also simply a product of modernisation.[10]

In complete concordance with this timing, Danish scholars usually place the emergence of a specific collective feeling of Danishness at the end of the eighteenth century. They believe that they can identify clear indicators of this development from the 1770s, with the Nationality Law of 1776 as the turning point, although as explained, this was more an expression of a patriotism to the united monarchy than a specifically Danish nationalism.

Some are more specific and date the development of the Danish nation state to around the time of the First Schleswigian War, 1848–50. They maintain that participating in this was particularly what made Danes Danish. As the infantrymen sang specially written patriotic battle songs as they marched to face the common foe – the Germans – they became aware for the first time that they were not just farmhands from Zealand, Fyn or Jutland, but Danes fighting a common enemy in a common cause.

There is thus broad agreement amongst Danish historians that the Danish nation state came into being in the first half of the nineteenth century, and that the inhabitants of the country became aware of themselves as being Danish at the same time. To this, the special characteristics which, as described, came to signal Danishness in the years after the defeat of 1864 must be added. No further comment on this will be made here. Instead, there will be an attempt to add an extra dimension to this understanding, starting from Sir James Mellon's tribal thesis outlined at the very start of this book.

The basis of the argument is a feeling that the time frame stated above for the emergence of modern Danishness is too restricted in some respects. In point of fact, it is exclusively based on the concept of nationalism adopted by the modernistic school, and is based on the 'them against us' perception as the key driving force. In the first instance, this was indignation at the overrunning of Copenhagen in 1801 and 1807 by the English and their rape of the navy – the pride and joy of booming Denmark as well as its very means of support. The second instance was the almost permanent antagonism towards Germany (and a baby-brother complex).

Certainly, these have a significant explanatory value, but not enough to explain the particular modern Danish self-perception and way of life which Sir James Mellon thought so typical – the tribal nature of the Danes. The type of Danishness which developed through the nineteenth century was a kind of reflected Danishness, which arose as a contrasting image to the enemies from outside. Figuratively speaking, it grew up in the hail of shells which rained down on Copenhagen and in the trenches during the Schleswigian Wars. It was a Danishness with clear front lines and a no less clear concept of the enemy.

The particularly Danish solidarity based on a tribal feeling which Sir James – clearly not uninfluenced by Grundtvigian ideas and the consensus approach of the Social Democrats and the Social Liberals – described, could perhaps be better compared to a campfire. All the members of the company assemble shoulder to shoulder around it, with their backs to the darkness outside the circle of light from the fire, and warm themselves with feelings of security and comradeship and the heat from the large communal bonfire. Such companionship is by its very nature not directed against any specific external enemy, but an attempt at common protection against all the unknown powers lying out in the darkness which might threaten the safety and unity of the community. There is no sense of an 'us and you' feeling, but of an introverted 'us–us' mentality. Such a postulated special 'campfire character' in Danish behaviour and ways of treating each other cannot easily be explained by the modernistic theories of nationalism and the related time frame for the emergence of Danishness in the first half of the nineteenth century.

In addition, the current schematics of nationalism have of necessity had to ignore a number of other indicators of the start of the development of a specific sense of Danishness. This applies to the phenomena already described at the end of the seventeenth century in the wake of the defeat by Sweden and the changes in the political system, which together suggest that something of an identity was already starting to ferment even then. Modern theories of nationalism are unable to accommodate these older traits, as they take their starting point from the French Revolution and the process of industrialisation. What is called the primordialist school of studies into nationalism, whose leading light is the British sociologist Anthony D. Smith, can, however, account for these traits.[11] Adherents of this school do not actually reject the conclusions of the modernists that modern nations are the result of the processes which mainly came to a head in the century after the French Revolution. They do, however, point out that these modern nations were very often modelled on previously existing, much older communities, which Smith calls *ethnies*.

These *ethnies*, according to Smith, are marked out by having a collective name, a myth of a common descent, an existing and normative history, a distinctive culture, a link to a particular territory and more or less developed forms of mutual solidarity. The primordialists also state that the study of these older communities can justifiably be included in forming the most satisfactory picture of the modern nations. This also heightens the awareness of the innate differences of modern nations. There are thus nations which have a historical starting point in the very process of building a nation itself, such as Brazil and the USA, which can accommodate very wide differences within their own boundaries. Then there are nations which have arisen on the basis of a single *ethnie* of considerable antiquity – such as Denmark after 1864 and Iceland – which cannot tolerate such wide differences. Between these two extremes lie a large number of mixed forms.

WHEN DID THE DANES BECOME DANISH?

Bringing this extended definition of a nation and the consequently extended time frame into the discussion of when the Danes became Danish, the question itself can be slightly reformulated – and the answer is then somewhat different to that of the modernists. Instead of asking when the Danes became Danish in contrast to the bordering Germans, and as opposed to being from Zealand, Fyn or Jutland, the question could be asked as to the nature of the older community – *ethnie*, to use Smith's terminology – which created the foundations for the twentieth-century Danish welfare model that, as stated before, can with good reason be described as the fulfilment of the Danish utopia.

The Danish welfare system differs in many ways from that of other countries, ignoring for the moment the other Nordic countries, which have adopted a rather similar welfare policy. These differences are the high level of general solidarity with the weaker sections of society and the universal nature, expressed by the fact that the welfare services are based on a legal principle and not means-testing and are financed through taxation. In this way, the system is a concrete expression of a concern for all the members of the community, which, according to Sir James Mellon, is one of the significant hallmarks of the Danish tribe. The Danish welfare system is virtually tailored to a broad political consensus, indeed this is also a prerequisite for its existence, and it strives to create uniformity and averageness, innate solidarity, exclusivity in regard to the outside world, and so on. In short, all the characteristics that Sir James identifies as typically tribal and which in current public debate are often described as 'the special Danish values'. All in all, therefore, the system reflects all the traits which constitute Danish society as a special community, whether one chooses to call it a nation or a tribe.

The postwar Danish welfare state was certainly the fulfilment of an old social democratic dream. But when all is said and done, it was a huge, common, political project which required – and still requires – wide political and popular support. Helped on its way by a strong and efficient state, it grew straight out of an agrarian society marked by shortage, where economic and social distress were everyday risks. It is here that a large part of the explanation for its special construction and final nature lies. What type of historical community lies behind the Danish welfare model which in the course of time has become synonymous with Danishness? Leaving out all the interim accounts presented in the previous chapters, the answer is that it is the ancient village community from the time prior to the agrarian reforms at the end of the eighteenth century.

In these village communities we find exactly the same exclusion of the outside world, the same duty towards the whole group and its members, the same need for innate solidarity, the same awareness of the necessity of being able to discuss issues without destructive confrontations and the same faith that the authorities at any given time – whether the church, the landowners or the state – would intervene and sort things out if everything went completely wrong. The village communities were social constructs and production collectives which arose to ensure their members the best possible chances of survival in a subsistence economy, exactly in the same way as the modern Danish welfare society had its origins in the experience of an economy of scarcity. The assertion here therefore is that the element which is first and foremost associated with being Danish – being a part of the welfare society – can to a great extent be understood as a modern manifestation and scaling up to a national version of a much older group – or *ethnie*, to use Anthony D. Smith's expression – composed of the old village collectives. Their origins go way back into the mists of the Middle Ages.

Yet an aggregation of village collectives in the flat, arable land of Denmark does not in itself constitute a nation. Rather the opposite, in fact, as the closed communities first and foremost exhibited internal solidarity, and only took any notice of others when forced to do so. True nation-building also requires the existence of a strong central power to take care of all the tasks which lie outside the scope of the collective, such as protection against threats from both within and without, care for those who do not belong to collectives, and so on. This starts to look like a description of Denmark in 1536, when the secular state took over the finely woven ecclesiastical net and the Church's function of *caritas* as part of the Reformation. From this very moment the comprehensive and long-lasting social disciplining of the king's subjects, which turned them into Danes, began.

The introduction of the absolutist system in 1660 and its deliberate striving towards uniformity and transparency in every sphere of its authority also produced the preconditions of power to create a state of law which would regulate people's behaviour towards each other and the state with a common purpose. This happened with the Danish Law in 1683. A central element of this, as described, legally enshrined the Danish model of contracts, that is, that the state would not interfere in agreements between two parties and that a verbal contract was just as binding as one in writing. This survival of the way in which things were done in the village collectives later also formed the basis for the modern Danish labour-market legislation, which left as much as possible to the parties involved themselves and continues to be an important condition for calm in the labour market, and so for the efficiency of the Danish welfare model.

The old agricultural collectives were dissolved in connection with the land reforms at the end of the eighteenth century, and so the self-managing village communities disappeared also. A few decades later the old *ethnie* – to continue with Smith's term – were no more than a legend. It was at this critical moment that Grundtvig appeared on the scene. In the rather hazy transition from absolutism to democracy in the 1830s and 1840s and precisely as a preliminary to the coming change to a democratic form of government, he formulated his thoughts with ever greater force and clarity, identifying *folkelighed* as the very fulcrum of the new democratic society. Although he took the idea from the world of German philosophy and terminology, he gave a special twist to the concept so that it fitted Danish circumstances and, as described previously, came to be one of the very key elements of Danish identity.

The duty of *folkelighed* in Grundtvig's interpretation, with the responsibility towards the whole and the obligation to involve all members of society in the national unit, was in fact Grundtvig's upgrading of the norms and values of the old village communities to a national utopia. As suggested, the hallmarks of this utopia corresponded very closely to the impressions Sir James Mellon formed and expounded in his tribal thesis in 1992. So the circle is closed, and on this basis it should be possible to decide whether the Danes are a nation or a tribe – to keep Sir James's distinction for now – and when the Danes became Danish.

The answer to the first question must be that the Danes are a tribe, which under the disciplining influence of the early modern state slowly developed into a nation, and under the pressure of the process of modernisation and the international events of the nineteenth century became a nation in the modern sense. The loss of the predominantly German duchies in 1864 created a completely unique situation, and from then on there was a more or less exact congruence of state, nation and people. This was brought to near-perfection when as a result of the plebiscite in 1920 the political border between Denmark and Germany corresponded to the linguistic border. This created the opportunity, somewhat unusual in the European context, for an exact identification of the state, the nation and the people, which became the true basis for developing the special national identity resulting from the violent disagreements about what Danishness was between 1864 and the First World War. The winning identity found its most pronounced expression in the modern Danish welfare model, where the fundamental aspects are clearly reminiscent of the patterns of the old village collectives.

On the basis of this hypothesis, that modern Danishness and the way in which Danes perceive themselves are especially constituted by the norms, values and rules of behaviour of the welfare society, it is possible to provide a tentative answer to the second question: when did the Danes become Danish in this sense? The answer has to be that in many respects, they have been since the seventeenth century. However, it was first with the impact of Grundtvig, towards the middle of the nineteenth century, when he transformed the old rules of conduct and norms of behaviour from the old agrarian society into a coherent national utopia, that the values of the ancient peasant society were promoted to common Danish values, and thus to an important element of identity – further defined and developed by politicians, artists and writers from the era of Romanticism onwards – which pointed the way forward to the modern welfare society.

This welfare society is today such an integral part of Danish identity that very few people could imagine a concept of Danishness capable of surviving without this welfare society and its especially Danish architecture. It is pertinent here that it is the protection of the welfare society which is one of the most frequently used arguments in the Danish public debate against further integration into the EU. To return to the image of the campfire, dismantling the welfare society in its current form would be akin to extinguishing the fire. All things considered, it makes little sense to sit in a circle around a fire that has gone out. This gives rise to a couple of concluding reflections about the future of Danishness in the form described in a globalised world.

DENMARK AND THE DANES IN 2000

At the turn of the millennium, Danish society was showing signs of breaking up. The situation in Denmark after the fall of the Berlin Wall in 1989 was no different to that in other European countries. The basis for the development of Europe had decisively changed. Denmark was perhaps, however, much more perceptibly affected, because the new global realities meant not only a marked change in foreign and security policy, but also in very important ways threatened the stability of the welfare society, and thus Danishness in the form it had taken during the twentieth century.

In terms of foreign policy, Denmark was no longer a front-line state, neither in regard to the defunct Soviet Union nor the resurrected Germany. All assessments of potential threats indicated that Danish territory would not be in danger from any outside enemies for the foreseeable future. From the point of view of security, around 2000 Denmark was safer than it had been since time immemorial. One result was that the Danish government involved the country more than ever in military peacekeeping actions far outside Danish borders. Danish army units operated under NATO and UN command in places as distant as Kyrgyzstan and Afghanistan. Similarly, a proactive foreign policy of a kind which would have been unthinkable just a few decades earlier was adopted, especially in regard to Eastern Europe. Indeed, it is necessary to look right back to the early eighteenth century to find anything comparable. Most recently, in the capacity of the EU chairmanship, Denmark made a significant and internationally recognised contribution in implementing the large expansion of the EU eastwards. In these areas, Denmark wholeheartedly took its place on the global stage as an active player.

On the other hand, the new globalised world order brought completely new and previously unknown contradictions and incongruities to the domestic debate about Danish society. In part this was due to the rapidly increasing immigration from the war zones of the world and poor developing countries, which placed a hitherto unknown pressure on the welfare system and is slowly transforming the previously highly homogeneous Danish nation, with its precise congruence between state, people and nation, into a multicultural society with all the conflicts that brings. Then there is the constantly growing pressure for integration from the EU, in the form of demands for harmonisation of laws, taxes and duties. Both areas contain clear threats to the Danish welfare model.

In the area of the law, many of the EU rules, based on Roman law, collide head-on with the traditions behind the Danish model of contract, which, as often mentioned, is the very foundation of the welfare society. This model rests on a web of written and unwritten agreements with deep historical roots, but is now coming under increasing pressure from the Roman law which holds sway in the EU and has its roots in quite different soil. This means that continued inclusion of EU law in Danish legal practice is not just a threat to the model of contracts, but by extension to the very welfare society in its present form.

The same applies to the efforts to harmonise taxation and duties. Putting these into practice will force the Danish government to lower the high levels of taxation which is in itself the basis for maintaining the universal welfare model, and surrendering this would be synonymous with abandoning the Danish utopia which is the cornerstone of the special national identity of the Danes. This model, which defines the national identity, is also threatened from the inside by the economic slowdown which has affected the Western economies, including Denmark, since the mid-1970s. This has meant that the rate of productivity increase has not been able, as it did in the 1960s, to keep pace with the growing demands of the welfare system. This has produced clear signs of crisis in the system.

From a longer perspective, it may well be that the twentieth- century welfare model in Denmark will turn out to have been nothing more than a short-term boom phenomenon which could only serve as the defining force of identity for a limited period. The future of Denmark and Danishness depends very much on how the Danes decide to react to these global challenges. Will the consensus-based Danishness perish, to be replaced by a new, more conflict-based identity, or will it be possible – as it has been so often before in Danish history – to find solutions to the current problems which will not mean abandoning the absolutely central quality and nature of the welfare model, namely the close linking of national identity and social responsibility? The amiably critical observer, Sir James Mellon, entertained no doubts:

> The public spirit and feeling of solidarity which exist in Denmark today will continue to exist and become a model which other European countries will look up to in centuries to come. The Danes will continue to be Danish, and the way in which their survival instincts and aspirations for progress will take them through the 21st century can serve as a sign to other European countries as to where their own future lies.[12]

If Sir James's prophesy turns out to be true, the saga of Denmark and the Danes will not just be limited to the 500 years covered in this volume. If he is right, then Europe needs Denmark just as much as Denmark needs Europe. This places an obligation on both.

POSTSCRIPT: DENMARK 2000–2010, A BRIEF ACCOUNT

With the publication of a revised edition of this book, it is natural to conclude with a continuation of the history of the Danes up to the present time and, in this postscript, it is intended to attempt a brief account of some of the most significant developments during this last decade, the period from 2000 to 2010. However, the normal task of an historian is to interpret events and phenomena of the distant past from a detached and long-term perspective, and it is a difficult and hazard-ous undertaking to evaluate a period that is so recent that it remains topical and part of continuing political debate, with all the differences of opinion that this entails in terms of a proper balance and insight. This update of developments in Denmark should therefore be read with some reservation and with an understanding that the importance and interpretation of these events will almost certainly be viewed quite differently at the end of this century. An account of the most recent developments in foreign and defence affairs has already been given in Chapter 2, and this postscript is therefore primarily concerned with internal issues.

Change of government – and a new political style

At the election in November 2001, the Social Democrat and Social–Liberal coalition government lost its parliamentary majority after nine years in power and, as a consequence, the government, led by Prime Minister Poul Nyrup Rasmussen, was forced to resign. The clear winner of the election was the Liberal Party, *Venstre*, which increased its mandate by 14 seats and became the largest parliamentary party and, for the first time since 1924, held more seats than the Social Democrats. It therefore followed that the leader of the Liberals, the 48-year-old Anders Fogh Rasmussen, should become the new Prime Minister. Together with the Conservatives and with the support of the Danish People's Party, *Dansk Folkeparti* – a right-wing party with a nationalist programme – he was able to form a government with a comfortable parliamentary majority. This latter political party, which was founded in 1995 by a splinter group of politicians from Mogens Glistrup's Progress Party, *Fremskridtspartiet*, won 22 seats in the election on a programme focused, in particular, on the question of immigration. In a number of ways, this shift of power altered the political climate in Denmark, and a number of commentators have gone so far as to describe it as a veritable change of system comparable with that of 1901 when, for the first time, *Venstre* came to power and transformed the political landscape.

Inspired by the example of the British Prime Minister, Tony Blair, and his 'New Labour', in the years that preceded the election in Denmark, Anders Fogh Rasmussen had gradually moved *Venstre* from an ideologically based, liberal platform to the political centre-ground with a programme that, to a large extent, reflected that of the Social Democrats and, it therefore follows, with an emphasis on the welfare state. This transformation was rewarded with electoral victory and the premiership.

The price for this transformation was that it was no longer possible to carry on with ideologically based politics in Denmark – and the usual practitioners had, in fact, already largely lost their importance at the time of the fall of Communism in Eastern Europe ten years earlier. In its place, and following the lead of Tony Blair on his election as leader of the Labour Party, Anders Fogh Rasmussen introduced a so-called 'contract with the people'. In simple terms, this consisted of a series of firm election promises that were so unambiguous that, in due course, the electorate would be able to determine to what extent they had been discharged. 'What we promise before the election will be fulfilled after the election', was the repeated assertion of the leaders of *Venstre* throughout the election campaign. This concept of a social contract has subsequently dominated Danish political life and it has been a contributory factor in keeping the centre-right government in power, up to now, for nine years. Until recently, it has been considerably helped by favourable economic conditions and by tight internal discipline within government circles.

The first challenge facing the new government was the extensive expansion of the European Union in Eastern Europe in 2002 at a time when Denmark held the EU presidency. The leadership of the summit meeting in Copenhagen was a baptism of fire for the new and untested ministers but, largely due to a strong personal involvement by the Prime Minister, the important decisions were taken without great difficulty. At the conclusion of the negotiations and with some sense of pride, he was able to announce to the world's media, 'we have an agreement'. It was the first occasion that Anders Fogh Rasmussen gave the appearance of statesmanship of European format, and it was a distinction that he was able to build on in the following years to such an extent that, in 2009, he was elected the Secretary-General of NATO – one of the most senior international appointments achieved by a Danish politician.

Rather more complex was the internal task of explaining to the public what had become of the ideologies that, until that time, had largely decided the political programme, and which had been replaced with a more pragmatic style of government. To resolve this and, at the same time, to distinguish itself from the opposition, the new government introduced a broadly based centrist policy which took the form of a general clear-out of the diffuse left-wing theories which, in its view, had dominated political discussion for too long. In his first New Year's address to the nation, on 1 January 2002, the Prime Minister also made clear his intention to bring to an end those state bodies and spin-doctors which, he believed, had become arbiters of public opinion and had enjoyed too much influence. In the following year he also put a stop to what he termed the insularity so often associated with smaller countries. The subsequent, more active foreign policy meant a Danish military involvement in Iraq and Afghanistan. The long-term plan behind all these initiatives was to drive the political agenda towards the centre, and thereby increase the readiness of society to accept more widespread liberal reforms within a centrist framework.

To some extent this course was only partly successful. Apart from introducing and maintaining an end to tax increases, the centre-right coalition made no significant changes to the structure and functions of the welfare state. In fact, in 2006, it came to a comprehensive agreement with the opposition which, in practice, approved of and enlarged the welfare state for the foreseeable future. The public sector has continued its relentless expansion, both in terms of the number of employees and the cost, throughout the present government's tenure, and it has only been able to get away with this without losing political credibility because, until 2008, the economic climate made it possible to finance this growth without an increase in taxation. However, there was a return to reality with the global financial crisis in 2008, to which Denmark was not immune, and at the present time, in a number of areas the government appears to have lost its grip.

The cartoon crisis

The so-called cartoon or caricature crisis of 2006 took the government and the public completely by surprise and sent shock-waves throughout the nation. The wider background to this crisis, which was probably the most serious in Danish foreign affairs since the Second World War, was the murder of the Dutch film director, Theo van Gogh, who had produced *Submission*, a film that was critical of Islam. This provoked much anger amongst radical Islamists and, in 2004, he was brutally murdered on the street by a fanatic. The murder caused a great international stir and, in Denmark, it also led to a persistent rumour that Danish artists had refused to illustrate a children's book about the prophet Mohammed for fear of reprisals.

This form of self-censorship was quite alien to the Danish tradition of freedom of expression – a concept enshrined in the constitution – and was also in conflict with the principle of human rights, which was something the government had attached importance to in its election campaign. One of the country's large centre-right newspapers, *Jyllands-Posten*, decided to put its toe in the water by inviting a number of cartoonists to depict the prophet Mohammed as they saw him. Twelve of these responded and, on 30 September 2005, the newspaper published the results of their efforts – including one that depicted the prophet wearing a turban containing a bomb – together with a leading article explaining that their action was not directed against Muslims, but should be regarded as an attempt to stimulate an open debate about an invidious tendency towards the self-censorship that, in the opinion of the newspaper, was beginning to infiltrate Danish culture and the media.

Apart from a few indignant comments from local Muslim leaders, there was an apparent calm for some months after publication. However, during that time, a group of 19 imams from the Muslim community in Denmark were busy preparing a response intended to force the government to intervene and to distance itself from this perceived insult to the prophet. To lend weight to this they contacted a number of ambassadors to Denmark from Islamic nations, with the Egyptian ambassador at the top of the list. In January 2006, these ambassadors requested a meeting with the Prime Minister and, in their communication, they made clear their expectation that, at the proposed meeting, he would dissociate himself from the newspaper's cartoons and undertake to ensure that there would be no recurrence.

That communication placed the Prime Minister in a difficult position. Freedom of the press was of fundamental importance in a democratic society and it would be outside the competence of the government to dictate to the media. In addition, any such intervention by the Prime Minister would have been in conflict with the liberal political programme that he had followed since coming to power. On the other hand, it could be said that the newspaper had abused the obligations imposed by this principle of freedom of the press, that it had been playing a very dangerous game or, at the very least, had acted naively. What was very clear was that, predictably perhaps, the governments of a large number of trading partners, with which Denmark enjoyed diplomatic relations, had been seriously offended. In the event, the Prime Minister decided not to meet with the ambassadors on the basis they had requested and, not surprisingly perhaps, this was interpreted by them, and by their governments, as a form of arrogance and an insult to Islam. From a local difficulty involving some possibly distasteful newspaper cartoons, quite suddenly it became a major issue setting Denmark against the entire Islamic world.

To make matters worse, at the end of January 2006, a group of Danish imams decided to visit the Middle East to present their account of events to governments and Muslim organisations there. They took with them documentary evidence intended to prove that Danish Muslims were subjected to systematic ridicule and persecution and, although some of this material was subsequently shown to have been fabricated, the effect was explosive. During a number of dramatic months in the winter and spring of 2006, the entire Muslim world from Indonesia to the Middle East was aligned against Denmark, and the Danish flag, together with photographs and effigies of the Prime Minister and ambassadors, were consigned to the flames. Danish goods were boycotted and exports to the Middle East plummeted.

So far as Denmark was concerned, it was a crisis on an international scale, and it was totally unexpected. No one in their wildest dreams had imagined that there would be such a violent reaction to a set of drawings which most people in Denmark regarded as rather foolish but otherwise quite harmless. Danish diplomacy was eventually brought into play in an effort to alleviate the worst consequences and to mobilise support from sympathetic governments, but it was not until the summer of 2006 that the situation began to improve and the sense of acute crisis slowly died down.

In many ways this course of events was a lesson for the Danes and for their government. It made it dramatically clear that, for better or worse, they were part of a global community and therefore inextricably linked in a fast communications network, which meant that a newspaper article in Aarhus could unleash a storm in the Middle East and an international crisis. It also served as a reminder that the democratic values on which Danish society is based are not universally accepted as a matter of course, but are under constant threat, both from abroad and from within the country, and must be constantly defended. Finally, it caused many to regard the growing number of Muslim immigrants with increased distrust and, for example, a number of otherwise quite reasonable people began to see the Danish imams as some kind of fifth column. This anger and suspicion was also directed at the very great majority of peaceful and loyal Danish Muslims, and there can be little doubt that the caricature-crisis was a considerable setback for the integration of Muslim immigrants – a setback from which the country has still not fully recovered.

The financial crisis and its consequences

Denmark was again reminded of its exposure to international events with the bank and financial crisis that began in the United States but became a widespread economic crisis in 2008–9. Like most other European countries, Denmark was badly affected, with banks collapsing and widespread bankruptcies. As in other countries, the government provided massive financial support for the banking sector to prevent economic meltdown and, at the same time, introduced a number of measures aimed at supporting business. Although this probably prevented a total financial crash, overall production fell and there was a sharp increase in unemployment. The bubble had burst and the situation had changed almost from one day to the next. From a situation of almost full employment, increasing production and a comfortable surplus in public finances, in common with most other western countries, Denmark was soon faced with spiralling unemployment, falling production and a massive budget deficit. Inevitably, this led to radical changes in the political agenda and, as it happened, it was also about this time that Anders Fogh Rasmussen, who had been Prime Minister since 2001, departed to take up an appointment as NATO's Secretary-General. His replacement was the former minister of finance, Lars Løkke Rasmussen. The new Prime Minister's primary responsibility was, and remains, to remedy the effects of this financial upheaval and to steer Denmark safely through the crisis.

This is by no means an easy task. Denmark's competitiveness in international markets is at a disadvantage because of high wage levels – a legacy from more affluent times – and the high levels of taxation that are unavoidable if the extensive public services within the welfare state are to be maintained. These two factors inevitably contribute to a reduction in employment – either because businesses have closed, or because production is moving to lower-cost areas elsewhere. The rise in unemployment and, as a consequence, the reduced tax revenue is increasing the strain on the welfare system and, at the same time, demographic changes mean that the number of elderly people is rapidly increasing and the working population is decreasing. Government finances are therefore, at present, under enormous pressure.

As we have stressed earlier in this book, a comprehensive welfare system has become a central element in the general perception of being Danish. Substantial changes or cuts therefore amount to an assault on a concept that binds the country together and gives it a feeling of identity. The government is therefore faced with the thankless task of having to square the circle – making Danish industry more competitive, and maintaining the welfare state in a shrinking economy. At the present time, in 2010, the signs are that substantial cutbacks in the welfare system will be unavoidable. What is less certain is the government's ability to survive any such cuts, although it may be able to derive some small comfort from the fact that, in the spring of 2010, and without much dissension, the trade unions approved a new two-year collective agreement that, in contrast with earlier settlements, does not contain any real provision of wage increases. There is therefore a sign that some understanding of the scale of the crisis is beginning to sink in, and this is essential if greater changes are to be made.

The crisis that Denmark faces in 2011, like so many other countries, is not just an economic predicament, but a crisis that embraces systems and values, and which raises a number of fundamental questions about, for example, the privileges and responsibilities of individuals within a society, and of the state's responsibility to its people. The answers to these questions remain unclear, and where they will lead Denmark in the longer term is unknown. However, from the viewpoint of a historian, Denmark has been through much greater crises in the past and has survived far greater changes in fortune – and survived in such a way that the country, as a whole, can still be regarded as amongst the most prosperous and peaceful of nations. At the same time, the Danes have a long tradition, which goes back to Grundtvig and the nineteenth century, of building a society that is based on collective strength, democracy and shared prosperity. If that tradition continues, the country will surely be able to maintain its position and make a worthwhile contribution in the global realities of the twenty-first century, without losing those special qualities that, with all their strengths and weaknesses, characterise Denmark and the Danes.

Notes

1 INTRODUCTION: WHAT IS DENMARK AND WHO ARE THE DANES?

1. The facts given here about modern Denmark are taken from the entry 'Danmark', in *Den store danske Encyklopædi*, vol. 4 (Copenhagen, 1996), which is the most recent national encyclopaedia.
2. H. G. Koenigsberger, *Early Modern Europe, 1500–1789* (London, 1987), p. 2.
3. Robert Molesworth, *An Account of Denmark as it was in the Year 1692* (London, 1694; repr. Copenhagen, 1976), pp. 98, 232. A broadly balanced assessment of Molesworth's *Account* is most recently presented in Hugh Mayo's unpublished PhD thesis, *Robert Molesworth's Account of Denmark: Its Roots and Impact* (Odense, 2000).
4. Sir James Mellon's account was translated into Danish from his original ms. and published under the title, *Og gamle Danmark. . . . En beskrivelse af Danmark I det herrens år 1992* (Århus, 1992). The quotations are translated from the Danish edn., p. 7.

2 FOREIGN AND SECURITY POLICY: FROM THE GATEKEEPER OF THE BALTIC TO A MIDGET STATE

1. For a brief introduction to the late medieval Baltic world order and the causes of its downfall, see David Kirby, *Northern Europe in the Early Modern Period: The Baltic World, 1492–1772* (London, 1990), pp. 1–73; and Knud J. V. Jespersen, 'Rivalry without Victory: Denmark, Sweden and the Struggle for the Baltic, 1500–1720', in Göran Rystad, Klaus-R. Böhme and Wilhelm M. Carlgren (eds), *In Quest of Trade and Security: The Baltic in Power Politics, 1500–1990* (Lund, 1994), vol. I, pp. 137–76. Readers who understand Danish might profit from reading the six-volume *Dansk Udenrigspolitiks Historie* (ed. Carsten Due-Nielsen, Ole Feldbæk and Nikolaj Petersen, Copenhagen, 2001–4).
2. For the importance of the Baltic in European great power politics in the early modern period, see the contributions of Anja Tjaden, Stewart P. Oakley, Ole Feldbæk and Andrew Lambert in Rystad et al. (eds), op. cit. (1994); and Derek McKay and H. M. Scott, *The Rise of the Great Powers, 1648–1815* (London, 1983), passim.

3. The Danish–Swedish rivalry has most recently been dealt with by Knud J. V. Jespersen, in Rystad et al. (eds), op. cit. (1994), pp. 137–76; and – in a wider East European perspective – by Robert I. Frost, *The Northern Wars: War, State and Society in Northeastern Europe, 1558–1721* (London, 2000). See also Stewart Oakley's contribution, 'War in the Baltic, 1550–1790', in Jeremy Black (ed.), *The Origins of War in Early Modern Europe* (Edinburgh, 1987), pp. 52–71, and Knud J. V. Jespersen's contribution, 'Warfare and Society in the Baltic 1500–1800', in Jeremy Black (ed.), *European Warfare 1453–1815* (London, 1999), pp. 180–200. The Danish involvement in the Thirty Years War is superbly described and assessed by Paul Douglas Lockhart, *Denmark in the Thirty Years' War, 1618–1648: King Christian IV and the Decline of the Oldenburg State* (Selinsgrove, 1996).

4. Denmark's dilemma during the Napoleonic Wars and after is treated by Stewart Oakley, Ole Feldbæk and Andrew Lambert in Rystad et al. (eds), op. cit. (1994), pp. 231 ff. The crisis of 1801 is thoroughly discussed in Ole Feldbæk, *The Battle of Copenhagen 1801: Nelson and the Danes* (London, 2002).

5. The growing national conflict in Schleswig-Holstein is treated in a balanced manner in Ulrich Lange (ed.), *Geschichte Schleswig-Holsteins* (Neumünster, 1997); and an equally balanced view is presented in W. Carr, *Schleswig-Holstein, 1815–1848: A Study in National Conflict* (Manchester, 1963).

6. There is a rich scholarly literature in Danish on the war of 1864 and its aftermath, most of which is listed in Johannes Nielsen, *1864 – Da Europa gik af lave* (Odense, 1987), but in European scholarship this first of Bismarck's decisive military campaigns is largely ignored in favour of his subsequent campaigns against Austria (1866) and France (1870–1). The general political context from a German perspective is presented in William Carr, *A History of Germany, 1815–1990*, 4th edn (London, 1991), pp. 89–96, while the British perception of the conflict is treated by Keith A. P. Sandiford, *Great Britain and the Schleswig-Holstein Question, 1848–1864* (Toronto, 1975).

7. Erik Scavenius, *Forhandlingspolitiken under Besættelsen* (Copenhagen, 1948), p. 9.

8. The place and role of the Scandinavian countries in great power politics in the early twentieth century is admirably covered by Patrick Salmon, *Scandinavia and the Great Powers, 1890–1940* (Cambridge, 1997); while Susan Seymour, *Anglo-Danish Relations and Germany, 1933–1945* (Odense, 1982), focuses on the difficult position of Denmark between Nazi Germany and Great Britain. Important aspects of Scandinavian policy during the Second World War are discussed in Henrik S. Nissen (ed.), *Scandinavia during the Second World War* (Minneapolis, 1983). The most recent treatment of the Danish armed resistance against the German occupation 1940–5 is Knud J. V. Jespersen, *No Small Achievement: Special Operations Executive and the Danish Resistance, 1940–1945* (Odense, 2002).

9. For an introduction to Danish post-war security policy, see the contributions by Rasmus Mariager and Poul Villaume in Jørgen Sevaldsen with

Bo Bjørke and Claus Bjørn (eds), *Britain and Denmark: Political, Economic and Cultural Relations in the 19th and 20th Centuries* (Copenhagen, 2003), pp. 535–93.

10. Aspects of the changes in Danish foreign policy in the late and post-Cold War period are analysed in Carsten Due Nielsen and Nikolaj Petersen (eds), *Adaption and Activism: The Foreign Policy of Denmark 1967–1993* (Copenhagen, 1995); Peter Viggo Jakobsen, *The Nordic Approaches to Peace Operations after the Cold War: A New Model in the Making?* (London, 2004); and Sten Rynning, *Denmark as a Strategic Actor: Danish Security Policy after 11 September* (Danish Foreign Policy Yearbook 2003, Copenhagen).

3 DOMESTIC POLICY, 1500–1848: THE ERA OF ARISTOCRACY AND ABSOLUTISM

1. Quoted from Bo Lidegaard, *Jens Otto Krag, 1962–1978* (Copenhagen, 2002), p. 687.
2. The 1536 revolution and its socio-political ramifications are briefly outlined in E. Ladewig Petersen, 'The Revolution of 1536 and its Aftermath, the Domain State', in E. I. Kouri and Tom Scott (eds), *Politics and Society in Reformation Europe: Essays for Sir Geoffrey Elton on his Sixty-Fifth Birthday* (London, 1987), pp. 475–86. A good survey of essential features and changes in early modern Denmark is presented by Paul Douglas Lockhart, *Denmark 1513–1660: The Rise and Decline of a Renaissance Monarchy* (Oxford, 2007).
3. On the changing position of the early modern Danish nobility, see Knud J. V. Jespersen, 'The Rise and Fall of the Danish Nobility 1600–1800', in H. M. Scott (ed.), *The European Nobilities in the Seventeenth and Eighteenth Centuries*, 2 vols (London, 1995); vol. II, pp. 41–70. The quoted statement by Herluf Trolle is taken from this article (p. 41).
4. The transformation of state finances from a system based on revenue from Crown lands to a tax-based system is most thoroughly analysed by E. Ladewig Petersen, who also coined the terms 'domain state' and 'tax state' to describe the nature of the transition. See E. Ladewig Petersen, 'From Domain State to Tax State: Synthesis and Interpretation', *Scandinavian Economic History Review*, 23 (1975), pp. 116–48. For a fuller discussion of the implications of the structural transitions, see Leon Jespersen (ed.), *A Revolution from Above? The Power State of 16th and 17th Century Scandinavia* (Odense, 2000).
5. The change of system in 1660 and its precondition in the emerging tax state is outlined in Knud J. V. Jespersen, 'The Revolution of 1660 and its Precondition, the Tax-State', in Kouri and Scott (eds), op. cit. (1987), pp. 486–501.
6. The administrative and social transformation described above is briefly outlined in Knud J. V. Jespersen's contribution to Scott (ed.), op. cit. (1995), pp. 55–62.

7. Griffenfeld's meteoric career and its context in early absolutism are discussed in Knud J. V. Jespersen, 'The Last Favourite? The Case of Griffenfeld: A Danish Perspective', in J. H. Elliott and L. W. B. Brockliss (eds), *The World of the Favourite* (New Haven, CT, and London, 1999), pp. 269–78.

8. The following appreciation of the Danish Law is based on Ditlev Tamm (ed.), *Christian 5.s Danske og Norske Lov* (Copenhagen, 1983).

9. The term was coined by Birgit Løgstrup in her dissertation on the administrative role of the large estate owners in the absolutist government, *Jorddrot og offentlig administrator: Godsejerstyret inden for skatte- og udskrivningsvæsenet i det 18. århundrede* (Copenhagen, 1983), with a summary in German, and further elaborated in her article, 'The Landowner as Public Administrator: The Danish Model', *Scandinavian Journal of History*, 9 (1984), pp. 283–312.

10. Quoted from the king's formal written reply, printed in *Collegialtidende* under the date 28 February 1835.

11. The term is coined by the Norwegian historian Jens Arup Seip, 'Teorien om det opinionsstyrte enevelde', *Historisk Tidsskrift* (Oslo), 38 (1958), pp. 397–463.

12. On Struensee, see Stefan Winkle, *Struensee: Artzt, Aufklärer, Staatsmann* (Stuttgart, 1983), idem, *Struensee und die Publizistik* (Hamburg, 1982); and Christine Keitsch, *Der Fall Struensee – Ein Blick in die Skandalpresse des ausgehenden 18. Jahrhunderts* (Hamburg, 2000).

13. A recent – though not uncontroversial – comprehensive interpretation of the agrarian reforms is Thorkild Kjærgaard, *Den danske revolution 1500–1800: En økohistorisk tolkning* (Copenhagen, 1991); English edn titled *The Danish Revolution 1500–1800: An Ecohistorical Interpretation* (Cambridge, 1994).

14. Knud J. V. Jespersen, 'Conscription and Deception: The Statute of Conscription 1788 and its Role as a Political Instrument in Non-Revolutionary Denmark', in Jean Delmas (ed.), *L'Influence de la révolution française sur les armées en France, en Europe et dans le Monde*, 2 vols (Vincennes, 1991), vol. I, pp. 307–16.

4 DOMESTIC POLICY, 1848–2000: DEMOCRACY AND THE WELFARE STATE

1. The 1848 Revolution has attracted rich debate among Danish scholars, but virtually nothing of this has found its way into the international debate on the last of the romantic revolutions; in Jonathan Sperber's masterly survey, *The European Revolutions, 1848–1851* (Cambridge, 1994) Denmark is hardly mentioned. A brief sketch of the basic events is presented in W. Glyn Jones, *Denmark* (London, 1970), pp. 44–71. The following discussion of the revolution and its roots and impact is based on Danish scholarly debate. See also Niels Clemmensen, 'The Image of Britain in the Danish Constitutional Debate, c. 1848–1870', in Sevaldsen et al. (eds), op. cit. (2003), pp. 39–59, for a discussion of the debate over the constitution after 1848. On the

Constitution of 1849 and its later amendments, see Royal Danish Ministry of Foreign Affairs (ed.), *Denmark's Constitution: 150 Years* (Copenhagen, 1999). For a recent general interpretation of Danish domestic politics after 1849, see Bo Lidegaard, *A Short History of Denmark in the 20th Century* (Copenhagen, 2009).

2. A more thorough discussion of the constitutional struggle can be found in Carsten Due-Nielsen, 'The Beginning of a Beautiful Friendship: Denmark's Relations with Britain, 1864–1914', in Sevaldsen et al. (eds), op. cit. (2003), pp. 171–97. Useful information can also be found in Carsten Holbraad, *Danish Neutrality* (Oxford, 1991).

3. The exchange between the King and Deuntzer is quoted from Søren Mørch, *24 Statsministre* (Copenhagen, 2000), p. 31.

4. The party system in the twentieth century is briefly outlined in the handbook on *Denmark* (ed. The National Encyclopaedia, Copenhagen, 2001) under the sub-heading 'The Political System'. See also Lidegaard, op. cit. (2009).

5. See Niels Finn Christiansen, 'Reformism within Danish Social Democracy until the Nineteen Thirties', *Scandinavian Journal of History*, 3 (1978), pp. 297–322.

6. For an introduction to the development and the present crisis of the Danish welfare state, see Niels Finn Christiansen and Klaus Petersen, 'The Dynamics of Social Solidarity: The Danish Welfare State, 1900–2000', *Scandinavian Journal of History*, 26 (2001), pp. 177–96. For a more general perspective on the relations between politics and welfare, see Gösta Esping-Andersen, *Politics against Markets: The Social Democratic Road to Power* (Princeton, 1985); and idem, *Welfare States in Transition: National Adaptations in Global Economies* (London, 1996). The Danish title of Hartvig Frisch's influential book is *Pest over Europa: Bolshevisme – Fascisme – Nazisme* (Copenhagen, 1933). For a more thorough assessment of his role, and that of the Social Democrats, in defending democracy and the parliamentary system against totalitarianism, see Lidegaard, op. cit. (2009), pp. 105–34.

7. Two different interpretations of the present crisis – that of a historian and that of a political scientist – are presented by Niels Finn Christiansen, 'Denmark: End of an Idyll', in P. Anderson and P. Camiller (eds), *Mapping the West European Left* (London, 1994), pp. 77–101; and Jørgen Goul Andersen, 'The Scandinavian Welfare Model in Crisis? Achievements and Problems in the Danish Welfare State in an Age of Unemployment and Low Growth', *Scandinavian Political Studies*, 20 (1997), pp. 1–37.

5 THE CHURCH AND CULTURE FROM LUTHER TO POSTMODERNISM

1. Jørgen I. Jensen, *Den Fjerne Kirke: Mellem kultur og religiøsitet* (Copenhagen, 1995).

2. The organisation of the Danish church and religious life in Denmark is outlined in the official handbook on *Denmark* (2001) listed above (ch. 4, n. 4).

3. Even though the modern debate among Danish scholars on the Reformation era is rich and varied, very little of it has been published in the major languages. However, a general impression of the chronology of the Danish Reformation and its wider context can be obtained from G. R. Elton, *Reformation Europe, 1517–1559* (Fontana History of Europe, London, 1963), especially pp. 125ff.; cf. also Petersen's above-mentioned (Ch. 3, n. 2) contribution to the Elton *festschrift* (1987). The modern standard work in Danish on the Reformation is Martin Schwarz Lausten, *Reformationen i Danmark* (Copenhagen, 1987); he is also the author of the magisterial survey of the history of the Danish Church, *Kirkens historie i Danmark: Pavekirke. Kongekirke. Folkekirke* (Århus, 1999). The account in this chapter is mainly based on those standard works.
4. Much of the modern Danish debate on the Reformation focuses on its role as a forerunner for the present welfare state. The most important work in this respect is Tim Knudsen (ed.), *Den nordiske protestantisme og velfærdsstaten* (Århus, 2000); see also Øystein Sørensen and Bo Stråth (eds), *The Cultural Construction of Norden* (Oslo, 1997), which has a similar perspective.
5. The wordings of the royal mottoes are taken from the list given in Benito Scocozza and Grethe Jensen, *Danmarkshistoriens Hvem, Hvad og Hvornår* (Copenhagen, 1994), p. 417.
6. On Grundtvig and his influence, see A. M. Allchin, D. Jasper, J. H. Schjørring and K. Stevenson (eds), *Heritage and Prophecy* (Århus, 1993).
7. On Grundtvig's ideas on education, see Eckhard Bodenstein, *Skolefrihed in Dänemark zur Entstehung eines schulpolitischen Prinzips* (Tønder, 1982).
8. The poem was first printed in Grundtvig's own periodical, Danskeren, on 30 August 1848. The verse quoted here is the seventh of the poem.

6 ECONOMIC CONDITIONS: THE OLD DENMARK, 1500–1800

1. Mellon, op. cit. (1992), pp. 98–9.
2. John P. Maarbjerg, *Scandinavia in the European World-Economy, ca. 1570–1625* (New York, 1995) offers a good introduction to economic life in Denmark (and in Scandinavia) around 1600. The best overall Danish survey of the pre-industrial economy is Ole Feldbæk, *Danmarks økonomiske historie 1500–1840* (Herning, 1993), from which most of the figures are taken.
3. The basic structure of the agrarian system is described in further detail in E. Ladewig Petersen, *The Crisis of the Danish Nobility, 1580–1660* (Odense, 1967).
4. E. Ladewig Petersen, 'The Danish Cattle Trade during the Sixteenth and Seventeenth Centuries', *Scandinavian Economic History Review*, 18 (1970), pp. 69–85.
5. Thomas Munck, *The Peasantry and the Early Absolute Monarchy in Denmark, 1660–1708* (Copenhagen, 1979) provides good insights into

agrarian conditions under early absolutism. The present account is based upon the voluminous Danish literature on the subject.

6. A *tønde hartkorn* was a Danish measure for as much land as could yield annually the value of one barrel of rye or barley.

7. Ole Feldbæk, *India Trade under the Danish Flag, 1772–1808: European Enterprise and Anglo-Indian Remittance and Trade* (Lund, 1969); and idem, 'The Danish Asia Trade, 1620–1807: Value and Volume', *Scandinavian Economic History Review*, 39 (1991), pp. 3–27; see also Hans Chr. Johansen, 'Scandinavian Shipping in the Late Eighteenth Century in a European Perspective', *Economic History Review*, 45 (1992), pp. 479–93.

8. For this and the following, see Kjærgaard, op. cit. (1994), and Claus Bjørn, 'The Peasantry and Agrarian Reform in Denmark', *Scandinavian Economic History Review*, 25 (1977), pp. 117–37.

7 ECONOMIC CONDITIONS: THE NEW DENMARK, 1800–2000

1. E. J. Hobsbawm, *The Age of Revolution, 1789–1848* (London, 1962).

2. Per Boje, 'The Standard of Living in Denmark, 1750–1914', *Scandinavian Economic History Review*, 34 (1986), pp. 171–9.

3. Translated from the *High School Song Book*, 17th edn (1990), no. 158.

4. To my knowledge, *The Penguin Complete Fairy Tales and Stories of Hans Andersen*, trans. Erik Haugaard (Harmondsworth, 1984–) is the latest complete English edition of Hans Chr. Andersen's works; his autobiography, *The Fairy Tale of My Life*, appeared in English (London and New York) in 1955.

5. There is no satisfactory account of the Danish co-operative movement in English, but Jens Christensen, *Rural Denmark, 1750–1980* (Copenhagen, 1983), may give an idea of the impact on rural society of that ideology, which revolutionised the Danish countryside in the late nineteenth century.

6. William Scharling and V. Falbe-Hansen, *Danmarks Statistik*, vol. 2 (Copenhagen, 1887), p. 99.

7. The figures on industrial development are taken from Hans Chr. Johansen, *Industriens vækst og vilkår 1870–1973* (Odense, 1988), table 8 (pp. 51–2) and table 90 (pp. 276–7). The larger context is presented in Lennart Jörberg, *The Industrial Revolution in Scandinavia, 1850–1914* (Fontana Economic History of Europe, London, 1970).

8. Early industrialisation is treated by Svend Aage Hansen, *Early Industrial-isation in Denmark* (Copenhagen, 1970); Ove Hornby, 'Industrialisation in Denmark', *Scandinavian Economic History Review*, 17 (1969), pp. 23–57; and Gunnar Lind, 'Development and Location of Industry in Danish Provincial Towns, 1855–1882', *Scandinavian Economic History Review*, 27 (1979), pp. 101–20.

9. See Tage Kaarsted, *Great Britain and Denmark, 1914–20* (Odense, 1979).

10. Jørgen Petersen, *Husmandsbruget* (Copenhagen, 1928), p. 196.

11. The Danish reactions to the world crisis are discussed in Seymour, op. cit. (1982), pp. 8–17; while the commercial relations between Denmark and Britain are treated at greater length in Patrick Salmon's and Bent Raymond Jørgensen's contributions to Sevaldsen et al. (eds), op. cit. (2003), pp. 231–49, 251–78. For the wider context, see Patrick Salmon, *British–German Commercial Rivalry in the Depression Era: The Political and Economic Impact in Northern Europe 1931–1939* (Newcastle, 1982).

12. *Rigsdagstidende*. Folketingets Forhandlinger 1932–3; 26 January 1933.

13. The Danish title of the manifesto is *Danmark for Folket*. It is printed in full in Claus Bryld, *Det danske socialdemokrati og revisionismen*, vol. 2 (Copenhagen, 1976), pp. 169–91.

14. On the Danish sailors and merchant ships in British service during the war, see Christian Tortzen, 'Danish Merchant Seamen and their Ships in British Service, 1940–1945', in Sevaldsen et al. (eds), op. cit. (2003), pp. 291–310.

15. Jespersen, op. cit. (2002), pp. 58 ff. The extent and importance of the economic collaboration with Germany is discussed in Philip Giltner, *'In the Friendliest Manner': German–Danish Economic Cooperation during the Nazi Occupation of 1940–1945* (New York, 1998).

16. Rasmus Mariager, 'Political Ambitions and Economic Realities: Anglo-Danish Relations and the US in the Early Cold War', in Sevaldsen et al. (eds), op. cit. (2003), pp. 535–73.

17. The account of the changes in agricultural life is mainly based on Svend Aage Hansen and Ingrid Henriksen, *Velfærdsstaten 1940–78* (Dansk social Historie, vol. 7, Copenhagen, 1980), pp. 166 ff.

18. This section is mainly based on Johansen, op. cit. (1988) pp. 267ff.

19. See the articles by Niels Finn Christiansen and Klaus Petersen mentioned earlier (ch. 4, n. 6). For a comparative discussion of the Danish and the British welfare models, see Carl-Axel Gemzell, 'The Welfare-State: Britain and Denmark', in Sevaldsen et al. (eds), op. cit. (2003), pp. 123–43. The figures given in this section are taken from the official statistics, *Statistisk 10-års oversigt*.

20. Denmark's road into the EEC, together with Britain, is treated by Peter A. Dalby, 'The First British and Danish Applications to Join the EEC, 1960–63', in Sevaldsen et al. (eds), op. cit. (2003), pp. 595–616; and Morten Rasmussen, 'How Denmark Made Britain Pay the Bills: Danish–British Relations during the Enlargement Negotiations of the European Community, 1970–72', in ibid., pp. 617–43.

21. A good introduction to the debate on immigration to Denmark and its consequences for society is Poul Chr. Matthiessen, *Immigration to Denmark: An Overview of the Research Carried Out from 1999 to 2006 by the Rockwool Foundation Research Unit* (Odense, 2009).

8 THE DANES – A TRIBE OR A NATION?

1. The role of the past in the creation of identity is discussed in the introduction to Bo Stråth (ed.), *Myth, Memory and History in the Construction of Community* (Brussels, 2000), pp. 19–46.

2. The radical tradition and its key concepts are subtly discussed in Jens Chr. Manniche, *Den radikale Historietradition* (Århus, 1981).

3. Quoted from Seymour, op. cit. (1982), pp. 153–4.

4. The term (in Danish: *Gårdmandslinien*) was coined by Thorkild Kjærgaard, 'Gårdmandslinien i dansk historieskrivning', *Fortid og Nutid*, 28 (1979), pp. 178–91, and has since given rise to much heated debate among Danish historians.

5. See, for instance, the admirable analysis by Linda Colley, *Britons: Forging the Nation, 1707–1837* (New Haven, CT, and London, 1992).

6. On the development of a specific Danish identity, see the many interesting contributions in Ole Feldbæk (ed.), *Dansk identitetshistorie 1536–1990*, vols I–IV (Copenhagen, 1991–2).

7. The following discussion is based mainly upon the subtle analysis of the discourses carried out by Niels Finn Christiansen in Flemming Lundgreen-Nielsen (ed.), *På sporet af dansk identitet* (Copenhagen, 1992), pp. 153–89.

8. Georg Brandes is usually regarded as the founding father of the subsequently very influential intellectual movement called 'cultural radicalism' which dominated Danish cultural life in the first half of the twentieth century. This movement can be seen as the intellectual parallel to the political line of the Social Liberalist Party, *Det radikale Venstre*. The main enemy of the cultural radicals was (and is) the Grundtvigian movement, rooted in the liberal party, *Venstre*. For an introduction to the intellectual landscape in twentieth-century Denmark, see Hans Hertel, 'Armstrong, Bogart, Churchill . . . Penguin: The Danish Turn to Anglo-American Cultural Values from the 1920s to the 1950s', in Sevaldsen et al. (eds), op. cit. (2003), pp. 431–75.

9. Quotation from his famous speech in the *Folketing* (1883) against the military budget. Quoted in Lundgreen-Nielsen (ed.), op. cit. (1992), p. 175.

10. Some important works from the modernist school are Benedict Anderson, *Imagined Communities: Reflections on the Origin and Spread of Nationalism* (London, 1983); Ernest Gellner, *Nations and Nationalism* (Oxford, 1983); and E. J. Hobsbawm, *Nations and Nationalism since 1780* (Cambridge, 1990).

11. Anthony D. Smith, *The Ethnic Origins of Nations* (Oxford, 1986), and idem, *National Identity* (Harmondsworth, 1991).

12. Mellon, op. cit. (1992), p. 178.

Select Bibliography

The list primarily includes works in English, though a few important titles in other languages are also included.

GENERAL

Danish National Encyclopaedia (Copenhagen, 2001).

Henningsen, Bernd, *Die Deutschen und ihre Nachbarn: Dänemark* (Munich, 2009).

Jones, W. Glyn, *Denmark* (London, 1970).

Kirby, David, *Northern Europe in the Early Modern Period: The Baltic World, 1492–1772* (London and New York, 1990).

—— *The Baltic World, 1772–1993: Europe's Northern Periphery in an Age of Change* (London and New York, 1995).

Lidegaard, Bo, *A Short History of Denmark in the 20th Century* (Copenhagen, 2009).

Lockhart, Paul Douglas, *Denmark 1513–1660: The Rise and Decline of a Renaissance Monarchy* (Oxford, 2007).

Mayo, Hugh, *Robert Molesworth's Account of Denmark: Its Roots and Impact* (PhD thesis, Odense, 2000).

Mellon, Sir James, *Og gamle Danmark . . . En beskrivelse af Danmark i det herrens år 1992* (Århus, 1992).

Molesworth, Robert, *An Account of Denmark as it was in the Year 1692* (London, 1694; repr. Copenhagen, 1976).

Oakley, Stewart P., *The Story of Denmark* (London, 1972).

Sevaldsen, Jørgen, Bo Bjørke and Claus Bjørn (eds), *Britain and Denmark: Political, Economic and Cultural Relations in the 19th and 20th Centuries* (Copenhagen, 2003).

Sperber, Jonathan, *The European Revolutions, 1848–1851* (Cambridge, 1994).

COMMERCIAL RELATIONS AND SECURITY POLITICS

Attman, Arthur, *The Struggle for the Baltic Markets: Powers in Conflict, 1558–1618* (Gothenburg, 1979).

Black, Jeremy (ed.), *The Origins of War in Early Modern Europe* (Edinburgh, 1987).

—— (ed.), *European Warfare 1453–1815* (London & New York, 1999).

Feldbæk, Ole, *India Trade under the Danish Flag, 1772–1808: Enterprise and Anglo-Indian Remittance and Trade* (Lund, 1969).

—— 'The Danish Asia Trade, 1620–1807: Value and Volume', *Scandinavian Economic History Review*, 39 (1991), pp. 3–27.

—— *The Battle of Copenhagen, 1801: Nelson and the Danes* (London, 2002).

Frost, Robert I., *The Northern Wars: War, State and Society in Northeastern Europe, 1558–1721* (London, 2000).

Giltner, Philip, *"In the Friendliest Manner": German–Danish Economic Cooperation During the Nazi Occupation of 1940–1945* (New York, 1998).

Hæstrup, Jørgen, *Secret Alliance: A Study of the Danish Resistance Movement, 1940–1945*, 3 vols (Odense, 1976–7).

Holbraad, Carsten, *Danish Neutrality* (Oxford, 1991).

Jespersen, Knud J. V., 'Henry VIII of England, Lübeck and the Count's War, 1533–1535', *Scandinavian Journal of History*, 6 (1981), pp. 1–33.

—— *No Small Achievement: Special Operations Executive and the Danish Resistance, 1940–1945* (Odense, 2002).

Johansen, Hans Christian, 'Scandinavian Shipping in the Late Eighteenth Century in European Perspective', *Economic History Review*, 45 (1992), pp. 479–93.

Kaarsted, Tage, *Great Britain and Denmark, 1914–20* (Odense, 1979).

Lengeler, Jörg Philipp, *Das Ringen um die Ruhe des Nordens. Grossbritaniens Nordeuropa-Politik und Dänemark zu Beginn des 18. Jahrhunderts* (Frankfurt a/M., 1998).

Lockhart, Paul Douglas, *Denmark in the Thirty Years War, 1618–1648: King Christian IV and the Decline of the Oldenburg State* (Selinsgrove, 1996).

Mckay, Derek and H. M. Scott, *The Rise of the Great Powers, 1648–1815* (London, 1983).

Nissen, Henrik S. (ed.), *Scandinavia during the Second World War* (Minneapolis, 1983).

Rystad, Göran (ed.), *Europe and Scandinavia: Aspects of the Process of Integration in the 17th Century* (Lund, 1983).

Rystad, Göran, Klaus-R. Böhme, and Wilhelm H. Carlgren (eds), *In Quest of Trade and Security: The Baltic in Power Politics, 1500–1990*, 2 vols (Lund, 1994, 1995).

Salmon, Patrick, *British–German Commercial Rivalry in the Depression Era: The Political and Economic Impact in Northern Europe, 1931–1939* (Newcastle, 1982).

—— *Scandinavia and the Great Powers, 1890–1940* (Cambridge, 1997).

Sandiford, Keith A. P., *Great Britain and the Schleswig-Holstein Question, 1848–1864* (Toronto, 1975).

Seymour, Susan, *Anglo-Danish Relations and Germany, 1933–1945* (Odense, 1982).

Tuxen, Ole, 'Principles and Priorities: The Danish View of Neutrality during the Colonial War of 1755–1763', *Scandinavian Journal of History*, 13 (1988), pp. 207–32.

GOVERNMENT AND DOMESTIC POLITICS

Anderson, P. and P. Camiller (eds), *Mapping the West European Left* (London, 1994).

Carr, William, *Schleswig-Holstein, 1815–1848: A Study in National Conflict* (Manchester, 1963).

Christiansen, Niels Finn, 'Reformism within the Danish Social Democracy until the Nineteen Thirties', *Scandinavian Journal of History*, 3 (1978), pp. 297–322.

Ekman, Ernst, 'The Danish Royal Law of 1665', *Journal of Modern History*, 29 (1957), pp. 102–7.

Elliott, J. H. and L. W. B. Brockliss (eds), *The World of the Favourite* (New Haven, CT, and London, 1999).

Jespersen, Knud J. V., 'New Technology versus Conscription: Some Reflections on Trends in Danish Army Organization during the First Twenty-Five Years of NATO Membership', *Militærhistorisk Tidskrift* (Stockholm, 1983), pp. 125–34.

—— 'Social Change and Military Revolution in Early Modern Europe: Some Danish Evidence', *Historical Journal*, 26 (1983), pp. 1–13.

—— 'Absolute Monarchy in Denmark: Change and Countinuity', *Scandinavian Journal of History*, 12 (1987), pp. 307–16.

Jespersen, Leon (ed.), *A Revolution from Above? The Power State of 16th and 17th Century Scandinavia* (Odense, 2000).

Keitsch, Christine, *Der Fall Struensee: Ein Blick in die Skandalpresse des ausgehenden 18. Jahrhunderts* (Hamburg, 2000).

Kouri, E. I. and Tom Scott (eds), *Politics and Society in Reformation Europe: Essays for Sir Geoffrey Elton on his Sixty-Fifth Birthday* (London, 1987).

Lange, Ulrich (ed.), *Geschichte Schleswig-Holsteins* (Neümünster, 1997).

Lind, Gunner, 'Military and Absolutism: The Army Officers of Denmark–Norway as a Social Group and Political Factors, 1660–1848', *Scandinavian Journal of History*, 12 (1987), pp. 221–43.

Løgstrup, Birgit, 'The Landowner as Public Administrator: The Danish Model', *Scandinavian Journal of History*, 9 (1984), pp. 283–312.

Petersen, Erling Ladewig, *The Crisis of the Danish Nobility, 1580–1660* (Odense, 1967).

—— 'From Domain State to Tax State: Synthesis and Interpretation', *Scandinavian Economic History Review*, 23 (1975), pp. 116–48.

—— 'Defence, War and Finance: Christian IV and the Council of the Realm, 1596–1629', *Scandinavian Journal of History*, 7 (1982), pp. 277–313.

Royal Danish Ministry of Foreign Affairs (ed.), *Denmark's Constitution, 150 Years* (Copenhagen, 1999).

Scott, H. M. (ed.), *The European Nobilities in the Seventeenth and Eighteenth Centuries*, 2 vols (London, 1995).

Winkle, Stefan, *Struensee und die Publizistik* (Hamburg, 1982).

—— *Struensee. Arzt, Aufklärer, Staatsmann* (Stuttgart, 1983).

CHURCH AND INTELLECTUAL LIFE

Allchin, A. M., D. Jasper, J. H. Schjørring and K. Stevenson (eds), *Heritage and Prophecy* (Århus, 1993).

Andersen, Hans Christian, *The Fairy Tale of My Life* (London and New York, 1955).

Bodenstein, Eckhard, *Skolefrihed in Dänemark zur Entstehung eines schulpolitischen Prinzips* (Tønder, 1982).

Haugaard, Erik (trans.), *The Penguin Complete Fairy Tales and Stories of Hans Andersen* (Harmondsworth, 1984–).

Lindhardt, P. G., *Kirschengeschichte Skandinaviens* (Göttingen, 1983).

MATERIAL LIFE AND THE WELFARE STATE

Andersen, Jørgen Goul, 'The Scandinavian Welfare Model in Crisis? Achievements and Problems in the Danish Welfare State in an Age of Unemployment and Low Growth', *Scandinavian Political Studies*, 20 (1997), pp. 1–37.

Bjørn, Claus, 'The Peasantry and Agrarian Reform in Denmark', *Scandinavian Economic History Review*, 25 (1977), pp. 117–37.

Boje, Per, 'The Standard of Living in Denmark, 1750–1914', *Scandinavian Economic History Review*, 34 (1986), pp. 171–9.

Christensen, Jens, *Rural Denmark, 1750–1980* (Copenhagen, 1983).

Christiansen, Niels Finn, Niels Edling, Per Haave and Klaus Petersen (eds), *The Nordic Welfare Model: A Historical Reappraisal* (Copenhagen, 2006).

Christiansen, Niels Finn and Klaus Petersen, 'The Dynamics of Social Solidarity: The Danish Welfare State, 1900–2000', *Scandinavian Journal of History*, 26 (2001), pp. 177–96.

Einhorn, Eric and John Logue, *Modern Welfare States: Policies in Social Democratic Scandinavia* (New York, 1989).

Esping-Andersen, Gösta, *Politics against Markets: The Social Democratic Road to Power* (Princeton, 1985).

—— *Welfare States in Transition: National Adaptations in Global Economies* (London, 1996).

Frandsen, Karl-Erik, *The Last Plague in the Baltic Region 1709–1713* (Copenhagen, 2010).

Hansen, Svend Aage, *Early Industrialisation in Denmark* (Copenhagen, 1970).

Hornby, Ove, 'Industrialisation in Denmark', *Scandinavian Economic History Review*, 17 (1969), pp. 23–57.

Johansen, Hans Christian, *Danish Population History, 1600–1939* (Odense, 2002).

Jörberg, Lennart, *The Industrial Revolution in Scandinavia, 1850–1914* (Fontana Economic History of Europe, London, 1970).

Kjærgaard, Thorkild, *The Danish Revolution, 1500–1800: An Ecohistorical Interpretation* (Cambridge, 1994).

Lind, Gunner, 'Development and Location of Industry in Danish Provincial Towns, 1855–1882', *Scandinavian Economic History Review*, 27 (1979), pp. 101–20.

Maarbjerg, John P., *Scandinavia in the European World-Economy, ca. 1570–1625* (New York, 1995).

Matthiessen, Poul Chr., *Immigration to Denmark: An Overview of the Research Carried Out from 1999 to 2006 by the Rockwool Foundation Research Unit* (Odense, 2009).

Mogensen, Gunnar Viby, *Det danske velfærdssamfunds historie: Tiden efter 1970*. Vols 1–2, with English summary (Copenhagen, 2010).

Munck, Thomas, 'The Economic and Social Position of Peasant Freeholders in Late Seventeenth-Century Denmark', *Scandinavian Economic History Review*, 25 (1977), pp. 37–61.

—— *The Peasantry and the Early Absolute Monarchy in Denmark, 1660–1708* (Copenhagen, 1979).

Nannestad, Peter, *Danish Design or British Disease? Danish Economic Crisis Policy in Comparative Perspective* (Århus, 1991).

Petersen, Erling Ladewig, 'The Danish Cattle Trade during the Sixteenth and Seventeenth Centuries', *Scandinavian Economic History Review*, 18 (1970), pp. 69–85.

Petersen, Klaus, *Legitimität und Krise: Die politische Geschichte des dänischen Wohlfahrtsstaates 1945–1973* (Berlin, 1998).

MENTALITY AND NATIONAL IDENTITY

Anderson, Benedict, *Imagined Communities: Reflections on the Origin and Spread of Nationalism* (London, 1983).

Colley, Linda, *Britons: Forging the Nation, 1707–1837* (New Haven, CT, and London, 1992).

Gellner, Ernest, *Nations and Nationalism* (Oxford, 1983).

Hobsbawm, E. J., *Nations and Nationalism since 1780* (Cambridge, 1990).

Smith, Anthony D., *The Ethnic Origins of Nations* (Oxford, 1986).

—— *National Identity* (Harmondsworth, 1991).

Sørensen, Øystein and Bo Stråth (eds), *The Cultural Construction of Norden* (Oslo, 1997).

Stråth, Bo (ed.), *Myth, Memory and History in the Construction of Community* (Brussels, 2000).

A Short Chronology
Since 1500

1523	Dissolution of the Kalmar Union. Christian II is deposed
1534–36	Civil war: The Count's War
1536	The Lutheran Reformation. Norway is incorporated
1550	The first Bible in Danish
1563–70	The Nordic Seven Years War (between Denmark and Sweden)
1611–13	The Kalmar War (between Denmark and Sweden)
1625–29	Christian IV's intervention in the Thirty Years War
1626	The King's army is defeated by General Tilly in the battle at Lutter am Barenberg in the Harz
1643–45	The Torstensson War. Some Norwegian border provinces and the province of Halland are ceded to Sweden
1657–58	The First Karl Gustav War. All the Scanian provinces are ceded to Sweden
1658–60	The Second Karl Gustav War. The cession of the Scanian provinces is confirmed, while the island of Bornholm is returned to Denmark after having liberated itself from the Swedish occupation
1660	Change of regime: Absolute monarchy
1665	The *Lex Regia*: The absolutist constitution
1670–76	The rise and fall of Chancellor Peder Griffenfeld. The older society of estates is replaced by a society of ranks
1675–79	The Scanian War between Denmark and Sweden. No territorial changes
1683	The Danish Law
1685	The Norwegian Law
1709–20	Danish intervention in the Great Northern War (1700–21). No territorial changes. Russia becomes the leading power in the Baltic region
1721	Frederik IV incorporates Schleswig
1733	The peasants are subjected to the bond of adscription
1770–72	Struensee's period in power: Enlightened despotism
1776	The Nationality Law
1784–88	The great agrarian reforms
1788	Reform of the system of conscription: The bond of adscription is abolished

1801	The Battle of Copenhagen: Lord Nelson forces Denmark to leave the League of Neutrality
1807	The British bombardment of Copenhagen. Britain confiscates the Danish Navy. Denmark allies with Napoleon
1807–14	War between Denmark and Britain
1813	National bankruptcy
1814	The Peace in Kiel. Norway is ceded to Sweden. The first national law on general basic education
1818	The National Bank is founded
1844	The first Folk High School is established (in Rødding)
1848–50	The First Schleswig War
1848	The Democratic Revolution brings 188 years of absolutist rule to an end
1849	The first democratic constitution
1864	The Second Schleswig War. The Duchies are surrendered to Germany
1866	Conservative amendments to the 1849 constitution
1875–94	The Conservative Prime Minister J. B. S. Estrup in power. Aggravated constitutional struggle
1882	The first co-operative dairy is founded (in Hjedding)
1891	The first national law on public old-age welfare is passed
1899	Widespread strikes and lock-outs lead to the normative September Agreement between the workers' unions and the employers
1901	Change of political practice into a system of cabinet responsibility. The Liberal Party comes into power
1914–18	Denmark neutral during the First World War. Increased state regulation of the economy
1920	Constitutional crisis. Northern Schleswig returns to Denmark after a referendum. The present border with Germany is established
1922	Economic crisis; the largest bank in the country fails
1924–26	The first Social Democratic government
1933	Cross-political agreement about anti-crisis measures: The collaborative democracy
1940–45	German occupation of Denmark. The government adopts a policy of appeasement and collaboration with the Germans
1943	Growing popular resistance to the German occupation leads to the August Rebellion, which ends the official policy of collaboration and appeasement
1944	Iceland denounces the personal union with Denmark
1945	Denmark is liberated by British troops and becomes one of the founding members of the UN
1949	Denmark signs the NATO Treaty
1953	A revised constitution is passed. Cabinet responsibility is made part of the constitution. Conditional female succession to the throne
1960	The welfare state becomes part of political practice. Denmark signs the EFTA treaty
1968	Youth rebellion at the universities

1973	Denmark enters the EEC together with Britain. The landslide election sends shock-waves through the political system. The first oil crisis
1979	Home rule in Greenland. Growing crisis in the welfare system
1982–93	Conservative–Liberal governments in office. Increasing stream of refugees from the Third World puts refugee question high on the political agenda
1989–92	The collapse in Eastern Europe sets a new agenda for Danish foreign and domestic policy
1993–2001	Social Democrat-led governments try to accommodate Danish policy to the new global realities
2001	A Liberal–Conservative government comes into power
2002	Denmark holds the EU presidency and hosts the summit on the EU-enlargement in Eastern Europe
2004	Military engagement in Iraq and Afghanistan
2006	The 'cartoon crisis' sends shock waves through Danish society
2008	The international financial crisis hits Denmark and sets a new political agenda
2009	Prime Minister Anders Fogh Rasmussen is appointed Secretary-General of NATO and is replaced by the former minister of finance, Lars Løkke Rasmussen. Denmark hosts the United Nations' climate summit, COP 15, in Copenhagen

Index

11 September 2001   33
1864 syndrome   198, 208–11

Aalborg   162
Aarhus   156, 162
absolutism   8, 69–70, 200, 204–8
  legitimising of   56–8
  opinion-driven   147
Act of Sovereignty (1661)   48
Act of Succession (1665)   48, 52,
    54, 58, 98
administration, reform of   49
adscription   61, 62, 142
advisory assemblies of the provincial
    estates   69
Afghanistan   222, 226
  US military operations in   34
agrarian reforms   8, 58–61, 138,
    140–3
agrarian revolution   129–30, 138–40
agricultural classes   134–6
agricultural commission   60
agricultural industrialisation   182
agricultural land (distribution of)
    127
Altona   155, 202
Amsterdam   14
Andersen, Hans Christian (1805–75)
    154, 207
Anti-Comintern Pact   28, 29
Antwerp   14
Archbishop of Lund   94
aristocracy, privileges of   42

Arup, Erik, historian (1876–1951)
    197
Askov   160
August laws (of 1914)   167
Austria   64, 191

Baltic region   3, 12–14, 15, 16, 19, 125
Baltic Sea   1, 2, 7, 13, 18
Baltic States   192
Bang, Gustav, historian (1871–1915)
    214
Bang, Nina, politician (1866–1928)
    214
Bastille, storming of (1789)   62
Bayle, Pierre   109
Beck, Wilhelm, church leader
    (1829–1901)   107
beef export   128–9
Belgium   67
Berlin Wall, fall of (1989)   30, 32,
    191, 222
Bernstorff, Andreas Peter, foreign
    minister (1735–1797)   59
Bible, first Danish translation of
    the   100–1
Billund   183
Bismarck, Otto von, German
    chancellor   23, 24, 25–6, 73,
    83, 196, 209, 210
Blair. Tony   225
Blixen, Karen, author (1885–1962)
    120
Board School Act (1814)   101

Bodin, Jean, French philosopher
(1530–1596)   45–6
Bohr, Niels, physicist (1885–1962)
120
Bohuslän (former Norwegian
province)   18
Borgbjerg, Frederik, politician
(1866–1936)   118
Bornholm   20
Brandes, Georg, man of letters
(1842–1927)   212
Brazil   217
Britain   29, 57, 58, 137, 150, 179
agriculture   138, 158, 174
assaults on Copenhagen   16, 21,
149, 197, 206
Corn Laws   150, 154
EEC membership   187
Empire   201
heavy industry   165
industry   158, 165
post- WW2 trade   179
social class   166
trade with Denmark   154, 179,
186–7
transport   155
Wall Street crash and   174
wars with Denmark   21–2, 147
WWI   168
Britishness   201, 202, 206
Brorson, Hans Adolph, bishop of
Ribe (1694–1764)   105
Buhl, Vilhelm   30
Burmeister & Wain, shipyard   163
Bush, George W.   34
Butterfield, Herbert, British
philosopher   200

caritas (charitable role of the
Church)   94, 104, 219
Caroline Mathilde, Danish queen
(1751–1775)   57
cartoon (caricature) crisis (2006)
227–9

Catholic Church   13, 38–40, 94–5,
104, 108, 201
arrest of bishops (1536)   39
becomes a national church   95
hymns   113
centrifuge, for production of
butter   158
Christensen, I.C., politician, prime
minister (1856–1930)   74,
76–7
Christian II, king of Denmark
(r. 1513–23)   15, 94
Christian III, king of Denmark
(r. 1534–59)   38–9, 98
coup (1536)   95
legislation on poor relief
(1539)   99
motto   110
Christian IV, king of Denmark
(r. 1588–1648)   17, 18, 25, 43,
51, 131, 197, 202
death of   45
motto   110
Christian IX, king of Denmark
(r. 1863–1906)   75
Christian V, king of Denmark
(r. 1670–99)   50
motto   111
Christian VI, king of Denmark
(r.1730–46)   105
motto   111
Christian VII, king of Denmark
(r. 1766–1808)   57
motto   111
Christian X, king of Denmark
(r. 1912–47)   75
Christian, duke; see Christian III
Christiansborg Palace   65
Christiansen, Gotfred Kirk, toy
manufacturer, founder of Lego
(b. 1920)   183 see also Lego
church land, confiscated   96
civil servants, increase in numbers
185

civil war (1534–6)   39 *see also*
    Count's War
Clausen, Mads, engineer, founder
    of Danfoss (1905–1966)   183
    see also Danfoss
clergy
    as servants of the state   97
    role in education   102
Colbiørnsen, Christian, agrarian
    reformer (1749–1814)   141
Cold War   30–2, 186
collaborative democracy   177
collective bargaining agree-
    ments   170
Common Market   186–7, 188, 198
    see also European Community
Communism   199, 225
Communist Party, Danish   28, 177
compromise between Liberals and
    Conservatives (1894)   74
    see also Højre; Venstre
Confessio Augustana (1530)   98
confirmation, ceremony of   101, 105
Congress of Vienna   148
conscription reform (1788)   61–3
consensus model   6, 36–8
Conservatives   207, 209–11, 214, 224
Constitution, amended (1866)   70–2
constitutional revolution (1536)
    40–1
co-operative movement   8–9,
    156–61
    dairies   157–9
    purchasing societies   159
co-operative workers   158–9
Copenhagen   1, 3, 5, 46, 49, 62, 65,
    176, 207, 209, 210, 225
    as port   137–8, 149
    blockade by Frederik III   47
    British assaults on   16, 21, 149,
        197, 206
    commerce   131, 149
    fortifications of   73–4, 210
    industry   131, 163

national theatre   109
population   127, 146, 162
siege (1536)   39
siege (1658–9)   45
transport   155–6
Copenhagen-Bonn Accord
    (1955)   30
Corn Laws (Britain)   150, 154
coronation charters (and the
    church)   98
Count's War (1534–6)   17 *see also*
    civil war
Cour, Poul la, high school teacher
    (1846–1908)   160
critical breakthrough   196
Crown lands   42, 60, 132
Crown of Denmark   40–1
customs reform (1797)   147
Customs Union (Germany,
    1834)   23
Cyprus   192
Czech Republic   192

dairies   157–9
Danfoss, manufacturing
    company   165, 182–3
Danish (social) Model   55, 122, 168
Danish Conservative People's
    Party   214
Danish Federation of Employers
    (founded 1895)   80
Danish Federation of Trade Unions
    (founded 1898)   80
Danish Freedom Council   29
Danish identity   201–2
Danish Law (1683)   51–4, 55, 69,
    80, 82, 133, 220
Danish nation state, emergence of
    216
Danish National Liberals   207
Danish National Socialist Party
    (DNSAP)   28
Danish People's Party (*Dansk
    Folkeparti*)   224

Danishness 123–4, 201–4
  absolutism and 204–8
  1864 syndrome and 208–11
demographic transition 161–2
Denmark for the People (Social
  Democratic manifesto,
  1934) 85, 176
Denmark of the Future (Social
  Democratic manifesto,
  1945) 184
Deuntzer, J.H., prime minister,
  professor (1845–1918) 76–7
dominium maris Baltici 15
double-track decision 31
dual revolution, the 148–51, 153, 215
duchies, the (ceding of) 24
dyarchy 41

Easter crisis (1920) 75
Edinburgh Agreement (1992) 191
educational system, national 121
EFTA 187
electricity generation 159
Elton, G.R., British historian 41
emigration 162
employment patterns 176, 180–1,
  182
England 3, 14, 16, 113, 125
  see also Britain
enlightened absolutism 57
Enlightenment 108–12
entailed estates 133, 170–1
  see also land reform (1919)
Erasmus, Desiderius, of Rotterdam,
  Dutch Humanist (1466–1536)
  95
Erik of Pomerania, king of Denmark
  (r. 1412–39) 125
Esbjerg 155
Estrup, Jacob Brønnum Scavenius,
  politician, prime minister
  (1825–1913) 72–3, 74, 210
ethnies 217–18, 220
euro, the (common currency) 192

Europe (early modern economic
  structure) 14
European Commission 190
European Community (EEC) 30,
  181
  Danish entry into 30, 187–8, 189
  see also Common Market
European Parliament 190
European Union 25, 87, 89, 198,
  222–3, 225
  Danish entry into 30, 189–92
Exchange Control Office (1932)
  175, 176, 177
Extraordinary Commission (1914)
  167

'farmers' approach to Danish history
  196, 200–1
'farmers' line' 200
farms
  decreasing number after World
    War II 181
  dissolution of 133
  forced sales of 174
Faroe Islands 1, 3, 22, 148
February Revolutions (1848) 64
financial crisis (2008–9) 229–31
Finland 187, 191
Folk High School 8, 114–16, 161,
  210, 214
  and co-operative movement 161
  Songbook 210, 214
Folkelighed 37, 117–19, 220
Folketing (Lower House) 67, 72,
  74, 86
foreign policy 34–5
four-party system
  emerges 78
  breaks down 86–7
France 19, 21, 25, 156, 186, 192,
  209
Franco-Prussian War 25
Frederik I, king of Denmark
  (r. 1523–33) 38, 94

Frederik II, king of Denmark
    (r. 1559–88)
    motto   110
Frederik III, king of Denmark
    (r. 1648–70)   45, 98
    becomes hereditary and
        absolutist   47
    motto   111
Frederik IV, king of Denmark
    (r. 1699–1730)
    founder of board schools   101
    motto   111
Frederik V, king of Denmark
    (r. 1746–66)
    motto   111
Frederik VI, king of Denmark
    (r. 1808–39)   56–7
Frederik VII, king of Denmark
    (r. 1848–63)   65
    motto   111
Frederikshavn   155
Free Schools   116
freeholders   42, 60, 128, 132
French Revolution   62, 110, 206,
    207, 217
Frijs-Frijsenborg, C.E., Count, prime
    minister (1817–96)   71, 72
Frikorps Denmark   28
Fyn (Funen)   1, 120

Gallop, Rodney, British
    diplomat   199
gatekeeper, Denmark as   14–16
Gaulle, Charles de, president of
    France   187
German Confederation   65, 66
German Democratic Republic   37
German occupation of Denmark
    (1940)   27, 198
Germanness   208
Germany   1, 7, 17, 64, 156, 199,
    208–11, 212, 216, 221, 222
    industry   164
    nationalism in   23

occupation of Denmark (1940)
    178
    policy of collaboration with   27
    Romantic movement   206, 207
    trade with Denmark   186
    unification of   2–3, 22–6, 30–1, 191
    Wall Street Crash and   174
    in World War One   168
Glistrup, Mogens, politician, lawyer
    (b. 1926)   87, 225
Gorbachev, Mikhail, last Head of
    State, USSR (b. 1931)   32
Gotland   3
grain export   128–9
Great Belt   27
Great Land Commission (1786)   141
Great Northern War (1700–21)   7,
    19
Greenland   1, 3, 4, 22, 27, 30, 148
Griffenfeld, Peder, chancellor
    (1635–1699)   50
Grundtvig, N.F.S., church leader,
    politician (1783–1872)   112–14,
    203, 206–7, 220, 221
    English influence on his
        thinking   113
    lectures on *Folkelighed*   117
    legacy   119–22
    philosophy of the popular
        116–19
    poem on *Folkelighed* (1848)   117
    unique discoveries   114
    views upon church and state   115
Grundtvigian Folk High School
    movement *see* Folk High School
Grundtvigianism   107–8, 113, 118,
    120
Gustav Vasa I, king of Sweden
    (r. 1523–60)   11, 15
Gustavus Adolphus II, king of
    Sweden (r. 1611–32)   17

Halland, province of   18, 197
Halle (in Germany)   105

Hamburg 57
Hanover 58
Hanseatic League 11, 12–13, 16–17
Hansen, I.A., politician
    (1806–1877) 71
Hansen, V. Falbe, political
    economist 162–3
Hansen Uhd, Niels, founder of
    cooperative dairy 160
Härjedalen (former Norwegian
    province) 18
Hedtoft, Hans 28
Helgesen, Povl, humanist
    (c. 1485–1535) 95 *see also*
    Catholic Church
Helsingør 126
Henry VIII, King of England 39
Hitler, Adolf, German Chancellor
    (1889–1945) 178, 198
Hjedding (in Jutland) 158
Hobbes, Thomas 110
Hobsbawm, E.J., British
    historian 148
Højre (Conservative Party) 74–5,
    78, 161, 211, 214 *see also*
    Conservatives
Holberg, Ludvig, philosopher,
    playwright (1684–1754)
    109–10, 203
Holst, H.P., poet (1811–1893)
    208–1
Holstein 3, 8, 64–5, 66, 139, 198
    loss to Prussia 198
    see also Schleswig-Holstein
Holstein, Duke of 292
Holy Roman Empire 3
Home Mission 107, 108
Hørup, Viggo, politician, journalist
    (1841–1902) 211, 212, 213
Hungary 192
Hussein, Saddam, President of Iraq
    (1937–2006) 123
Hvidt, L.N., politician, minister
    (1777–1856) 65

Iceland 3, 22, 27, 148, 203, 218
immigration, impact of 87, 189
    Muslim 93
independent farmers 143, 144, 146,
    154, 158, 161, 171–2, 200
    see also farms
Indfødsretten 205
Industrial Revolution 148
industrialisation 9, 217
    in Europe 148
    first wave 164
    impact of late 165
    pattern of 164
    second wave 182–4
    third wave 184
Ingemann, B.S., hymnodist, author
    (1789–1862) 207
Iraq 226
    invasion of Kuwait 32
    US-led invasion of 34
Islam 121
Italy 186

Jämtland (former Norwegian
    province) 18
Jensen, Jørgen I, church historian 91
Jutland 1, 10, 14, 21, 24, 27, 39, 97,
    105, 119, 129, 135, 159, 179,
    216, 218
Jyllands-Posten 227

Kalmar Union (dissolution of, 1523)
    7, 11, 12, 13, 15
Kalmar War (1611–13) 17
Kanslergade Agreement 176
    see also World Crisis (1929)
Karl Gustav Wars (1657–60) 18, 203
Karl X Gustav, king of Sweden
    (r. 1654–60) 18
Karl XII, king of Sweden
    (r. 1697–1718) 19
Kattegat 1
Kauffmann, Henrik, diplomat 30
Kiel 66, 155–6

Kiel Canal 26–7
Kiel Treaty (1814) 149
Kierkegaard, Søren, philosopher (1813–1855) 111–12
King, Dr William, British philanthropist (1786–1865) 158
Kingo, Thomas, bishop, hymnodist (1634–1703) 203
Koenigsberger, H.G., British historian 2
Kold, Christen, school reformer (1816–1870) 114
Kongeå (national boundary 1864–1920) 24
Korch, Morten, novelist (1876–1954) 182
Korsør 155, 156
Krag, Jens Otto, politician, prime minister (1914–1978) 36–7, 78, 88, 90, 186, 187
Kronborg 126
Kuwait, Iraq invasion of 32
Kyrgyzstan 222

labour movement 166
land reform (1919) 170–3
Landmandsbanken (1922) 173
landslide election (1973) 36, 86, 88
Landsting (Upper House) 67, 72, 76
Lauenburg 22
law on elementary education (1814) *see* Board School Act
Lego (toy company) 165, 182, 183
Legoland (amusement park) 183
Lehmann, Orla, politician, minister (1810–1870) 65, 68, 209
Lex Regia see Act of Succession
Liberalist movement 69
Liberty Stone 62
lock-outs 167
London 14
London Peace Treaty (1852) 66
Louis XIV, king of France (r. 1643–1715) 19

Lübeck 12, 14, 17, 39
Luther, Martin, German theologian (1483–1546) 93, 94, 95, 96, 100–1, 105
Lutheran Church, impact of 102–4
Lutter am Barenberg (battle at, 1626) 25, 197

Maastricht Treaty (1992) 190
Maersk Mc-Kinney Møller 188
Magnussen, Arne, antiquarian (1663–1730) 203
Malling, Ove, minister, author (1747–1829) 206
Malta 192
manor farms (decree on, 1682) 132–3
March Government (1848) 65–6 *see also* Revolution: February (1848)
Marshall Aid 180
Marx, Karl, German political theorist (1818–1883) 213
Mellon, Sir James, British diplomat, author 5–7, 8–10, 37, 123, 124, 193, 216, 218, 220, 223–4
merchant navy (in Allied service 1940–5) 178
military conscription 61–3 *see also* conscription reform (1788)
military revolution (in the sixteenth century) 43
military service 67
'mini-ice age' 130
Ministry for Religious Affairs 92
Molesworth, Sir Robert, British diplomat, author (1656–1725) 4–5
Møller, A.P. (shipping company) 138, 165
Møller, John Christmas, Conservative People's Party politician (1894–1948) 28
Møller, Poul Martin, poet (1794–1838) 153

Moltke, A.W., prime minister
  (1785–1864)   65
Monarchy
  becomes hereditary (1660)   46–7
  becomes absolute (1661)   48
Monrad, D.G., politician, prime
  minister (1811–1887)   65, 208
Montesquieu, Charles-Louis de
  Secondat, French philosopher
  (1689–1755)   67, 110
Moth, Matthias, civil servant
  (1649–1719)   203
mottoes, Royal   110–11
Munch, P., politician, minister
  (1870–1948)   174

Napoleon I (Bonaparte), emperor of
  France   21, 22, 137
Napoleon III, emperor of France
  25, 209
Napoleonic Code (1804)   52
Napoleonic Wars   20, 22–3, 57, 61,
  63, 68, 106, 113, 137–8, 147,
  148–9, 153, 154, 206
national assembly (for preparation of
  the Constitution, 1848)   67
National Bank   152, 167, 175, 179
national bankruptcy (1813)   150, 174
National Conservatives   210
National Liberals   65, 68–70, 207,
  209
National Romantics   211
nationalism   207, 215–18
  modernist school   215–17
  primordialist school   217
nationalist movement   69, 210
  in Germany   23
Nationality Law (1776)   205, 215
NATO   30–2, 34, 198, 222
Nelson, Horatio, British admiral
  (1758–1805)   21
Netherlands   2, 14, 16, 18–19, 20,
  57, 109, 125, 128–31, 137, 138,
  150, 165

neutralism   196, 198
neutrality   21, 198
neutrality pact (with Russia and
  Sweden)   21
New Zealand   208
Nielsen, Carl, composer
  (1865–1931)   120
Nielsen, L.C., engineer
  (1849–1929)   158
nobility
  loss of privileges   49
  titled   49
Nordborg (in Als)   183
Nordek (plans of a Nordic free
  market)   187
Nordic Seven Years War
  (1563–70)   17
North America   156 see also
  United States of America
North Schleswig   24
North Sea   1, 7, 188
Norway   2, 3, 15, 17, 21, 22, 24, 27,
  50, 102, 129, 148–9, 150, 178,
  187, 197, 202, 204, 206
Novo Nordisk (medical company)
  165
Nyborg   156

occupation by Germany (1940)   178
Odense   154
OECD   122, 180
Oehlenschläger, Adam, poet
  (1779–1850)   206
oil crisis (1973)   86, 160, 188,
  189–90
Oldenborg Monarchy   201
Oldenborg State   23, 201, 205
Oldenborg, Royal House of   3, 12, 23
open field system   59, 136, 140
Order of the Dannebrog   50, 51
Order of the Elephant   50
Øresund   3, 14, 15, 18, 21, 46, 125–6
Owen, Robert, Welsh social reformer
  (1771–1858)   158

pacifism 198, 196–7, 198
parish registers (introduced 1646) 97
Parliament 67 *see also Folketing, Landsting*
parliamentarianism 75–8, 210
parliamentary responsibility (of ministers) 67
Peace of Westphalia (1648) 20
peasant farms 136 *see also* farms
peasants 127, 129, 132–4 *see also* independent farmers
Persian Gulf 15, 19
Peter I the Great, Tsar of Russia (1672–1725) 20
Petersen, Jørgen, political economist 172
Pietism 104–8
'pig tickets' 175
plebiscite (1920) 24, 221
Poland 192
policy of regulation (during World War I) 167–70
Poor Law (1708) 100
Popular Church (*Folkekirken*) 92, 93, 116
population (size and composition) 1, 14, 127–8, 145, 149, 151–2, 161
in different European countries 127–8
Portugal 187
privileges for counts and barons (1671) 133
Progress Party (*Fredskridtspartiet*) 87, 225
provisional financial budgets 73
Prussia 23–4, 66, 71, 97, 196, 198
Prussian Seven Years War (1756–63) 21, 141

radical tradition (in Danish historiography) 196
Radikale Venstre, Det (the Social-Liberal Party) 77–8 209, 211, 213, 214

railways 155, 156
Rasmussen, Anders Fogh, prime minister (b. 1953) 33, 34, 224, 225, 226, 229
Rasmussen, Lars Løkke, prime minister (b. 1964) 229
Rasmussen, Poul Nyrup, politician, prime minister (b. 1943) 33, 53, 224
rationing 169, 179, 180
Reagan, Ronald, US President (1911–2004) 32
reformation of the Church 94–6
Reformation, the 8, 201, 219
reformatory movements 94
Renaissance 202
Reventlow, Christian Ditlev Frederik, politician, agrarian reformer 59, 141
revivalist movements 106
revolution
of 1660 46–7
agrarian 129–30, 138–40
constitutional (1536) 40–1
dual 148–51, 153, 215
February (1848) 64
French 62, 110, 206, 207, 217
industrial 148
military 43
Tudor 40
Reykjavik 203
Rochdale 158
Rødding (in Jutland) 114
Rode, Ove, politician, minister (1867–1933) 167
Romanticism 221
Rome Treaty (1957) 187
Roskilde 155
Rousseau, Jean-Jacques, French philosopher (1712–1778) 56, 58
Royal Copenhagen Porcelain Manufactory 205
Rubin, Marcus, historian (1854–1923) 147

rural class system   146, 160
Russia   20, 21, 22, 32, 156, 169,
    172, 173, 198
  population   127
  see also Soviet Union

Scanian provinces (*Skåne*)   3, 18,
    197, 203
Scanian War (1675–9)   19
Scavenius, Erik, politician, prime
    minister (1877–1962)   26,
    212–13
Schimmelmann, Heinrich Ernst,
    politician, minister
    (1747–1831)   59–60
Schleswig   3, 7, 24, 64–5, 66, 204,
    213
  loss to Prussia   198
  see also Holstein; Schleswig-
    Holstein
Schleswig-Holstein   23, 65, 66,
    208
Schleswigian Wars (1848–50;
    1864)   7, 23–4, 65, 211, 216
Schlüter, Poul, politician, prime
    minister (b. 1929)   190, 191
schools (founding of)   101
Schumacher, Peder; see Griffenfeld
Scotland   3
Scott, Walter   207
September 11, 2001   33
September Agreement (1899)   80
Single European Act (1986)   190
Skagen   125
Slovakia   192
Slovenia   192
Småland   18
smallholders   9, 60, 107, 135–6,
    143, 145, 152, 158, 160, 171–2,
    181, 211, 213
Smith, Adam   145, 175
Smith, Anthony D., British
    sociologist   217, 218, 219, 220

Social Democrats   31–2, 78–80,
    81–2, 93, 118–19, 169, 171,
    184, 213, 216
Social Security Act (1976)   85
social security reforms   82–3, 85,
    176
socialists   209
Social-Liberal Party   171, 216
  see also Radikale Venstre, Det
Sound Dues   3, 125–7
sovereignty (new concept of,
    1536)   40
Soviet Union   31, 180, 222
  collapse of   33
Special Operations Executive
    (SOE)   28, 178
St Petersburg   20
State Council   38, 39, 40
  as *alter rex*   45
  crisis of   44–6
state mercantilism   131
state power
  and civil society   54–6
  'leasing out of'   134
Statute Book (1643)   51
Stauning, Thorvald, politician, prime
    minister (1873–1942)   81, 84,
    173–5, 176
steamboat routes   155–6
Steincke, K.K., politician, minister
    (1880–1963)   176
Stockholm Bloodbath (1520)   15
strikes   167
Struen see, Johann Friedrich, German
    physician, political reformer
    (1737–1772)   57–8, 61, 205
Submission (film)   227
superintendents   96
suspension of gold standard   174
Sweden   2, 7, 11, 15, 20, 21–2, 24,
    25, 29, 77, 119, 125–7, 187
  education system   102
  in European Union   191

Halland ceded to 148, 197
Scanian provinces and 132, 203
union with Norway 197
war with Denmark 16, 17–19, 43, 46, 202, 217
Switzerland 187
syndicalists 169

taxation (changes in) 43, 44, 223
tenancies 129, 132, 133, 134
tenants 60, 71, 133, 134, 135, 139–40
Teutonic Order 11, 13
Thirty Years War (1618–48) 17, 18, 43, 197, 202
Thisted 158
Tilly, General (1559–1632) 25
Torstensson War (1643–5) 18
trade routes (changes in) 13, 14
trade under neutral flag 137
trade unions 80, 170, 230
trading companies 131
Trolle, Herluf, Lord Admiral (1516–1565) 42–3, 201
Trondheim Fjord 50
Tscherning, A.F., politician, minister (1795–1874) 65
Tudor Revolution 40

unemployment 2, 83, 169, 174–7, 179, 184, 188–9, 229–30
United Left Party 72 see also Venstre
United Nations 222
United States of America 16, 27, 30, 217
emigration to 162, 180
invasion of Iraq 34
World War One 168
University of Copenhagen 100, 120

urban middle class (emergence of) 147

van Gogh, Theodore, film director (1957–2004) 227
Venstre (Liberal Party) 72, 73, 74–5, 84, 86, 119, 161, 171, 173, 174, 175, 176, 196, 209, 210, 211, 224, 225
Versailles Treaty (1919) 24
Vienna Congress (1815) 23, 148
village collectives 138, 139, 143–6, 219–21
village land (redistribution of) 141
villeinage 60, 128, 133, 134, 139, 141–3

welfare model 193, 218–19, 221–3
welfare state (the Danish model) 9, 82–6, 184–6
and Danishness 218–19
world economy 186–9
Western Defence Alliance 30
Westphalia (peace negotiations in) 18
Westphalian system 23
Wittenberg 96
women
in labour market 184
right to vote 67
Workers' Songbook 214
working class 81, 166, 208, 209
world crisis (1929) 173
World War I (1914–18) 27, 167–9, 214, 221 see also England
World War II (1939–45) 27–30, 199

Yugoslavia, break-up of 33

Zealand 1, 60, 203